Allen O. Abbott

Prison Life in the South

At Richmond, Macon, Savannah, Charleston, Columbia, Charlotte...

Allen O. Abbott

Prison Life in the South
At Richmond, Macon, Savannah, Charleston, Columbia, Charlotte...

ISBN/EAN: 9783744757669

Printed in Europe, USA, Canada, Australia, Japan

Cover: Foto ©Suzi / pixelio.de

More available books at **www.hansebooks.com**

PRISON LIFE IN THE SOUTH:

AT

RICHMOND, MACON, SAVANNAH, CHARLESTON, COLUMBIA,

CHARLOTTE, RALEIGH, GOLDSBOROUGH,

AND ANDERSONVILLE,

DURING THE YEARS 1864 AND 1865.

BY A. O. ABBOTT,
LATE LIEUTENANT FIRST NEW YORK DRAGOONS.

With Illustrations.

NEW YORK:
HARPER & BROTHERS, PUBLISHERS,
FRANKLIN SQUARE.
1865.

TO THE

OFFICERS OF THE FEDERAL ARMY

WHO HAVE BEEN CAPTURED ON THE

BATTLE-FIELD,

AND WHO HAVE SUFFERED, WITH HIMSELF,

THE PRIVATIONS OF A LINGERING CAPTIVITY

IN SOUTHERN PRISONS,

These Sketches are Respectfully Dedicated by

THE AUTHOR.

PREFACE.

The following pages are offered to the reading public, with the hope that they will throw some light upon the barbarous treatment we received at the hands of the Rebels.

They do not claim to tell *all* the story of Prison Life, only a part. Others are filling it up, dark and gloomy as is the picture; yet pen and tongue both fail to tell it *all*.

I had no intention of writing a book till we had been several weeks at Columbia, S. C. Having kept both a diary and journal since my capture, upon reading portions of it to some of my fellow-prisoners, they persuaded me to write it out in full. The rough manuscript was mostly written in a brush shanty, sitting flat on the ground, writing on my knee. A portion of that manuscript was brought through the lines by Lieutenant Krohn, 5th New York Cavalry, in December, 1864, by secreting it in the back of his coat. The rest came through in a cotton pillow, in possession of Colonel Warren Shedd, 30th Illinois. The Appendix is principally the work of J. O. Goodrich, Adjutant 85th New York Veteran Volunteers, a Plymouth capture.

To these, as well as those officers who have so kindly furnished me with their experience, I return my sincere thanks. Should these pages serve to throw any light upon the question "What shall we do with the Negro?" I shall feel that my labor has not been in vain.

A. O. A.

Portageville, N. Y., August, 1865.

CONTENTS.

CHAPTER I.
Capture, and Arrival at Libby Prison.................................. 13

CHAPTER II.
In Libby 22

CHAPTER III.
From Libby to Macon, Georgia... 42

CHAPTER IV.
At Macon, Georgia.. 58

CHAPTER V.
At Savannah, Georgia... 81

CHAPTER VI.
At Charleston, South Carolina.. 102

CHAPTER VII.
At Columbia, South Carolina—Camp Sorghum 124

CHAPTER VIII.
At Columbia, South Carolina—Asylum Prison............................ 150

CHAPTER IX.
Homeward Bound... 176

CHAPTER X.
At Andersonville. (By Ira E. Forbes, Corporal 16th Connecticut Volunteers.) 192

CHAPTER XI.
Among the Negroes. (By H. B. Seeley, Adjutant 86th New York Volunteers.) 207

CHAPTER XII.

IN SEARCH OF LIBERTY. (By ——, Major, —— New York Volunteers.) 219

CHAPTER XIII.

IN THE HOSPITAL NEAR CHARLESTON, SOUTH CAROLINA. (By A. F. Tipton, Lieutenant, 8th Iowa Cavalry.) 239

CHAPTER XIV.

AN ADVENTURE. (By F. Murphy, Lieutenant, 94th New York Volunteers.) 241

CHAPTER XV.

IN THE CELL AT LIBBY. (By A. C. Litchfield, Lieutenant Colonel, 7th Michigan Cavalry.) 257

CHAPTER XVI.

ESCAPED AND RECAPTURED. (By Professor J. Ogden, Lieutenant, 1st Wisconsin Cavalry.) 260

CHAPTER XVII.

FIVE WEEKS AMONG THE LOYAL LEAGUE AT CHARLESTON, SOUTH CAROLINA. (By W. H. Telford, Captain, 50th Pennsylvania Veteran Volunteers.) 296

CHAPTER XVIII.

REBEL BARBARITIES. (From *Harper's Weekly*.) 303

APPENDIX.

Containing the Name, Rank, Regiment, Date, Place of Capture, and Post-office Address of the 1500 Officers who were confined at Columbia, South Carolina, 1864 and 1865 317

LIST OF ILLUSTRATIONS.

1. Tunneling.. *Frontispiece.*
2. Captured .... Page 16
3. Fresh Fish.. 58
4. Camp Oglethorpe, Macon, Georgia............. 59
5. Washing... 65
6. Shoulder-straps on Police Duty.................. 67
7. "Bucked".. 71
8. Filling up the Sinks at Savannah, Georgia... 96
9. Washing—under Difficulties....................... 99
10. Jail-yard, Charleston, South Carolina......... 105
11. Work-house, Charleston, South Carolina..... 110
12. Roper Hospital, Charleston, South Carolina. 114
13. Burnt District at Charleston, South Carolina. 120
14. Capture of the Fugitives............................ 130
15. Hauling Wood, Camp Sorghum................... 137
16. Drawing Meat Ration................................ 147
17. Shanties, Columbia, South Carolina............ 148
18. Asylum Prison, Columbia, South Carolina... 153
19. Dividing Wood 156
20. Sutler's Establishment.............................. 158
21. Delivering the Mail 163
22. Skirmishing... 185
23. Passing the Line for Exchange, North Carolina 188
24. Pursuing Knowledge under Difficulties....... 271
25. Recaptured 289
26-33. Rebel Barbarities................................ 304-313

SKETCHES OF PRISON LIFE.

CHAPTER I.

CAPTURE, AND ARRIVAL AT "LIBBY PRISON."

THE morning of the 3d of May, 1864, was an eventful one to the Army of the Potomac; for on that day began the grand movement, which, it was hoped, would finish the rebellion. General Grant had been called from his victorious Army of the West, placed in command of the ill-fated Army of the Potomac, and of all the forces of the East. He came with the prestige of a success which had an excellent effect upon the soldiers who had been so long trying, but unsuccessfully, to take Richmond.

For nearly five months active preparations had been going on in both the Federal and Rebel armies, each determined to strike a telling blow for its interest; the *one* for a Nationality and Republican institutions, the *other* for an Oligarchy founded upon human slavery. From December till May these two armies had confronted each other, both picketing the line of the Rapidan and Rappahannock Rivers, each waiting the signal of settled weather to begin the forward movement which was to drive its foe back upon Richmond or Washington. The public feeling, both North and South, had been wrought up to its highest pitch. Much confidence was reposed in General Grant by the loyal ones, and many prayers ascended daily for him and his noble army.

My brigade broke camp from the base of Pony Mountain, near Culpepper, Va., on the morning of the 5th of May; took the Stevensburg Road, and encamped at night three miles from Germania Ford. The infantry had preceded us, and, as is always the case at the commencement of a spring campaign, the roads were strewn with blankets, overcoats, knapsacks, etc., cast off by the soldiers to lighten their load. As our train did not come up that night, we had to content ourselves with such rations as we chanced to have in our haversacks or could borrow, not an unusual thing in a campaign.

We crossed the Rapidan at Ely's Ford by fording, the pontoons being used by the infantry and artillery; took the old Chancellorsville Road, and picketed it for three miles beyond Chancellorsville. As we passed over the battle-field, I could see very plainly the marks of the terrible struggle of last year. The tops of the trees looked as though they had been measured and trimmed by a skillful hand, while their trunks and limbs were scarred and broken. But little of the *débris* of the battle remained on the ground, it having been picked up and carried off by the inhabitants of the vicinity last year, for the benefit of the Rebel government, who made a practice of sending out agents to collect all such spoils from the inhabitants. This I learned from one of the residents near Ely's Ford.

We had no fighting to do until Saturday, being kept on picket on the Fredericksburg Road. On that day (the 7th) we were ordered, at 12 M., to Todd's Tavern.

The weather was intensely hot, and the clouds of dust through which we rode almost suffocated us. After a halt of a few moments at Todd's Tavern were ordered out on the Spottsylvania Road to discover the position and movements of the Rebels; soon found they were advancing down the road, supported by two brigades of dismounted cavalry, intending, no doubt, to drive us from our possession of the roads leading to Richmond, and, if possible, thus turn the left flank of our army. Colonel Gibbs, of the 1st New York Dragoons, who was in command of the third brigade, first division, at once comprehended the situation, and ordering the 6th Pennsylvania to dismount, sent them in on the right of the road, while my regiment, Lieutenant Colonel Thorp in command, took the left. We at once opened on them with our "seven-shooters," and sent their skirmish-line tumbling back to their supports. As we charged up a little rise of ground, we at once discovered them intrenched behind some bushes that hid them from our view. We held our position in their front till they brought down five times our numbers, when they made a dash on our line, and, just as our support was coming in sight, "scooped out" six officers and about forty men. I was in a thick piece of underbrush, closely watching matters in my front, when I heard a shouting behind me, and, as I turned round, a Rebel captain confronted me, and, presenting a loaded revolver at my breast, said, "Do you surrender?" Looking him calmly in the face, after a moment's reflection, I replied with a smile, "Of course I do. I don't see any sight for any thing else right here." "Give me up your sabre, then." I did so, and then the captain ordered two men to take me to the rear on the double-quick.

Captured.

"Come out of them boots," said one, as soon as he saw that I had on a pair of good ones. "Give up them boots." "I want them ar boots." "You 'Yank,' leave them boots." "You d—d son of a ——, take them boots off, or I'll blow your brains out," as he prepared to fulfill his threat. Such and like expressions greeted me upon my first introduction to Southern chivalry. I kept my boots, however, but had to appeal to an officer to save them. After the boot question had been settled, they turned their attention to arms, and found I had a belt and pistol, which they then took from me. They marched me back about half a mile, where I found Lieutenants West and Lewis, of my regiment, and soon after we were joined by Captain Britton also, 1st New York Dragoons, Captain Carpenter and Lieutenant Hazel, of the

6th Pennsylvania. We were tired completely out, had had nothing to eat since breakfast, and no immediate prospect of getting any thing for some time, and were nearly sun-struck. While sitting by a tree, an officer rode up to Lieutenant West, and, without saying a word, reached down and snatched a good new hat from off his (Lieutenant West's) head, put it upon his own, and replaced it by an old worn-out cap, which was so small it could with difficulty be kept upon his head at all, and then left. While awaiting orders, an officer rode up to me, when the following conversation took place between us:

Reb. " What regiment do you belong to?"
Fed. " A cavalry regiment, sir."
Reb. " What one?"
Fed. " One just over there, sir."
Reb. (*A little nettled*). " What is the *name* of it?"
Fed. " First New York Dragoons."
Reb. " Whose division is yours?"
Fed. " The first, sir."
Reb. " Who commands it?"
Fed. " I don't know, sir."
Reb. " Where is Wilson's division?"
Fed. " I don't know, sir."
Reb. " Where is Gregg's division?"
Fed. " I don't know, sir."
Reb. " Were we fighting Wilson's division this forenoon?"
Fed. " I don't know, sir."
Reb. " What are your folks going to do over there?"
Fed. " We are going to *fight* you, sir."

While we were resting a little while, our people sent

over their compliments in the shape of a shell, which at once started us, with our guards, farther to the rear.

We had not remained there long before we could see that the tide of battle had turned, and that our gallant boys were driving them. Back they came pell-mell, horses, artillery, and ambulances, drivers and skulkers, crying out, "The Yankees are coming—the Yankees are coming;" and *we* said, "Let them come, for *we* are not afraid of them."

While moving back, Captain Britton and myself in company were overtaken by a Rebel soldier, a mere boy, who was greatly excited. Seeing we were Yankees, he at once cocked his carbine, and, bringing it to his shoulder, swore that "these two Yanks should pay for the life of his brother just slain;" and, had not the guard interfered, there is no doubt but that he would have carried his threat into execution.

They marched us back, with their train and lead horses, till nearly dark, when we went on ahead to Spottsylvania Court-house, about five miles from the battlefield. We halted a few moments in a large field on our way, and here, for the first time, we began to comprehend our situation. We could hear the sharp firing of the carbines of our own brave comrades, and we hoped that soon again we might strike telling blows for our holy cause. But this privilege was to be denied us. We were no longer to campaign, march, fight, and win glorious victories with the "Army of the Potomac." We were torn away from them by *traitor* hands, and were now powerless and under their control. With sad hearts and bitter tears, we bade "good-by" to our brave comrades in the distance, regretting deeply that we could no longer share their toils and trials, and, as we *expected also*, their triumphs over Lee, and the downfall and capture of Richmond.

On our way we saw a rebel bearing one of the guidons of my regiment, which had been captured at the same time I was. We all noticed it, and kissed our hands to it as it passed out of sight, and bade it a long, last "good-by." One corporal had been killed, and the second one was shot through the arm, when the Rebels wrenched it from his hands.

We arrived at Spottsylvania Court-house soon after dark, and, after some delay in trying to find us quarters, they turned us out into an old orchard, backed us up against a board fence, put a guard around us, and told us we would stay there all night. We asked the sergeant of the guard who had us in charge for something to eat, as we had had nothing since breakfast; but he very politely informed us that "they could not get enough to eat for themselves," consequently could not divide with prisoners.

The night was cold and damp, and, as we had no blankets or extra clothing, the guards built us a small fire out of rails. I remarked to them that "they need not be so afraid of their rails, for our boys would be along there next week, and *they* would not spare *many* I was very sure."

"No," said Johnny Reb," "you'ens army will never come here, and by next Wednesday we will have Grant back across the Rapidan."

After an hour's talk over our condition, we prepared for our night's rest; but the air was too cold and damp for us to sleep much, and we welcomed the morning light as the harbinger of warmth, and more comfortable circumstances.

We started at daylight for Guinea's Station, twenty miles distant, without a mouthful of breakfast or any thing to appease our hunger, having been up to that time twenty-four hours without food. As the sun came up, the day began to be very hot; and, being cavalrymen, we were not much accustomed to marching on foot, our feet soon got sore and we tired out, so that the latter part of the distance we could not march over half a mile without stopping to rest. The guard marched us *very* fast, would not even allow us to stop at the creeks long enough to wash our faces. We reached the railroad at about 12 o'clock, so much exhausted we could not sit up, but threw ourselves upon the ground while the sergeant went to get us some rations. After a few moments' rest we were ordered on board the train. Soon after the sergeant came back and told us that, as it was Sunday, he could get nothing for us, but that when the train arrived at Hanover Junction rations would be put on board for us, and our wants would then be supplied.

The train left Guinea's Station at 2 P.M. for Richmond, but no rations did we see at Hanover. As we passed Ashland Station, a number of *ladies* (I suppose they called themselves such) came up to the train with delicacies for their sick and wounded, and, although we told them how long we had been without food, yet not one of them deigned to give us a particle, but made up faces at us, called us " Yankee thieves," murderers, scoundrels, etc.; and one, more bitter than the others, threw a handful of water in our faces, saying, " Take that, you miserable wretches." Some of the old men asked, "What you'ens all want to come down here and steal we'ens' farms, and run off our niggers, and burn our houses for?" As we did not feel in an argumentative mood, I suppose they were left in ignorance of the matter.

We arrived in Richmond about 4 30 P.M., just as the churches were out. The streets were filled with people, whose countenances betokened anxious hearts in regard to the terrible struggle that was then going on in the Wilderness. As we were the first prisoners sent to Richmond from the Wilderness, I suppose we were regarded with unusual interest. Guards were at once placed around us, with orders to allow no one outside to hold any intercourse with us. They marched us first to General Winder's office, detained us a few moments while a gaping crowd satisfied their curiosity, and then we passed on through some of the principal streets of the city. As we marched along we could hear the doors and windows open around us, while men, women, and children looked out upon us as Yankee prisoners. A troop of boys followed in our rear, hooting, hallooing, and calling us names.

After a walk of a mile or more we came up before a large three-story brick building, dark and frowning, and from the corner of which hung an old weather-beaten sign, "Libby & Son, Ship-chandlers." All at once I comprehended the fact that this was the *in*famous "Libby Prison," and we were to be confined in it as prisoners of war. I confess I did not like the idea of being a "ship-chandler" so far from home, but their arguments were too powerful, and we all entered the prison Sabbath, May 8th, 1864, to come out when—Ah! that was an interesting question to us.

CHAPTER II.

IN LIBBY PRISON.

As soon as we were inside the prison the officers were separated from the enlisted men, and we were not permitted after that to be near enough to them to hold any conversation with them. We were then marched into the office of the prison, where were registered our names, rank, company, and regiment, when and where captured. While waiting for my turn, I looked around the office, and through an open door in the rear I saw the battle-flag of the 25th Missouri, filled with bullet-holes and stained with blood. I gazed upon it with intense interest, for I thought it might be a long time before I should again see the "dear old flag" that I had followed for nearly two years, and for which so many precious lives had been given. My eyes filled with tears as I looked upon it, and, as I marched out of the office, I said to myself, "Good-by, old flag, till I see you again." We were then taken into the hall in the rear of the prison, and were politely requested to give up all the United States money we had in our possession. If we gave it up voluntarily they would keep it for us, and perhaps we might get it again, and perhaps not. If they searched and found it upon us, they would confiscate it. We gave it up at once, when they ordered us to strip for a search, which we did, and they *went through* us till they were satisfied. The sergeant then led the way, and we followed to the third story of the building, and, taking us to the northeast corner of the upper west room, told us "that place would be our quarters for the present." We then asked him for some rations, as it had been thirty-six hours since we had eaten any thing. He politely informed us "that it was past prison ration hours, and we would have to wait till next day." He then left us "alone in our glory." One remarked, "Well, boys, we are *here*," to which we all replied "we thought that was so beyond a doubt." "What are we to do?" said another. "*Stay here*," replied the third; and then we began to look around to see what we could find.

We had expected to find in prison some of the conveniences of a soldier's camp life, but we were sadly mistaken. We found not, in all the prison, a bunk, table, blankets, conveniences for eating, or any thing of the kind. Bare walls and a wet floor greeted us whichever way we looked.

The eight hundred Federal officers who had been confined there during the winter had, on the 7th inst., been sent to Georgia. The order that came to them the night before was to prepare to march twenty miles, to Petersburg. It was subsequently shown that the order was thus given, not because they were actually to *march* that distance, but because it would oblige the *Rebel officers*, if the prisoners had to leave behind a large quantity of the delicacies that they had received a short time before by "flag-of-truce boat" from kind friends at the North. But the Yankees were too sharp for them, for, upon consultation, it was decided to destroy what they could not carry. Accordingly, coffee, sugar, flour, butter, lard, soap, candles, tobacco, ham, every thing they had, was broken up, cut up, feather and cotton pillows ripped open and contents scattered over them, and then the whole trodden under foot. The bunks and benches they had made of their boxes were also destroyed, thrown in a pile, and, when they left the next morning, some venturesome fellow, not having the fear of Major Turner or the Rebel authorities before his eyes, set the pile on fire, but, *unfortunately*, it was discovered in time to save the building from any material damage.

"Libby Prison" takes its name from its former owner, who carried on the ship-chandler and tobacco business in it. It is located in that part of the city known as the Rocketts, it being in the southeast corner, on the bank of the "James River Canal," near the James River. From its windows we could look out across the river and see the green fields, leafy forests, and the beautiful summer residences of Manchester, a small village opposite Richmond.

The prison stands on such ground that it has three stories front and four in the rear. It is about 130 feet in length and 100 in width, built of brick, and contains six rooms, each 40 by 100 feet. The partitions are of brick, two feet thick. The lower west room is partitioned off and used for offices to the prison. The lower middle room was furnished with stoves, and was used for a kitchen. In one corner of this kitchen was a room or cell, in which were confined "General Kilpatrick's raiders."*

The lower east room was the prison hospital. The sashes from all the windows had been removed, and the places supplied by grates made of one-inch rods of iron, passing through three cross-bars, two and a half by three

---

* See Colonel Litchfield's experience.

fourth inches; the whole firmly imbedded in the walls. A flight of stairs led from each room to the one above, but at night those leading to the lower story were taken down, and sentinels were stationed to prevent any attempt to escape that way. A hydrant in each room supplied us with water from the river, and an apology for a bath-tub was placed in each for our use. A line of guards were stationed around the outside of the prison, with orders to shoot any who approached the windows from the inside. It was not an uncommon occurrence for them to send up a bullet to us when one ventured near to get a breath of fresh air.

It is generally known that Brigadier General Winder was Commissary General of Prisons, and we were under him, but the immediate command of the prison devolved upon Major Turner, one of Winder's pets. Dick Turner, a cousin of the major's, had the control of the inside of the prison, kept the records, counted us, issued orders governing us, acted as sutler, and robbed the officers generally, so far as he could do it, under any pretense whatever. I think he was one of the smoothest and most polished villains I have ever known. Several times I sent out money by him to purchase articles, and he usually kept any change that might be due, without even saying it was to pay charges.

Our rations while in "Libby" consisted of corn bread, beans, or cow pease, or, in lieu thereof, rice and bacon. The bread was made of unsifted meal mixed with water, without salt, and baked in cards of twelve loaves; each loaf being two and a half inches square by two inches thick, a single loaf constituting a ration. The beans were small, red or black, a little larger than a pea, with

B

a tough skin, a strong bitter taste, emitting a flavor very much like an old blue dye-tub. It was almost impossible for one to eat them *at first*, but hunger soon brought us to it. Those we got while in "Libby" were generally filled with black bugs which had eaten out the inside and then died. It was not an uncommon thing to see the pail of soup they brought up to us with the top spotted over with their cooked carcasses. When we got bacon, it was strong, rancid, and maggoty, and we received about two ounces per day. We had been there about a week before we received any meat, and when they brought in this, we were so rejoiced to get it that we gave it a hearty welcome.

We were put upon half rations as soon as we arrived, and before we left were reduced to quarter rations. Dr. Ferguson, of the 8th New York Cavalry, who was with us a short time, gave it as his opinion, that "the quantity of food we received there was not sufficient to keep one in good health." We were very hungry all the time, and often, when the bread came in on the wheelbarrow, did we crowd around it to snatch the crumbs that might chance to fall from it. What we did get was usually eaten at once, and then we went without till the next day. Before we left, some officers came in who were fortunate enough to have saved some of their money, and enlisting the services of the negroes who came in to sweep and mop the floors, managed to get something "*extra*" to eat. They allowed us papers, provided we would pay for them in advance; yet they had taken all our money from us, and there was little prospect of our getting it back, but we managed to get a paper somehow every day.

During the first week of our stay in "Libby," we were much elated at the prospect of Sheridan with his cavalry coming into the city and taking us out. Thursday morning, May 12th, we got the "*Examiner,*" and from its editorial news column we learned that Sheridan was indeed near the city, with a good prospect of capturing it. The authorities were very much alarmed, for the governor issued at daylight the following address:

"To the citizens of the state and people of Richmond:

"The enemy are undoubtedly approaching the city, and may be expected at any hour, with a view to its capture, its pillage, and its destruction. The strongest considerations of self and duty to the country *call every man to arms*—a duty which none can refuse without dishonor. All persons, therefore, able to wield a musket will immediately assemble upon the public square, where a regiment will be found in arms, and around which all can rally, and where the required direction will be given for arming and equipping those who respond to the call.

"The governor confidently relies that this appeal will not be made in vain.

"WM. SMITH, Governor of Virginia."

Upon this the "*Examiner*" remarked editorially as follows, viz.:

"Nor was the appeal in vain. In a short time the entire arms-bearing population of Richmond turned out, and repaired to the capitol square, where they awaited information from the enemy before they should march to the field. In a few hours came the following dispatch from General Stuart, at Ashland:

"'Headquarters, Ashland, May 11th, 1864, 6 30 A.M.

"'To General Bragg:

"'GENERAL,—The enemy reached this point just before us, but were promptly whipped out, after a sharp fight, by Fitz Lee's advance, killing and capturing quite a number. General Gordon is in the rear of the enemy. I intersect the road the enemy is marching on at Yellow Tavern, the head of the turnpike, six miles from Richmond. My men and horses are tired, hungry, and jaded, but *all right*. J. E. B. STUART.'

"Sheridan within six miles of Richmond, and pressing on!!"

When we read that, and saw the commotion in the streets—troops marching each way; a citizen guard put around the prison; officials of the prison looking sour and cross — we *rejoiced* over the prospect. "Will he come?" "Will he succeed in capturing the *hated* city?" passed from lip to lip, and, with intense anxiety, we waited for farther developments; at the same time we could hear the booming of Butler's guns—all of which served to keep us excited, and to while away the lonely hours of prison life. So great was our anxiety concerning the situation we could scarcely sleep, and when we got a morning paper, nothing was done till it was read aloud to *all*. There was about the prison a force of about twenty negroes, the most of whom had been free in the North; had entered the service as waiters for officers, and had been captured, and were kept to do the dirty work of the prison. These were always our friends, and kept us posted as to the situation, so far as they were able. Sometimes the rumors they brought us were of the wildest kind, but in the main they were more or less correct. The next day after this stir in the city they were more excited by the news of a raid upon the Danville Railroad by General Kautz and Colonel Spear. The "*Examiner*" thus whistled to keep its courage up:

"The situation is unchanged. The said situation is that precise state of things which has been predicted in this journal repeatedly during the last four months. The enemy is making a most determined effort to capture Richmond, and is employing extraordinary means to accomplish that purpose. They have collected several armies of the largest size known in modern times, and set them in motion from different points to attack this city, with peremptory injunctions to the generals that they do not return unless the main order is accomplished. To do this, every other enterprise has been abandoned. Since the commencement of the year, troops have been in motion toward Virginia from every corner of the United States. * * *

"If Richmond stands the storm, the whole military power of the United States is beaten, and the war is virtually ended. Perhaps the Confederate government has not been alive to the extent and reality of the grand fact; but nothing has been lost, and all will turn out well if it is never infected with the spirit of panic which seized upon the Southern Congress and Southern Executive when the true nature of the similar, though less dangerous crisis of 1862 became slowly palpable. Richmond is in no real danger so long as the authorities keep their heads and hold their hearts firm.

"In 1862, Congress adjourned at the first appearance of danger. Their last sessions were secret, and a bad rumor grew out of them, that they had been discussing a law to change the seat of government. Then commenced the irresolution of the executive. Congress adjourned on the 21st of April. On the 27th arrived the news of the fall of New Orleans; on May 5th Yorktown was evacuated; on the 11th Norfolk was deserted, and then the Merrimac was blown up. What followed is well remembered. The departments were all moved; the families of members of the government, with all their household goods, followed; and the train was kept in readiness for the government itself. Had it gone, the Southern Confederacy would now be not only *non extant*, but *forgotten.* * * *

"It is hoped that the recollection of these things will prevent the recurrence of some incidents in the history of these times. The Confederate authorities were inexperienced then, they are not so now. They know now where lies the true road to safety. They have vast forces at their command. The enemy, powerful indeed, has been firmly held at bay for a week, and can be kept back at bay for weeks more by the magnificent troops and splendid officers in the front. Time, fixed resolution, and energetic action by the central authorities, are all that the occasion requires to render Virginia the grave of those armies which now menace her capital. * * *

"The aim of the enemy in the neighborhood of Richmond is evidently to cut the railroads; but, even if they succeed, the effect will be temporary and trivial. Cavalry can not stay, and roads can be repaired."

The first intelligence from the "Army of Northern Virginia" was received in an "extra" from the office of the "*Enquirer*," headed as follows, in leaded capitals:

"Latest from General Lee's Army!!!
"Our Troops Victorious!!!
"Great Slaughter of the Enemy!!!

"Saturday, May 14th, 2 P.M.,
Guinea's Station, May 12th.

"Very little of interest transpired yesterday. Heavy skirmishing occurred at intervals during the whole of last night. This morning at daylight, the enemy, having massed heavy forces in front of Johnson's division, made a most vigorous assault upon Jones's brigade. For a while our line of battle was broken, and the enemy pressed over our breast-works, gaining possession of several pieces of artillery, and capturing a number of prisoners.*

"Forces were quickly sent to the relief of those thus engaged, and the enemy was driven back.

"About 10 o'clock this morning, the enemy made most vigorous and repeated assaults upon Field's division, but were driven back with great slaughter. At 2 P.M. the enemy are making a most desperate fight in Ewell's front, but all accounts agree that we are driving them back and punishing them with great slaughter. The musketry firing to-day was the heaviest of the war.

"The battle has extended along the whole line to-day, and has been fought by the Yankees with more *vim* and *bravery* than any other fought on Virginia soil. We captured 2000 of the enemy's wounded, left by them at the Wilderness. Yankee papers of the 7th instant contain letters written from Grant's head-quarters acknowledging a loss of 20,000 men in the Wilderness fight. Yankee

---

* Their account of the capture of Johnson's division by the 6th and 9th Corps.

prisoners say General Grant is putting fresh troops in the fight to-day. At 2 o'clock severe and continuous fighting has occurred all along our lines, but had every where been repulsed, and, *in some cases, we have driven the enemy before us.* * * *

"Our men are buoyant and resolute, and we have achieved grand results, but the enemy are still pressing the battle with desperation. Our loss to-day is not heavy, as we have been fighting mostly behind breast-works. The enemy are fighting in the open field, and their loss must be *terrible.* Hill's whole corps has been engaged all day recovering, in some instances, the ground lost by other troops; and Mahone's and Law's brigade, about 2 o'clock, made a most gallant charge, capturing about 300 prisoners, and a number of stand of colors.

"Second Dispatch!

"Battle-field, Spottsylvania Court-house,
May 13th, *via* Guinea's Station, May 14th.

"The battle yesterday lasted all day and late into last night. Our men, after a temporary repose in front of Johnson's division, successfully resisted every onset of the enemy, who repeatedly assaulted our lines with troops massed in, as some say, as many as ten columns deep. Our boys stood nobly to their work, piling the enemy's dead thickly before our breast-works. The lowest estimate of the enemy's loss in the battle of yesterday is 20,000. These figures are corroborated by a Yankee colonel wounded and in our hands. Our losses are estimated at 2000. There was continuous fighting for ten hours on one point yesterday, and so severe was the musketry fire that trees were cut down by it. Prisoners say that General Grant expressed a determination not to re-cross the river while he has a man left.

"Our troops fought yesterday with more than usual bravery and gallantry, and the enemy fought more stubbornly than ever. Our men are as resolute as ever, while accounts from the Yankee side show that their troops are growing dispirited."

The following article I copy from the "*Examiner*" of May 16th, to show their appreciation of General Grant's tactics, and their manner of figuring up our losses. In speaking of the battle of the 12th instant, it says:

"Grant had received a full corps of fresh troops, kept back up to that moment to defend the trenches of Washington, and risked, with the recklessness of a true gambler, on the cast of a die. He attempted no manoeuvre, he relied on main strength, bringing up his ten lines at a run, each one close behind another, and dashed them, like the waves of the sea against the rocks, on the breastworks of the South.

"By these tactics, either a perfect victory is won or an attacking army is lost. The first rush was successful on one point. The enemy broke through the blaze of the living volcano upon Johnson's men, leaped the works, took 2000 men and 10 guns. But reserves were ready, and a charge of greater fury than their own drove them out in brief time. On all other parts of the line they were entirely unsuccessful; they were *utterly repulsed!* with scarcely any loss to the Confederates, who fired with the advantages of rest, aim, and cover, but with a slaughter of the foe which is represented by universal testimony to have been the most terrible of modern warfare.

"In these two battles the Army of Northern Virginia has enjoyed the advantage of firing into the enemy with grape and rifle-balls from lines of substantial breast-works; and, if one may judge from the high spirits and unbounded confidence of the wounded who have come to this city from the battle, it has been highly gratified by the new position. 'We just mowed them every time.' Such is the only account they give of the struggle.

"The Confederate loss, killed, wounded, and missing, in all these battles, beginning with the Wilderness, and including that of last Thursday at Spottsylvania Courthouse, was under 15,000. The *Washington Chronicle*, the organ of Lincoln, that sees all these things in the rose's color, announces the depletion of Grant's army, by the battle of the Wilderness and 'other causes,' to have been on Tuesday evening ascertained at 35,000. To this awful figure must now be added the two days of unsuccessful assault on the breast-works of Spottsylvania—assault without manœuvre, full in front, with deep columns, each forcing the other on the muzzle of the guns, wherein the carnage and the loss *must*, in the necessity of things, have been many times greater than in the open battles of the Wilderness and succeeding days. Putting the two data together, it is impossible to doubt the deduction that Grant's depletion by killing, wounding, and 'other causes'—that is to say, by straggling, desertion, etc., has *surpassed* 70,000. * * *

"Nevertheless, we have no idea that Lee and Grant have yet settled their accounts in full. Grant will get up the last rakings of the Northern army, and try again. He is said to have made every body about him understand that he will not recross the river while he has a living man under his orders.

"There are butchers of humanity, to whom the sight of their fellow-creatures' blood affords an intoxicating pleasure. They are indifferent whose blood it is, so it does not come from their veins. And Grant is one of those charming individuals. His government and his generals will not balk him in the present instance. A large part of the army now in his hands is composed of the regiments enlisted for three years, and their time expires in this coming summer. They have resisted every inducement to re-enlist, and have formally notified the Secretary of War that they will obey orders so long as they are legally given, *but no longer*. The government is entirely willing that Grant should save it the trouble and mortification of giving the discharge to these veterans. He *will* use them, and he is using them."

Such was the *news*, the kind of lying trash we had to read from one of the leading journals of the capital of the Southern Confederacy.

Begging pardon of my readers for copying so much, I wish to show them one more article from this same paper, and, read in the light of the developments from the time it was written to the present, May, 1865, it proves just what it says: *They hate the Northern people.* It is entitled "*The Price of Liberty.*"

"The Yankee warfare is becoming desperate. The press reports from North Georgia declare that, in their advance through the country, they levy contributions as they march, and burn all the mills, factories, and *residences*. One can imagine the devastation. What stealing of spoons and forks; what chopping of pianos; what burning of libraries, appropriating of pictures and wearing apparel; women taking shelter, cowering and shivering in the woods, with their homeless little ones, and looking out from their covert upon the blazing roof-trees of their own houses.

"Such is the great feature of this campaign *every where*. On the Peninsula also, and on either bank of the York and James Rivers, destruction of private property and outrages upon peaceful citizens have been reduced to a more perfect system than ever before; and the constant employment of negroes in these operations of war has given them an additional character of brutal ferocity which is grateful to the Yankee soul in its present mood. Seeing that they can not subjugate the South, they mean to make it a desert, and a wilderness of ruins and ashes. They are happy in the thought that they can revenge the slaughter of their troops in open battle by torturing the unarmed and helpless people along their line of march. If they can not trust their negro brigands to *fight*, they can at least trust them to burn, murder, crucify, and ravish. This we call desperation. It must be they have given up all hope of conquering these Confederate States, and that, feeling the effort is a failure, their malignant hearts can devise nothing better than to hurt and harm us to the utmost extent in their power, and make our independence cost us dear. And the cost is the very bitterest we could be called on to pay—the agonies and terrors of our unprotected people. If it be any pleasure or glory to them, we may freely avow that we have been deeply hurt in our affections and in our pride, on the continually recurring tale of our noble and devoted people, subjected to the brutal atrocities of that offscouring of creation which makes up the Yankee armies. It is sad enough to have our people burned out and pillaged, our women bullied and insulted, but it is doubly humiliating to suffer such evils at the hands of a people we have *always* despised. It does, indeed, cost us heavily to rid ourselves of all connection with the Yankee nation; but then this riddance is worth the cost, and perhaps we should never have set the right value upon the independence we fight for, if it had not cost us so dear. We might never have been so fully and deeply conscious of the great necessity that was upon us, for our honor and our children's well being, to cut off that abandoned nation from our society, if it had not been permitted to develop and display, at so many points, and for so long a time, all the dark depths of its hateful character—all its dastard cruelty, and mean thievery, and unparalleled fertility of falsehood.

"Now we know fully from what a rotten carcass we have cut ourselves loose; and, to escape its pollution, no price is too great.

"Rather than submit to that foul embrace again, we would bid higher, and still higher, until nothing was left to the few survivors of us but bare life.

"In this sense, we may almost be said to be under some sort of obligation to the Yankee nation. It has more than justified our secession, and has left in the regions of our country which have once fallen within its military lines certain bitter and burning memories, which, in ages to come, will cause mothers to teach their little children to thank God in their nightly prayers for the rescue of their native land out of the clutches of an evil generation. The many unmistakable symptoms of desperation visible in this year's campaign; the employment of Grant himself with absolute dictatorial powers, because he was known to be the man who would either effect his purpose or throw away his army, the insane drunkenness with which he drowned the senses of his troops before he hurled them against the muzzles of Confederate cannon, the reckless and unsparing ferocity with which quiet country places are devastated, and covered with smoking ruins, and soaked with the blood of unresisting people; all these things *ought* to encourage us. They consist well with what the enemy's public press has plainly avowed, that if the grand combined movement of '64 should fail, then *all* was lost; that armies could no longer be raised to continue the invasion, that anarchy and financial ruin would break up their whole social system, and that the United States would be no more a nation!

"And that campaign, may we not already say, HAS failed; its force is expended and broken. Of its four grand armies, one in the Trans-Mississippi is no longer an army; another at Bermuda Hundreds has no care save to protect itself from destruction; in front, by intrenchments; in rear, by a fleet. The two other armies, and the two greatest, have advanced indeed, with tremendous waste of men and material, to the points at which Lee and Johnston, at the head of fresh and eager troops, say to them, 'No farther hitherto shalt thou go!'

"All the *elan*, all the drunken vigor of the opening campaign is gone; the pluck is taken out of it, and the invincible Yankee hosts, or what is left of them, can do no better than to turn upon the already plundered population in their rear, rob a few houses, ravish a few women, crucify a few '*secesh*' planters, and go home. * * *

"On the whole, we can afford to make the rogues welcome to all the profits they have got out of their invasion, especially as with the last day of the campaign, our cost ends and theirs begins. Nations, having no future state, always expiate their crimes in this world, and no nation ever run up such an account of crime, or so richly deserved a hell upon earth. 'There shall be weeping and gnashing of teeth.'"

In keeping with the above is the following, clipped from the same paper of March, 1864:

"Goodies for the Ghouls.

"The last 'flag-of-truce boat' brought up several tons of precious freight for the prisoners confined at 'Libby' and Americus, Ga.

"Boxes of fine raiment for the scabs and riff-raff of Germany and the North; hampers of cured meats and delicacies for the blue-bellied and gold-braided officers who commanded the '*scabs.*' The Confederate government is the consignee, and the United States government the consignor. Happy commercial relation! At the time these boxes were being gingerly handled by the official stevedores at City Point, unclean hands were plundering the boxes sent to our poor prisoners at Point Lookout and other places. At the same time a portion of the vandal horde were rearing and pitching over the unprotected portions of the Confederacy, burning mills, houses, barns, destroying property, stealing horses, and insulting God and man by their high-handed deviltry and outlandish vandalism.* Truly we are a Christian people, and our rulers the most exemplary of all the earth."

About 10 o'clock this forenoon we had a large re-

* Kilpatrick's raid.

enforcement to our number. Hearing an unusual noise in the street, while one watched for the guard, another determined to look out of the window and learn its cause. Soon he reported that a long row of officers and men had just come in. The officers were soon sent up to us, numbering twenty-one, among them a brigadier general. We were all driven into the middle and east rooms, and the doors connected with the west rooms nailed up, and the enlisted men were confined there. From these officers we learned that Grant had not been whipped as badly as the Rebel papers represented, but was still on the move toward Richmond.

The armies seemed to be in good spirits, and confident of final success. Even the prisoners were jubilant, for soon after being put into "Libby" they began to sing "Rally round the flag" and other patriotic pieces. From these officers also we obtained two Northern papers, the "*Baltimore American*," of the 14th inst., and the "*Springfield Republican*." We read and reread them with interest, till there was nothing left of them. Upon the arrival of these "boarders," it was found necessary to divide ourselves into *messes*, which we did at once. I was appointed commissary of the prison inside, and my duties consisted in bringing up stairs the corn bread, beans, rice, and whatever we had to eat, and then dividing it, giving each his portion. When these twenty-one came in, they did not issue them any thing to eat till the next day. We divided our little all with them, and went without supper and breakfast till we drew again. And this was common; for often prisoners would be brought in after having been marched twenty-five or thirty miles without any thing to eat, and then kept twenty-four hours more without receiving rations.

About this time the Rebel commissary informed me that we could draw our rations raw if we chose, and cook them on the stoves in the kitchen below. We concluded to try the rice and beans raw, and let them bake the bread. I experimented all one day in trying to cook a mess of the beans, and make them fit to eat. I first looked them over very carefully, throwing out the "buggy" ones, which took over one half. I then washed them three times, boiled them, pouring off the water as many more times, and yet, when done, they were about as bad as ever. The water, or soup, was thick, strong, and almost black; very unpleasant to smell, much more so to eat. I concluded to give up the beans till I was starved more than I yet had been. Daily we found our strength failing, for we were hungry, *hungry*, HUNGRY all the while. We had no lights in the prison, and, consequently, we retired soon after dark, and often you would hear one in the morning tell of his dream of home and plenty, which, alas! *was all a dream.*

About a week after this, in the kindness of their hearts, they brought up to us some old lousy pieces of blankets, rusty tin plates, and a few old knives and forks, or pieces of them, articles left by the other officers. We were glad to get even these, for we had been eating with our fingers, and bits of sticks, or any thing we could find, and sleeping on the bare floor. A few days before we left, they gave us a little bacon in lieu of the beans. So rejoiced were we to get it, we paid our respects to it by giving it hearty cheers, maggoty and rancid though it was. Dick Turner promised us the use of our money nearly every day, but not a dollar of it could we get. It seems that they cared little for our comfort or convenience, and tried to fret and annoy us in all the ways they possibly could.

CHAPTER III.

FROM RICHMOND TO MACON.

On the morning of the 31st of May we were aroused at 5 o'clock by the sergeant, and ordered to get ready to go South at once. We had barely time to roll up our blankets when the drum sounded, and we were ordered to fall in and march down stairs in single file. As we passed out of the front door of the middle room we each received half a loaf of corn bread, and a slice of bacon one fourth of an inch thick and one and one half inches square, for a day's ration.

I had been an inmate of "Libby" but three weeks; yet when my feet struck the pavement I nearly fell, and many of those who had been confined there six or eight months could scarcely stand when they first reached the ground.

On both sides of the street was formed the guard, standing about five paces apart, who were to go with us to Danville. There were at this time but sixty-two officers in Libby, and one of these, who was too sick to accompany us, was left behind and sent to the hospital.

While waiting for orders to march, they brought up in the rear of our column 700 enlisted men, who were to go on the same train with us. They marched us over the James River to Manchester, and halted us alongside of the Danville Railroad, made up a train of box-cars and loaded us in, putting forty enlisted men in a car; but to the officers they were a little more generous, giving us two cars. They were very filthy, and had no seats or any thing for us to sit on, yet we got along very comfortably. Before we left we could hear the dull, heavy thunder of Grant's guns, and knew he was not far from the city; and we interpreted the move as one to place us in a safer prison. We had not been in Libby forty-eight hours before they began to talk "*exchange*" to us; and when we spoke of sending for boxes, they told us we would not be prisoners long enough to receive them.

When we found we were to go South our hearts sunk within us, for it seemed to us that we were going beyond the reach of "exchange; but there was no help for it, and here we were on our way. We had an opportunity to see some of the enlisted men who had spent the winter on Belle Isle. They looked as though they had had a hard time to live, for they were pale and sickly looking, and very many of them, from long suffering with the chronic diarrhœa, were so weak that they could scarcely walk.

The weather was intensely hot, and the guards would allow but one of the car doors open at a time; so these poor, and many of them sick men, had to ride for twelve hours, suffering for the pure air of heaven; but this was only the beginning of sorrows.

When we parted from our Libby Prison officials, they promised that our money, boxes, and letters should all be sent through to us with as little delay as possible. How well they kept their word the sequel will show.

We left Manchester at 7 30 A.M., the 31st of June, just as the battle of Cold Harbor was opening. We soon found that traveling on a Rebel railroad was very different from what it would be on one in our Northern States. Their rolling stock was nearly worn out, the rails broken, splintered, and battered, the ties rotten, and, altogether, it was a dangerous matter to ride at all upon them, to say nothing of speed. For greater safety, their fastest trains were limited to twelve miles an hour by Act of Congress. Their stops are frequent, for their wheezy old engines use double the fuel they would if they were in good repair; and their wood and water stations are separate, thus making a stop every four or five miles.

During this ride we suffered for water, for the day was intensely hot, and we had nothing to get it in, but had to drink it from our hands or from the holes by the side of the track. The stations along this route are not villages such as you find on our Northern roads, but consist of five or six houses dignified with a name high sounding enough for a corporation. The dépôts are small, unpainted buildings, with but few conveniences and much dilapidation.

About twenty miles from Richmond we passed the scene of Kautz's and Spear's raid. The track had been repaired, but tanks, dépôts, and wood-piles were wanting. While waiting a few moments, I politely inquired of a gentleman standing by the name of the place.

"Coal Fields, sir," he replied.

"Ah, indeed! this is near the place of Kautz's raid a few days since," I said.

(*Reluctantly speaking*), "Yes; but I guess some of his rascals won't raid it any more."

"Grant is raiding it *now*," said I, "in front of Richmond; we heard his guns this morning as we left the city."

"Well," he said, "he never can take Richmond if—"

"*Baa! baa!*" from a hundred voices as the train moved off.

The country through which we passed was very poor, the cultivated portions of it being planted to corn by the negroes. Here we saw the practical benefit of the Emancipation Proclamation. Very few white men were to be seen. The negroes were the power that supplied the Rebel armies with food, and our noble President reasoned well when he proposed to cripple them by inducing this class to run away from the South.

We obtained a little relief from the oppressive heat in the cars by kicking off some of the boards, thus letting in fresh air.

We arrived at Danville about one o'clock the next (Wednesday) morning. We were not allowed to leave the train till seven, when we were marched to another train in waiting to take us to Greensboro', North Carolina. After we were on board they issued to us half a loaf of corn bread warm from the oven, and a small piece of cooked bacon, in quality much better than any we had ever received at Libby. Here our old guard was relieved by some Virginia militia under command of Lieutenant Gay, 3d Virginia Infantry (Hampton's Legion).

Danville is situated on the south side of the Dan River, one hundred and forty-eight miles from Richmond, and had at this time a population of about five thousand. It had increased in numbers since the war, many of the refugees from Northern Virginia coming here with their families to escape from the immediate horrors of the battle-field. It had several government hospitals, and at times Federal prisoners have been confined here, but at this time nearly all had been sent farther South. It was also a dépôt for supplies *in transitu* from Georgia and North Carolina.

The road connecting Danville with Greensboro' is a new one, built in 1863, '4, by the Rebel government, and we were among the first that went over it. The train did not make over eight miles per hour. We met several negroes, who said they were on their way to Richmond to work on the fortifications. They were on foot, and carried whatever they had in bags or packs on their backs.

We arrived at Greensboro' about 1 o'clock P.M., and were ordered from the train and marched to a little grove to rest and wait for a train to be made up for us. As soon as we were bivouacked there began a sharp business in trading. Some of the inhabitants came around with something to eat. Our rations received at Danville were barely sufficient for a single meal, and the sight made us very hungry. Watches, knives, rings, jewelry, pocket-books, any thing that could be spared, was sold for rations. We paid for onions five dollars per half dozen, scallions at that; bacon, four dollars per pound; crackers, homemade, two dollars per dozen; biscuit, three dollars and fifty cents per dozen. Many of us took a nap, while the enlisted men spent a portion of their time in *skirmishing*, a duty all prisoners soon learn, while several ladies strolled by and watched the process.

Night came, and, there being no prospect of a train, we composed ourselves to rest. About eleven o'clock we were aroused, to take the train at one. After some delay we were marched to the cars, and halted before an old rickety thing with two large holes in the bottom, and ordered to embark. About forty succeeded in getting into the car, when the lieutenant in charge of us was told that the car was full. He said it was *not*, and more should ride there. Ten or twelve more were crowded in, when it was declared that no more *could* ride there. The lieutenant then ordered in two of his guards, and told them to use their muskets in driving the men back, *for the whole sixty-one must and should ride in that car*, no matter what the consequences might be. After a good deal of swearing on his part, and no little grumbling on ours, the whole sixty-one *were* crowded into the car; but for more than one quarter of us to sit down at the same time was out of the question, to say nothing of trying to sleep in that condition; but this was not all of our trouble, *for the guards must ride with us.* They attempted to get standing room near the door, but could not; and finally, referring the case to the lieutenant, he gave permission for four of the officers to ride on top of the car, thus leaving room for the guard, and in that packed, suffocating condition, we were to ride to Charlotte, North Carolina. We finally started from Greensboro' about two o'clock the next morning, ran about ten miles, then came to a dead stand. The engine was unable to draw us. It was uncoupled and started off to get up steam, and after an hour returned, and we went on at the rate of about eight miles per hour.

"The night, the long dark night, at last
Passed fearfully away.
* * * * * *
We hailed the dawn of day,
Which broke to cheer the suffering crew
And wide around its gray light threw."

A drenching storm came on during the night, which,

though uncomfortable to those on the outside, seemed to cool the atmosphere, and make it more tolerable to us inside.

This morning we found ourselves passing through a low, flat country, but little cultivated, and at nine o'clock crossed the Yadkin River, and arrived at Salisbury, North Carolina. While waiting here for a train to pass, I learned that the town contained about five thousand inhabitants, and was the site of the State Penitentiary, which has been occupied more or less during the war by Federal prisoners. Lately a stockade had been built, where many more were confined—another of those "*hells*" where the Rebels have murdered so many of our brave men. Salisbury was also a place of punishment for Rebel deserters, who were brought here to serve out the balance of their time with ball and chain attached to them. They were kept at work breaking stone, carrying wood, or some such duty, which their punishment did not prevent them from doing with some freedom.

Here, for the first time, we saw a Rebel flag floating in the breeze from the top of a staff, and we treated it with *contempt*. While we were thus waiting for the train, a citizen came and inquired for Colonel White, 55th Pennsylvania Volunteers. Colonel White immediately responded to the call, and, stepping out of the car, stood within two feet of the door. While thus engaged in earnest conversation with his friend (an old acquaintance), with guards all around him, a boy, by the name of Arnold, sitting on the top of the car, being one of the train guards, chanced to spy him, and, standing up, ordered him into the car, with the threat that, if he did not go *at once*, he would come down and beat his brains out with his musket. The colonel did not hear him, or at least did not pay any attention to the threat, when the boy came down from the car, and, seizing him roughly by the arm, gave him a push toward the car door, saying, "Go in there, you d—d Yankee son of a ——."

Captain Belger (of Belger's Battery, 1st Rhode Island), who was looking out of a hole that had been made to let in the air, and who chanced to see the proceeding, very quietly remarked to another officer standing by, "that he thought that rather rough for a boy." The boy heard the remark, and, calling for his musket, cocked it, and, bringing it to his shoulder with his finger on the trigger, said, "He would learn a Yankee how to talk to him." Captain Belger dodged back, and the villain was about to shoot into the loaded car, when Captain Carpenter, 6th Pennsylvania Cavalry, who was sitting on the top of the car, remarked "that he saw no cause for such treatment as that." "I'll show you," said the young Rebel, pointing his gun at him.

"Please point that gun the other way," said Captain Carpenter, in the politest manner possible.

"D—n you, don't you talk to me in that way," said the Rebel, and, letting down the hammer of his musket, he came up to Captain Carpenter, and struck him three times on his feet and legs, when the captain drew them up out of his way. Supposing the matter was all over, he took no farther notice of it; but the young villain climbed up on the car, came behind the captain, and struck him twice over the back of the head with his musket, knocking him senseless upon the car, and then walked off with a "*There, d—n you, take that!*" A rush was made by the officers for the captain, and he was saved from falling from the top of the car. Water was brought, and he was soon restored to consciousness, but suffered from the injury for several days.

There was a moment when all felt like killing young Arnold on the spot, but better judgment prevailed, and no violence was offered—much the safest and best way for us under the circumstances. Shortly after, Lieutenant Gay came round, and, learning there had been some disturbance between the officers and the guard, went to Arnold and inquired into the matter, and he told him his story. Without asking any farther questions, he stood in front of us all, called the attention of his guard, and addressed them as follows: "I have heard of this affair of Arnold's. He did just right. I don't want any of you to take a word from the d—d Yankees. If they don't mind you at the first word, put a bullet through them, d—n 'em. Arnold did just right." He then came up where Captain Carpenter was lying, to see if he was much hurt.

While there, one of his guards, who was sitting close by Captain Carpenter all the time that Arnold was talking to him, attempted to tell Lieutenant Gay that Captain Carpenter was not to blame *at all*, for he did not insult the guard; when the lieutenant turned around, and told him to shut up his d—d head, for he (the guard) knew nothing about the matter. We began to think that our lives were not worth much in his hands.*

We left Salisbury at 12 M., passing through a wet, marshy section of country, interspersed with pine groves. After we left Salisbury, Lieutenant Gay allowed six or

---

* A citizen standing by remarked that such things would not continue long; that we had friends even there.

eight more to ride on the top of each car. At one of the stopping-places, permission was given to four enlisted men to climb to the top. Three of them had succeeded in reaching it safely; the fourth one was a sickly, weakly boy, hardly able to walk. The lieutenant, in company with a guard, was watching him, when the whistle blew, and the train started. Instead of leaving him to make his way up alone, as he was likely to succeed in doing, he at once ordered the guard to shoot him, which he did. The poor fellow dropped upon the track, and the cars passed over him. We received no rations till dark that night, being thirty-six hours with nothing to eat.

We arrived at Charlotte about four o'clock in the midst of a rain-storm; but we were very glad to get out of the packed cars, for we felt almost dead. We were then marched to a little grove, and waited patiently for our rations till dark, when we received, for two days, four hard tacks, four inches by six, made of bran and middlings, black, mouldy, and rotten, and one fourth of a pound of bacon.

We made sure of *one* full meal, that is certain, and then lay down on the wet ground to sleep. My chum and I each had a blanket, so we slept comfortably, till about half past two the next morning, when it began to rain very hard. It awoke us, and we discussed the question as to what we had better do, but finally concluded to *let it rain*, and sleep what we could. We covered up our heads, and finally awoke at daylight, to find ourselves wet to the skin, and four inches of water in the centre of the bed; but we found no fault with that, for we were used to rough weather.

We started soon after daylight for Columbia, the capital of South Carolina, and found our accommodations no better than on the other train, except that a few more were permitted to ride on the top of the cars. Of Charlotte I shall have occasion to again speak. A few miles' ride brought us into the notorious State of South Carolina—the one which led the van in the *hellish work* of secession, and, up to this time, had eaten the least of its fruits. We had anticipated seeing much of the spirit of hatred manifested toward us in our passage through this state, but we were most happily disappointed. At no point along our route had we found the people so willing to attend to all our wants as they were in this. At almost every station we found white people or negroes with snacks* to sell, at moderate prices to what some had obliged us to pay. In fact, had we not possessed the means of thus buying food, we must have suffered very much on the road. I know the poor private soldiers did not get half enough to eat any day they were with us. The people seemed more anxious to obtain "greenbacks" than any we had seen before—quite a significant fact.

During this day's travel we passed through some very pleasant little villages, Chester and Winnsboro' being the principal ones. At the latter, a young lady flaunted in our faces a little Rebel flag; but each one treated the act with silent contempt, not deigning to notice it by making a single remark.

We reached Columbia at dark, and changed cars again, but from bad to worse. The car to which we were transferred had been used for transporting cattle

---

* A snack consisted of a piece of bread and meat, or cold potatoes, cake, pie, any thing you could take in your hand to eat.

and mules, and had not been cleaned out. The guards were dirty, lousy, and abusive, and the air was damp and thick. We had but one door open, and that was filled by the guards, and orders were issued to *allow no one to leave the car under any circumstances whatever.* Many of the officers were sick with diarrhœa, and we were literally packed into the car. All of these things made the night one of horror, long to be remembered by us all.

Morning found us at Branchville, the junction of the South Carolina Railroad with the Charleston branch. It consists of one very good house, used as a dépôt and hotel, three or four others much inferior, and the usual number of negro huts. As we passed on toward Augusta, the country began to look better, and more cultivated.

Lieutenant Gay gave us another specimen of his notions of chivalry to-day in ordering the guard to shoot one of our privates who had gotten off the train to attend the calls of nature, and was likely to be left. The guard had more humanity than the wretch who commanded him, and refused to shoot; whereupon the train was stopped for the poor sick man to come up, and then orders were issued to *shoot the first man who attempted to get out on the ground.*

The day was quite pleasant, and passed off without much occurring worthy of record, except that some of the privates jumped from the train while it was running, and the guards would shoot at them, but did not hurt one of them. We finally arrived at Augusta, Georgia, about 4 o'clock P.M., so tired and hungry we could scarcely stand up. As soon as we crossed the river we were ordered to leave the cars, and were placed in an old cotton-shed, to remain till the next day. It was, indeed, a relief to us to have the prospect of a night's rest after our long journey. We were turned over to Captain Bradford, son of ex-Governor Bradford, Maryland, provost marshal of the city, and glad were we to get out of the hands of the villain Gay. A citizen guard was placed around us as we were marched to our quarters.

The people flocked around to see the Yankees, and we had reason to believe that some of them were disposed to do us all the good they could. A hose was at once attached to a hydrant near by, and plenty of water was furnished us, of which we availed ourselves immediately, taking the first wash we had had since leaving Libby Prison. They then brought in to us a sufficient ration of hard bread and bacon, of splendid quality, to which we did ample justice. The enlisted men had the same issued to them. Supper over, we lay down, and had a good night's rest.

Augusta, the capital of Richmond County, is the second town for size in the state. It stands on the southwest bank of the Savannah River, one hundred and twenty-seven miles from Savannah. The town is well laid out. The streets are wide, crossing each other at right angles, and ornamented with trees. Many of the houses are spacious and elegant. The public buildings are, a city hall, a masonic hall, academy, court-house, jail, theatre, arsenal, hospital, female asylum, building for free-schools, two markets, five banks, and seven houses for public worship. Steam-boats can run up to the city.*

* This description of Augusta is taken from the *Georgia Gazette* of 1860.

Sabbath morning dawned upon us bright and beautiful, yet we were still prisoners of war. As we listened to the "sounds of the church-going bell," memory went back to many a little church in the Northern States in which were gathered loved ones; but, alas! the circle was broken, we were not there. About nine o'clock visitors commenced flocking around the shed, peeping through the cracks at us, and watching all our movements; yet they treated us with a kind of respect that softened, in some degree, the horrors of our situation. They seemed anxious to converse with us about the war, and wished to know the popular feeling at the North concerning it, and we were not slow in telling them the truth. I had the substance of the following conversation with a lawyer who was on guard near the gate. After a little desultory conversation concerning my capture, where I lived, etc., he asked,

Reb. "Do you think Grant will ever take Richmond?"

Off. "Most assuredly I do; just as much as I expect to go to Macon, and I am almost there now. A few hours will complete the journey if nothing happens."

Reb. "Well, what are you'ens all fighting for? What do you'ens all want to come down here and steal our niggers, destroy our property, and ravish our women for? You never can whip us; we never will submit to be governed again by Yankees." And then, waxing warm, he continued, "You'ens have conducted this war as no other nation ever did a war before. Such barbarity, such cruelty, such meanness as burning our private property, stealing our niggers, arming them and sending them down to butcher us, to incite insurrection, and drive us from our own homes and country. *No, sir!*

you may kill us, you may *annihilate* us, *but you never can* SUBJUGATE US."

Off. "Very well, sir, if annihilation is the word, you need not complain if we accept the terms. *You* are to pay the price, not we, and you can bid just as high as you choose. It does not take long to annihilate a man when you once get at him."

Reb. "But how long do you intend to fight over this question?"

Off. "This summer's campaign."

Reb. "Do you think the war will close this year?"

Off. "I do, sir."

Reb. "But what if you do not accomplish what you think you will this summer? What then? General Lee and Johnston may hinder your plans somewhat."

Off. "Then we will fight next summer; and if that does not whip you into the traces, we will try the third one; in short, we will fight you as long as we live; and if the war does not close before we are too old and disabled to fight, our little children will be trained to bear arms and fight you too; and *that*, sir, I believe, is the sentiment of the *majority* of the Northern people. Fight you? Yes, sir, we intend to fight you till rebellion is crushed and treason punished; and, to accomplish this work, it is the policy of our government to use *all* the means within its reach, the use of public and private property, destroying what it can not use, any and every thing that you use, directly or indirectly, to support the war. Yes, thank God! we *will* use the negroes, for they love this kind of work, and are our most faithful allies. Unless you repent soon and return to your allegiance, something worse than the loss of property may overtake you. Our people North have suffered much to bring you back again; but beware, sir, that you do not go beyond the limit of our forbearance, and that public sentiment does not cry out 'let them alone,' 'let *just* punishment be meted out to them,' for 'they are joined to their idols.' You may yet feel the *power* of that government you have aimed to destroy.

"Before we will consent, sir, we will *multiply* the blood and treasure that has been so freely offered. Our glorious old flag, it *must*, and it SHALL, yet wave over a united people North and South."

Here the officer of the guard interrupted us, ordering me away, and not to talk with the guard any more, dispersing the crowd which had by this time gathered around us of both citizens and prisoners.

At 12 M. they issued us another day's rations of hard bread and meat, and then marched us into the street, where a large crowd was waiting to see us; but, after standing a little while, we were sent back again, and remained till 5 P.M., when we were marched to the dépôt in a most drenching shower, while the enlisted men remained behind, to come up on Monday. They furnished us with two large, clean, nice box-cars, and the guard put in seats for us, a luxury we had not enjoyed before since we started. They were uniformly kind and obliging, and treated us with great respect. This was, by far, the most pleasant part of our journey. Monday morning, at nine o'clock, found us at Macon, Georgia, our point of destination. As we came in sight of the prison stockade my heart sunk within me, for it seemed like being buried alive to go inside of it; but there was no relief, and here we were at the office, waiting for the calling of the roll.

CHAPTER IV.

AT MACON

AFTER standing a few moments at the office of the prison, the roll was called, and in squads of five we were marched through the gate, inside the stockade, where we were at once greeted with cries of "Fresh fish!"* "Give

Fresh Fish.

* The first six months of prison life one is called a "fresh fish," the next four months a "sucker," the next two a "dry cod," and the balance of his time a "dried herring." After exchange he becomes a "pickled sardine."

CAMP OGLETHORPE, MACON, GEORGIA.

'em air!" "Don't take his blanket away from him!" "Keep that louse off from him!" etc.—remarks which astonished us, coming as they did from United States officers; and our astonishment being discovered by them, turned a good hearty laugh upon us.

This prison, or stockade, was built in May, 1864, and was located three quarters of a mile east of the city, on what was known as the old Fair Ground. It embraced two acres and seven eighths inside of the "dead line," by actual measurement. It was surrounded, or inclosed rather, by a stockade built of boards, twelve feet high, and so tight we could not look through the cracks even.

On the outside of this, and at sufficient height to enable the guards to overlook the camp, was built a platform for the guard line. Upon this were posted sentinels at intervals of about ten yards, whose duty it was constantly to watch us and see that we did not attempt to escape. At the northwest corner, near the gate, and also on the east side, were posted two 12-pounder brass pieces that could sweep the camp; and, a few days before the 4th of July, three others were posted on a little hill in the rear of the camp, but, fortunately for us, they did not use them while we were there.

Inside of this stockade, and about twenty feet from it, was the *in*famous "dead line," which, in this case, was an ordinary picket-fence three and a half feet high. Often it is only a line of stakes, and sometimes a single board nailed to posts. It is called the "dead line," for it marks the limit of the camp, and any attempt to cross it was death, or at least a shot from the guard. We were not permitted to hang clothes or any thing upon it, or even to touch it.

QUARTERS.

The Rebel authorities pretended to furnish materials for the building of quarters, but at no time while in Macon were there less than 200 officers without any shelter at all. Near the centre of the camp was the shell of an old building, used for the general officers' quarters, and in part for a hospital. A roof of another like it stood near the east side of the camp. As fast as the Rebels furnished the materials, sheds were erected, from seventy-five to one hundred feet long by twenty feet broad, ends and sides left open for two reasons, viz., we could not get the lumber to close them up, and we needed the air.

Many dug holes in the ground under the large building, and lived there, getting along tolerably well except when it rained, and then they would find their excavations full of water. A few had succeeded in bringing blankets with them, and they used them for building tents.

ARRANGEMENT.

The officers were divided into "squads" of 100 each, one of whom was the commissary, and the senior was the chief of the squad. Each squad was subdivided into "messes" of 20, one of whom was a commissary. One of the officers also received rations from the Rebel commissary, and he was denominated the "chief commissary of the prison."

RATIONS.

It was the duty of the chief commissary to receive the rations in bulk from the Rebel authorities as they sent them into the prison. He issued them in bulk to the squad commissaries, dividing them equally among them. The squad commissaries, in turn, issued them to their mess commissaries, who issued them to the individual members of their several messes.

It no doubt would have amused our friends at home could they have seen the straits to which we were often put for something to draw our rations in. We could not do without them; we were *obliged* to draw them that we might have something to live on, but what to draw them in was an important question. One came with a bag made from one of the legs of his drawers (and his only pair at that) for his corn-meal; another had a coat-sleeve lining for rice, a stocking for salt, a chip for soft soap, his hat for beans; while another, who has been robbed before getting into prison, is obliged to take his only remaining shirt to put *his* rations in.

The fact is, when an officer is captured it is usually in battle, when he has no extra clothing about him, and, as a consequence, when he gets into prison he is about as destitute in this respect as he can be.

They issued to each squad of 100 five iron skillets with covers; fifteen iron skillets without covers; ten tin pails or buckets, holding about six quarts each; ten small tin pans for mixing our meal in; five wooden pails or buckets.

As for any thing to eat with, such as plates, knives and forks, etc., I have never known of their issuing any thing of the kind, except to a few of the officers who were in "Libby" just after the eight hundred left, and the articles then issued were those that were left there by the eight hundred. "Borrow and lend" was one of the first and principal rules of our prison life.

Our rations at this time consisted of the following articles, issued once in five days, viz.: Seven pints coarse corn meal; one half pint sorghum; one seventh pound of maggoty, rancid bacon; two table-spoonsful of beans (black and wormy) or rice; two table-spoonsful of salt.

The cooking utensils were not sufficient for our use, and we were obliged to wait one for the other. It was often ten o'clock before we could get breakfast, for want of something to cook it in.

For bread, we would mix our meal with water and a little salt, and, putting it in a skillet with the cover on, build a little fire under and on top of it, and in about twenty or thirty minutes you had what was called a "pone"—not very good, yet eatable to us.

Of our beans we made soup, putting in a little meat when we had any. For variety we would make mush, or, instead of pone, bake the dough as griddle-cakes. The more experienced learned to have a little of the meal mixed up and "soured," which, being put into a pone, with a little soda, made it quite light, and more palatable. We ate the sorghum on the mush, rice, and pone.

The bacon was maggoty more or less, and had been preserved in ashes in lieu of salt. At home we would not consider it fit to eat.

For wood, a detail of two from each mess of twenty was allowed to go out, *under guard*, to the wood-pile, and bring in all they could at one time for their mess, and this was for twenty-four hours. They issued, each morning at nine o'clock, at the gate, something they called *axes*, and spades, with orders to have them returned at six in the evening, upon penalty of being deprived of them the next day.

I think a Yankee would feel insulted by offering him such tools to work with as they sent in to us.

The axes resembled two iron wedges put together, with a hole through them, and a straight stick in them for a helve. The steel is not over half an inch deep, and invariably breaks off after two or three days' use, and one could scarcely *chop* with them at all.

For water we had a fine spring* near the south side

Washing.

---

* It was near this spring that Lieutenant Grierson, 45th New York Volunteers, was shot by the guard, early in the evening of June 12th. He was full twelve feet from the dead line, and was simply standing by the spring enjoying a season of meditation. Those who were near could centre of the camp, and in July they dug three wells, and put in wooden pumps, which supplied us with abundance of water.

A little brook ran through the rear of the camp, in which we used to bathe and do our washing. Our conveniences for washing were not very ample, but we got along better for something to wash *in* than we did for something to wear. While we were engaged in the work, the most common plan was to go without till our garments got dry again; here it was not an uncommon sight to see officers around the camp *minus* some *very necessary* articles of clothing.

Extra garments were out of the question, and it was necessary for one to be as economical as possible; so we went barefooted during the summer, and those who had drawers wore them in place of pants during the hot weather.

SHOULDER-STRAPS ON POLICE DUTY.

The Rebels pretended to police the camp daily, yet if it was cleaned once a week they did well. Large piles of filth would often be collected, and when the police

---

assign no reason for the act but the intention to commit a deliberate murder, as he was not near the dead line. It was not an unusual thing for officers to be down there at that time of night. The senior officer in camp wrote to Captain Gibbs, requesting an investigation of the circumstances, and the communication was returned with the following indorsement: "Such investigation as may by me be deemed proper will be made in this case; and it shall be more complete than in the cases of Confederate officers murdered by negro troops at Fort McHenry and elsewhere." The guard who committed the murder was at once promoted to sergeant, and furloughed for thirty days; at least so some of the members of his regiment *informed* us.

Shoulder-straps on police duty.

carts did come in, we were so anxious to get the camp clean that many of the officers helped to load them up.

ROLL-CALL.

We usually had roll-call at 9 A.M. each day, after the following plan, viz.:

A company of the guard was brought in, and deployed across the yard near the centre of it, while half a dozen more were sent through one half of the camp to drive out the officers across this line formed by the guard. When one side had been emptied, an opening was made, and all were counted through; the guard who drove them out at first being required to see that none staid back in their quarters, and were not counted.

It usually took from one and a half to three hours;

for we generally had to be counted through twice or three times before they were satisfied with it.

An attempt was made to count us by squads through the building, but was abandoned after a short time; for many would not be particular and get counted in their own squads, but fall in where it was the most convenient, which would make too many in *that* squad, while their own would lack one.

They finally divided us up into divisions, and counted us much quicker, and all at the same time.

AMUSEMENTS, ETC.

Time would not drag so heavily on a prisoner's hands if he had something to busy himself about; but we had so little to do, and so little to take up our time in the way of reading matter, studies, etc., that the days were long and wearisome. There were, however, classes in German, French, Logic, Rhetoric, Butler's Analogy, and in some of the higher mathematics.

For meetings, we usually had preaching on the Sabbath by one of the chaplains present, at 11 A.M. and 7 P.M. The forenoon services were usually held under the large tree on the west side of the old building that was near the east line of the camp.

Prayer-meeting on Thursday nights, prayer and conference meeting on Saturday nights. The meetings were usually well attended, and profitable to many. There was such a tendency to demoralization in prison, that whatever tended to keep our spirits up and counteract evil influences was truly refreshing.

And while speaking of meetings, I am reminded of an incident which transpired in camp the night before I arrived there, but which was related to me by one of the parties concerned. It is too good to be lost, and was as follows, viz.:

Religious service had been held in the forenoon, for the first time in the stockade, and as was the custom of the chaplain (White, 4th Rhode Island Battery) who made the prayer, he prayed "for the President of the United States, and for our army," etc. During the day word came to the commandant of the prison, Captain Tabb, that "the prisoners were praying for Abraham Lincoln, Grant, and Sherman!"

Services had commenced in the evening, and the congregation were singing the first hymn, when in came Captain Tabb, accompanied by the officer of the day. They at once inquired who had charge of the meeting, and being informed that it was Chaplain White, came up to him, and, entering into conversation, told him "he (Captain Tabb) could not allow any praying in there for the President of the United States."

Meanwhile the hymn was concluded, when Chaplain Dixon (16th Connecticut) at once stepped forward and began to pray, asking God to "bless all in authority, especially the President of the United States, his cabinet and Congress, and all his advisers." Also, that "he would bless General Grant and his glorious army; that he might be successful in capturing Richmond, the capital and strong-hold of the rebellion; that he would also bless *Sherman*, spare his life, give him wisdom to carry out his plans, that his army might be a victorious one all through its campaign; that treason might be crushed, and traitors punished; that the time might speedily come when our 'dear old flag' should wave over every village, town, and city of the United States, and we enjoy peace again."

Captain Tabb staid till after the prayer was finished, and then withdrew from the crowd, with the remark, "D—d smart prayer, but I don't believe it will amount to any thing;" and that was his last effort to crush free speech in the Federal officers' prison.

Once before this, however, he gave us a specimen of his hatred of Yankees and *his* notions of justice.

At the request of a prisoner, he took a watch and chain to sell for four hundred dollars—not less. After a considerable time, when questioned as to the matter, he said he had sold them for two hundred dollars; and upon being asked how he came by the chain which he was then wearing, said the purchaser gave it to him. After such an explanation the officer demanded the return of his property, or the four hundred dollars, threatening to expose the affair unless it was complied with; upon which Captain Tabb abused him most shamefully, and then had him "bucked" for several hours, after which the articles were restored. We were all very glad when we were relieved from the petty annoyances to which he subjected us by his being superseded by Captain Gibbs, a gentleman who, although very strict, made us no promises he did not intend to fulfill.

For the amusements, cricket, wicket, base-ball, and sword exercise, for the more active; while cards, dominoes, and checkers were of the more quiet kind.

The 10th of June fifty officers were sent to Charleston, including all the general and field officers down to about one half of the majors. It was surmised they were to be exchanged, and we all hoped it was to be so. Certain it was, they started off in good spirits, feeling that an exchange would not punish them much.

"Bucked."

About this time, some of the other squad, who had been occupying the old "shell," had so far completed their quarters as to move in, and squad 12 was ordered to take their places. We had no lumber to build bunks, so we made sand-hills for a bed, by piling up a bed of sand a foot high, four feet wide, and six feet long. By this means we kept out of the water when it rained, for there was no floor to the "shed," and the water was six inches deep during the hard showers. This month was, indeed, the rainy one, for we generally got a shower every day; and such showers—regular *drenchers*.

Exchange stock* run very high about this time, and often we were the victims of willful lies, both by the Rebels and also by some of our own party, upon that

* Rumors of an exchange.

subject; and, although we had been deceived a hundred times before, yet even a *rumor* would raise our hopes more or less. Sometimes they were of the most extravagant kind; and, although the whole camp would profess not to believe it, yet the greatest excitement would prevail till the report was "run down," when we would find ourselves, as we had a hundred times before, "sold."

One of the most exciting rumors we ever had, and that seemed to affect the crowd most, came to us the evening of the 18th of this month. Report said that "Johnson had been driven across the Chattahoochee by Sherman with great loss, and that Atlanta was on fire. Johnson had determined to evacuate it (Atlanta), as he could not hold it any longer, and that one of the guards had thrown in a paper containing the news." A chase was at once instituted to find the "lucky paper." Many had *heard* of such a paper being in camp, but not an officer could be found who had read the paper or even seen it himself, yet he could tell you of several who *had;* and thus you might chase for an hour or two, only to find at last you were humbugged.

But, for all this, we used to enjoy such rumors, for they influenced our exchange stock. Every officer invested, more or less, in that question, and every fresh rumor raised or depressed it in his own mind as well as in others.

On the 22d we were visited by a Catholic priest, who had been at Andersonville, and had seen our men there. The story he told of their sufferings touched every heart, and we each inquired, "Can not something be done for them by the officers?" A meeting was called to consider the question. The plan advised was that a committee should be appointed, who should address the Rebel Secretary of War upon the subject, asking permission for five of the officers to be paroled to visit Andersonville and other prisons, and then be permitted to go through to Washington and report the facts to our government.

The objections raised to this procedure were twofold, viz.:

First, It was asking the government to do what it had not seen fit to do before. As loyal and true men, it was our duty to believe that the government *was* doing, and *would* do, all it could for us, consistent with its plans and purposes in carrying on the war, and we ought not to embarrass it by any action we might take.

Our authorities knew perfectly well the condition of our brave men at Andersonville, and would not forget them at all; and, although *humanity* might demand that they be exchanged at once, "grim-visaged war" said otherwise, and ours was now a state of war.

Second, In the request to the Rebel Secretary of War, the committee stated that these "delegates are to proceed to Washington to represent that our men are dying at Andersonville from *other* causes* than the inhuman treatment they were receiving at the hands of the Rebels."

The address was signed by only a small minority, and was finally sent out to the Rebel authorities, and that was the last we ever heard of it.

On the 23d some officers arrived from Sturgis's command, captured by Forrest in Mississippi. They had

---

* The representations they proposed to make were, "that the suffering was caused from change of climate, and the hopelessness of exchange."

D

been robbed of every thing, clothing, money, watches, rings, diaries, and even the photographs of their friends at home, and, not content with robbing them *once*, every time they changed hands they were plundered again.

They were destitute indeed, yet were cheerful-looking, and only asked to be exchanged that they might settle up their accounts with the villains who had thus treated them.

They were kept on board of a train of cars for three days without any rations being issued to them, having nothing to eat except what they could buy from the Rebel guard; and at length, when they did get any thing, it was dry corn meal, and only one skillet to cook it in for 100 men. I have never known an instance where the Rebels have ever fed a prisoner under two or three days after capture.

The 27th was a day of considerable excitement among us, and eventually the blasting of many hopes. The evening before, five of the officers had made a plan to escape by crawling under the stockade at the point where the little brook ran under it. It was a dark night, and several trees shaded that corner, which facilitated operations. The first had succeeded well, but the second one was less fortunate, and, in passing out, made a little noise which attracted the attention of the guard, who at once fired in that direction, but hurt no one.

The long roll was at once sounded in the Rebel camps, the men turned out under arms, the artillery manned, and every thing put in order to quell a general outbreak. We enjoyed the alarm *very much;* but soon the officer of the day came in and ordered us all to our quarters, and not to leave them till daylight the next morning, for the guard had been instructed to fire upon any one they could see in the streets.

Very soon we heard the howling of the dogs, which were brought down to the place on the outside of the stockade and started on the trail, and, after about an hour, they succeeded in treeing—not a Yank, but a veritable *coon*.

They were finally obliged to give up the chase till daylight, when they came on again, and spent half the forenoon, but were finally obliged to give up the job, no doubt to their chagrin, but *much to our joy*.

Roll-call came on, and we soon found out there was something terrible on the minds of the authorities of the prison. As soon as they had counted us all through on one side, they searched the other for tunnels.

After three hours' close searching, they succeeded in finding *three;* one leading from the northeast corner of the old shell occupied by squads 12 and 13, another leading under the hospital, the third commenced under the second shed from the left, on the west side of the camp. They were nearly completed, and the parties who made them were only waiting for a dark stormy night to spring them, and thus make their way to freedom again. But alas! hope was now gone, and sorrow sat upon the countenances of all. The frontispiece represents the process of

TUNNELING AT MACON, GEORGIA.

The plan was usually as follows, viz.: A party of from six to twelve was made up, who were the principals in the matter. Selecting a site, usually under a bunk, as near the dead line as possible, they sunk a shaft or well about four feet deep, large enough in diameter for a man to work in comfortably.

To avoid detection, pieces of boards were fitted in the

mouth of the well a foot from the top, and, when the men were not at work, these boards were put in and the mouth of the well filled up, the dirt carefully swept over the cracks to obliterate all traces of it, the bunk replaced, and then it was ready for inspection.

About three feet below the surface would be dug the tunnel proper, making it large enough for a man to work in handily. The men would be divided into reliefs, and change work often. One would dig; another would haul the dirt to the mouth of the tunnel in an old sack drawn by a string; another would take it in a haversack or any thing he could get, and carry it to the sink and empty it; another would be out on picket, watching for any body they did not wish to know of it; while another would be around in the camp on a scout.

The work had to be done in the night, which made it very tedious. Yet, so long as it promised a hope of success, many were willing to try it with all their might.

The tunnels being discovered, the bunks over the tunnels were ordered torn up, a detail sent in to open the excavations, and thus they were left for five days, the guard being instructed to shoot any one who attempted to come within five feet of them. At the end of that time the guard was taken out, and the officers permitted to return to their quarters. In the afternoon, Captain Gibbs, commandant of the prison, sent in an order stating "that in the future all tunneling *must be stopped; if it was not,* all the sheds and buildings would be taken down and removed, the shade-trees would be cut down, and we should be left without shelter or shade."

The order farther stated that "all the bunks and boards should be *at once* removed to the gate, and from there he would send a detail to remove them outside." We considered this order as *inhuman;* for many, very many of the officers, were suffering from diarrhœa, and lying on the ground was one of the worst things they could do for it; and farther, when the rain-storms came, the ground was flooded with water for hours at a time. Some of the field-officers got permission to see Captain Gibbs, and finally persuaded him to rescind that part of the order relating to the bunks—a comfort to those who had them, but many of us were without any thing between us and "mother earth."

Forty prisoners from the Army of the Potomac, brought in on the 28th, gave us the joyful information that General Wilson's cavalry had reached and torn up twenty-five miles of the Danville Railroad, and we had quite a rejoicing time over it. Days passed on, bringing to us our glorious

FOURTH OF JULY.

We kept it as never before we had. How, the following letter, written soon after, will show:

"Federal Officers' Prison, July 5th, 1864.

"My dear M——,—Our nation's birthday has passed, and I doubt if any of our people at the North celebrated the 4th of July with greater profit than did the officers confined at Macon. For variety the Rebels gave us four roll-calls in the morning, as if to prevent any thing on our part like a celebration, but without effect, for ere the last one was over, Captain Todd, 8th New Jersey Infantry, displayed a little silk flag four by six inches in the midst of the crowd, which was at *once* greeted with rousing cheers.

"This little flag has a history. It was presented to him by a patriotic young lady, a Miss Paradise, of Trenton, New Jersey, and the captain had carried it ever since in his pocket-book, and, when captured, he secreted it to prevent the Rebel guard from taking it from him. After the cheers were given, another officer sang the 'Star Spangled Banner' with effect, while the glorious emblem was held up to the view of all, and then the song was cheered. I think the guard trembled a little, and were fearful of an outbreak, judging from the haste with which they left the yard. Without any previous arrangement, the crowd adjourned to the large building, when Chaplain Dixon, of the 16th Connecticut, was called out, and who made a most excellent and patriotic prayer, remembering our generals and our brethren in the field and on the sea, our sick and wounded, our noble President, his cabinet, and Congress, and our dear ones at home.

"Captain Ralph Ives, of Rochester, New York, was called for, and, mounting the table, gave us a sharp little speech touching 'the day we celebrate.' He was followed by Lieutenant Ogden, 1st Wisconsin Cavalry, in a speech of fifteen minutes, concerning the history and purpose of our government. 'Our Country' was then sung by the audience. Lieutenant Lee, Captains Lee and Kellogg, Chaplain Whitney, 104th Ohio, and Chaplain Dixon, also followed the singing with telling speeches right to the point.

"We then sang 'Rally round the Flag,' and we sang it with a *will*, I assure you. Lieutenant Colonel Thorp, 1st New York Dragoons, was then called out, who added fuel to the flame of patriotism already burning high in our hearts in a speech of half an hour. The points of his speech were, 'the right of the people to crush this rebellion;' 'the *necessity* of closing this work, and doing it *thoroughly*—not turning back a single moment till every traitor was subdued or ANNIHILATED.'

"It was *masterly* in its effect, and the audience showed their appreciation of it by frequent and prolonged applause. In fact, it seemed to tell *too* much for the feelings of our Rebel commandant outside, for he sent in his officer of the day to stop the proceedings and to break up the meeting. Over us all this while floated our little starry banner, the emblem of freedom, and many an eye was dimmed by a tear as it gazed upon it for the first time in long, weary months.

"Of course the speaking was stopped, and the crowd quietly dispersed, but not till we had given three rousing cheers each for President Lincoln and the little flag, the Proclamation, Grant, and Sherman.

"I heard many officers say that it was the best 4th of July they had ever spent, and it would long be remembered.

"I have often asked the question myself, How do those officers feel about our country and government who have been so long in prison? Are they still true to the principles that led them first to take up arms against the Rebels? Has not their long imprisonment and hardships dampened their ardor and chilled their affections for the 'red, white, and blue?'

"The experience of yesterday fully satisfied all my questionings upon that subject, and I doubt if there lives upon the face of the globe a more true, loyal, and patriotic band of men than the officers confined here at Macon."

In the course of the afternoon the following order was posted on the bulletin-board. It will best explain itself.

"*Special Orders No. 6.*
"C. S. Military Prison, Macon, Ga., July 4th, 1864.

"I. Lieutenant Colonel Thorp is relieved from duty as senior officer of prisoners for a violation of prison rules, and Lieutenant Colonel McCrary will again assume that position.

"II. The same order and quiet will be observed on this day as on any other.

"III. A disregard of this order may subject offenders to unpleasant consequences.

"GEO. C. GIBBS, Captain commanding."

But the order came too late. We had had our celebration, and nobody wanted to have another, so we were all quiet as need be the rest of the day.

After the meeting was over, Colonel Thorp was called out to headquarters, when the following conversation took place between Captain Gibbs and himself:

G. "What's your name?"

Col. "T. J. Thorp."

G. "Were you addressing the officers in the prison?"

Col. "I was."

G. "What did you mean by it?"

Col. "It was the desire of the officers that I should address them, *which I did*, as is the custom in our country on the 4th of July."

G. "*Sir*, I shall put you in *irons*, and send you to jail."

Col. "Very well, you can do so; but such treatment will not ameliorate my feelings toward you or the Confederacy in the least. We deem it not only a privilege, but a duty, to commemorate the 4th day of July as the birth-day of a great nation, for whose defense and perpetuity we are willing to *suffer*, and *die* if need be."

At this the captain became more quiet, and commuted his verdict to solitary confinement in the jail *without irons;* but, before the guard arrived, the order was entirely revoked, and Colonel Thorp was sent back inside the stockade, with threats of summary treatment if he persisted in addressing the officers again on *any subject.*

The following "Poem" was written on that day, and presented to the officers by Lieutenant Ogden, 1st Wisconsin Cavalry, formerly Professor Ogden, of the Wesleyan University, Delaware, Ohio. It has never been published before:

THE FOURTH OF JULY IN PRISON.

I.

The light of that glorious morning is breaking,
And night's sable curtains are folded away;
For the sons of Columbia, all harnessed, are waking
To the battle of freedom that lowers to-day.
On the day of the nation's convulsive emotion,
When she breathed her first breath in the pangs of her birth,
Then she shook with the thunder of war's dread commotion,
And the wail of her anguish was heard round the earth.

II.

But the God of the down-trodden people was with us,
And he heard the deep wail of that sorrowful time;
Then his arm was made bare, and his angel, to save us,
Sped swift as a sunbeam o'er country and clime,
Till he came to the "Hall" where our councils assembled,
Were struggling to bring the new nation to light;
And he touched those brave hearts, and two cherubims trembled
Upon the "old flag" that hung full in their sight.

III.

Then a thrill of delight was sent through the nation—
To life it sprang up, but an infant at first;
But soon it grew strong, and the whole world's libation
Was poured at its feet from the sea and the earth;
And wide through the valley far southward and westward,
The emigrant sought for his kindred a home;
And the wilds echoed joyous the songs of the woodman,
And were dressed in the garb of their prophetic bloom.

IV.

Then I saw, while the cherubim soared o'er the mountains,
That a serpent was coiling its folds in the soil;
And he left his foul slime on the land—in the fountains—
For the slave sweat and bled, unpaid for his toil;
And the land that was blooming like roses in Eden,
Grew sick and forsaken in valley and plain,
For the death-worm was there at its vitals still feeding,
And it writhed like a giant in death-throes of pain.

V.

Then I looked, and the Maid of our Freedom was weeping
By the tomb of our Washington buried so long,
For the hearts of our fathers in glory were sleeping,
And their deeds and their valor lived only in song;
But even in the North, where the storm and the tempest,
Beats wildly and loud 'gainst the war-eagle's nest,
Her fledglings screamed fiercely, and flew to the contest
From the North, from the East, and the echoing West.

VI.

Now bellow the thunders of Mars' rolling chariot,
And the blood of the martyr gushes out from its wheels;
For the sage and the sire, the son and the patriot,
Are marshaled in fight on the red battle-field.
The contest is fearful, while onward, *right onward!*
The flag of our country—the war-eagle's cry—
Exults in the smoke and the loud shriek of battle,
And are borne o'er the ramparts of freedom on high.

VII.

Oh, day of our birth and our glad exultation,
Lift high the "old flag!" let it flaunt to the sky!
The hope of the country, the pride of the nation,
The "Flag of the Free," on the "FOURTH OF JULY!"
Let thy Ægis of glory be lifted in battle
To-day, where the cohorts of freedom shall stand,
Where the loud cannon's roar, and the musket's fierce rattle,
Hurl the hosts of rebellion from out this good land.

VIII.

This day shall exalt thee, thou emblem of glory,
A terror to traitors—the hope of the slave;
In thy folds are still lingering the legend and story
Of the sons of Columbia, the true and the brave.
And as WASHINGTON bore thee in triumph and glory,
When the pangs of our birth shook the earth and the sea,
So now in our baptism, all blood-streaked and gory,
Shall ABRAHAM bear thee, "*thou Flag of the Free!*"

CHAPTER V.

SAVANNAH.

On the morning of the 27th of July, Lieutenant Davis at roll-call notified the first division to be ready to move to Charleston at 5 P.M. It was a busy time till that hour. Clothes were washed, pones baked, haversacks made ready and filled for *emergencies.**

Judging from the extensive preparations being made in that direction, it was evident that many intended to escape if possible. Lieutenant Davis began to call the roll at 5 o'clock P.M., passing the officers through the first gate into the space between the "dead line" and the stockade.

Soon after dark, those who remained, and who had particular friends in the party designated to go, determined not to be separated from them, and, after working a while, succeeded in joining them by pulling off some of the pickets from the "dead line," so that when Lieutenant Davis counted them through the outer gate he found over fifty more than he had called for.

These were accordingly sent back inside of the stockade, while the others, after sleeping on the ground till 3 A.M. the next morning, were marched to the train, and at four o'clock started for Charleston *via* Savannah. This

---

* An emergency to a prisoner was an opportunity to escape, and hence we held ourselves in readiness for all opportunities whenever we were moved.

was the last we saw of them till we joined them, seven weeks after, at Charleston.

The next morning we received a re-enforcement of 111 officers, captured both from Sherman's and Grant's army. Those from Sherman informed us that Hardee's great victory of the 22d was a dear one to the Rebels; that he had been unable to maintain his position, and was obliged to fall back to his former one, suffering a terrible loss both in his advance and retreat.

About this time we obtained a paper, and found the news column headed, in leaded type:

"The Raid into Maryland!!"
"Early within Four Miles of Washington!!"
"He throws Shells into the City!!"
"Great Consternation among the Inhabitants!!"
"Probability of its Capture!!"
"The City left Defenseless!!!"

As might be supposed, these items caused great excitement in camp, and we waited impatiently for farther news, not knowing the truth of the matter. A few days after we got another paper, containing a dispatch from General Grant, in which he says "that Washington will take care of itself, for he must attend to Richmond." This quieted our fears, and we felt that Grant would take care of the Rebels and their army.

On the 28th 600 more left, being marched to the cars at 3 A.M. the 29th. Several embraced the opportunity to get *under* instead of *into* the cars, and thus managed to escape. Many of us had determined to escape while running from Savannah to Charleston, and we were quite busy cutting holes with saw-knives in the bottoms of the cars. As we reached the road leading to Charleston we noticed that something was wrong, for, instead of going to Charleston, we were run into Savannah. I afterward learned that we were stopped by an order of the commanding general of the department, and that we could be better cared for in Savannah than Charleston.

As we arrived in the city, a crowd collected around the train to see the "Yankee prisoners," the majority of whom were colored people. They seemed to understand our feelings, and had respect for them, saying very little to us, while many of them manifested an interest in us such as we had not seen before in any city of the South. We were escorted by a company of the City Battalion to the old United States Marine Hospital, and turned loose into the yard. It appeared that all the preparations for our reception had been made since seven o'clock in the morning, and they had nothing ready for us but the "stockade" or "pen." We found inside several boards, which we at once appropriated for bunks; and, to destroy them for any other use, early the next morning we cut them up the right length for our beds, and thus managed to obtain boards to sleep on.

The yard or pen contained about one and a half acres, surrounded on three sides by a brick wall eight feet high, and on the top of this was a board stockade or fence of four feet more, while the third side was altogther of boards, same height as the other. Two sentry-boxes graced each side, and from which the guards overlooked the camp. There were several large trees in the yard, under the shade of which we passed many a long, wearisome hour.

The next morning they brought us in some small "A" tents, issuing sixteen to ninety-six men. These we pitched in regular streets, first cutting them open to the peak, that we might spread them wider and make them cover six of us comfortably. They also issued to each squad of 100 a large iron pot, holding sixteen gallons, for washing purposes; eight tin kettles or pails, holding twelve quarts each, for cooking; eleven small iron skillets for baking our bread in and frying our meat; sixteen tin pans, each holding six quarts, for mixing our meal in; four wooden buckets or pails, two axes, and two hatchets.

For rations they issued to us daily one pound of fresh beef five days of the week, one half pound of bacon the other two days; one quart of corn meal; one pint of rice; one fourth of a gill of vinegar; one tea-spoonful of salt, and a small piece of hard soap. The rations were of very fair quality, and, had the bread been any thing but corn, we would have got along tolerably well. Once the rice that was issued to us was musty, and, upon its being shown to Colonel Wayne, he ordered it to be gathered up and returned to the commissary, with instructions to replace it by good rice; the only instance I have known or heard of where the Rebels have taken back an issue of any thing, no matter how bad it was.

The wood was drawn into the yard each day and issued the same as the other things were, and was of sufficient quantity to do our cooking, which was all we needed, as the weather was warm and pleasant.

We were guarded by the 1st Georgia Regulars, Colonel Wayne commanding. The officers of his regiment were gentlemanly, and uniformly treated us with respect.

His character will best be illustrated by the following anecdote:

A few days after we had become somewhat settled, to

prevent tunneling and facilitate inspections, he claimed to have issued an order requiring the tents to be raised three and a half feet from the ground, and the bunks two and a half feet, and ordered an inspection for that day at 2 o'clock P.M. Unfortunately for us, the order never had been sent in; and farther to hinder us, the axes were not allowed to come in that morning till after nine o'clock. Many of the officers had not been able to get any lumber, and he refused to let any more be brought in; consequently, at two o'clock, when he made his inspection, he found some sixteen tents that were not raised as he claimed to have ordered. Without receiving a word of explanation, he called for a detail of the guard and took those tents out of the yard, thus leaving nearly one hundred officers without any kind of shelter. A terrible rain came on that night, and as the other tents were all crowded full, the sufferers were exposed to all the severity of the storm, and, as a consequence, took cold, from which they did not recover for weeks afterward.

The attention of the surgeon in charge was called to this state of things, and he made a report of the case to the medical director, who ordered the tents restored to these officers; and two days afterward they were returned.

Such kind of treatment did not increase our love for Confederate rule or for Confederate officers very much. Some mornings he (Colonel Wayne) would get a *fit* on, and would not let the commissary have an ax to cut up the beef till after roll-call, thus keeping six hundred officers out of the principal part of their breakfast.

The mornings were usually hot and sunny, and the

green flies swarmed in abundance, and at such times it would turn black before we received it.

The guards generally treated us well, with few exceptions. One day a party of us were engaged in building an oven near the "dead line," and as was natural, without thinking, we would occasionally touch it. After one or two warnings from the sentinel in the box near by, we heard the click of a musket, and some one looked up just in time to warn one of his comrades (who had thoughtlessly touched the "dead line"); for the guard had brought his musket to his shoulder, and was about to fire. After that, one of the officers kept watch while the rest were at work.

In contrast with the above, another of the guard, who was an Irishman, was inside the camp one night to attend to the fires, when he came up to a group of the prisoners, and, with his good-natured brogue, asked,

"How things wint inside?"

"Oh, very well," replied one.

"Do you want any hard tobacca?"

"Yes, we are all out," said several.

"Here, take that, and God bless yees," said he, giving us a good-sized plug—all he had.

"How are matters going outside?" we inquired.

"Goin' bully; Sherman is after Atlantha, and, I tell yees, we Irishmen are glad of it. I have a wife in Atlantha, and I wrote her a letter the other day, telling her not to lave the city when Sherman comes in, but to stay there with the childers, and then I will come home to stay with her. We is all your friends here in Georgia. Every Irishman will help yees to get off, if yees can only get out of here. Why don't yees burrow out? If yees can get out fifteen rods from the wall yees are all right. I am not a Rebel, and never was; and there are twenty-three in my company who are with me. We are going to *disart* the first opportunity. They dasent send us to the front, for they know us. They watch us very close. If they knew I talked so, they would kill me before mornin'. I will do all I can for yees. I must be gone, or I shall be misthrusted. Good-night; God bless yees!"

He was true to his promise; for he *did* help us to nearly all the papers we had while we were there. He would wrap them around a stone, and, watching his opportunity when the other sentinels did not see him, throw it over the "dead line."

It was not long after our arrival here before the tunneling commenced. Two tunnels were in process at the same time. One on the west side of the camp was dug through an old vault, which was a great help in secreting the earth that was dug out of the excavation. Arrangements had been made to go out on a certain dark rainy night, and all that remained was to *spring* the tunnel, that is, to open the outer end. One of the party went down into it, and, after a few moment's work, succeeded in opening a hole large enough to let out his head, when the sharp cry, "Go back dar, you Yank, or I will shoot; cawpal of de gaud, post No. 17," made him draw in his head, and back out to inform his companions of the discovery.

The truth at once flashed upon their minds that they had been outwitted by the Rebels this time, for they had posted a guard of sentinels *outside* of the wall, watching for just such developments, and one of them chanced to be close by the opening made in the tunnel. The officer of the day came in at once with a guard, found the tent where the tunnel started from, drove out the inmates, placed his guard over it, and the next day Colonel Wayne sent two of the occupants of the tent to jail for tunneling, but they were returned after a few days. At the time we left Savannah two other tunnels were being dug, with a fair prospect of success.

Between the "dead line" and the wall were built five stands four feet high, something after the fashion of those used at Methodist camp-meetings. On the top of these were built every night pitch-pine fires, and were kept up till daylight, thus lighting the camp and making it very pleasant, besides conducing much to our health; and it also enabled the sentinels to see all that was going on in camp. During the pleasant evenings it was not an uncommon occurrence to see groups of the officers sitting near these fires, engaged in reading, studying, or playing games.

An effort was made to get books or pamphlets to read. Contributions of Confederate money were solicited in all of the squads, but only two of them succeeded in getting any thing. The sutler, who was to buy the reading matter, said that, since the war, the bookstores and periodical men had not been able to get any additions to their stock, and, consequently, they had *nothing* on hand. Paper had been so scarce, they had used up all of the old books and pamphlets for waste and wrapping.

They would not allow us to have their own city papers, consequently we were obliged to go without much reading matter; but, to the honor of some one, however (I never could find out who), we received as a *gift* one day a dozen English Testaments, and half a dozen Hymn-books, published by the South Carolina Tract Society at Charleston.

We usually had preaching Sabbath evening by one of the chaplains while they staid, and, after they left, one of the officers officiated; for there were several present who had formerly been ministers.

We had prayer meetings Thursday and Saturday evenings. Lieutenant Ogden, 1st Wisconsin Cavalry, formerly of the Wesleyan University, Delaware, Ohio, formed a class, and each morning, immediately after roll-call, gave them very interesting and instructive lectures on Literature and the English Language. We also had here, as at Macon, students in Moral Philosophy, Logic, Rhetoric, and the Languages.

About this time we began to learn something of the destitution of the Rebel army. We learned that many of the regiments had not been paid for over a year, and that the small amount per month that was *promised* the enlisted men proved insufficient to keep one of them a single day in one of their cities; that those regiments away from the front drew very little clothing, and the poorest kind of rations; that their regiments were being fast depleted, and could only be filled up by old men and boys; that their mercantile interests were suffering severely from the stringency of the blockade.

A knowledge of all these things tended to keep up our spirits, and caused us to look for the more certain overthrow of the rebellion.

The 28th of August the Rebels brought in a slip of paper purporting to be an offer from their government to exchange man for man, rank for rank, until all were exchanged; *but the black soldiers* they said nothing about. This occasioned much discussion among us, whether our government would or *ought* to accept such terms. A few days after, a part of the correspondence between Judge Ould, then Commissioner of Exchange, and General Butler, was sent in to us and posted on the sutler's shop; in fact, it was nothing but Ould's letter, in which he attaches all the blame of non-exchange to the United States government. We took some hope from these things, for it was evident that there was agitation on the subject. We hoped and prayed for deliverance, yet we asked not for it at the sacrifice of any principle which the government claimed would be violated by acceding to our wishes at once.

The 2d of August brought some hope to our discouraged hearts; for on that day went out from us, to be sent through the lines, two chaplains and seven surgeons, and we read it as an omen of good to us, saying that the government wishes to get out of the way all the non-combatants, the sick and wounded, and then would commence the general work.

As soon as the chaplains were notified that they were to leave the next morning, a desire was manifested by many to have religious services once more before they went away. Accordingly, word was circulated through the camp that there would be preaching by one of the chaplains at dark on the green.

The appointed hour came, and with it a large attendance of the officers, for it was a lovely evening. The circumstances all combined to make the services very solemn and impressive. We had been many months together as prisoners. They had been *our* pastors, *we* their people; *they* the shepherds, *we* the flock. Now our relation was to be broken up. They were to leave us in bonds, and return to enjoy the freedom of a prosperous and happy country. It seemed also that God would make us mindful of His presence, for, during the services, He rolled up a thick black cloud, from behind which we could occasionally hear the mutterings of His voice, while ever and anon He parted it in twain, that we might behold the flashing of His eye for an instant, and then it was hidden again, only to be revealed in brighter splendor.

Chaplain Dixon preached from Luke xv., 25: "Lord help me." The text was short, and so was the sermon; but it was also timely and to the point, and was listened to with marked attention. Chaplain White followed him in exhortation, bringing out some most beautiful thoughts drawn from our situation and circumstances.

As he closed, he said he hoped to get to heaven when he died, and asked all those present who would try to meet him there to raise their right hands, when up went all of them. I trust, when the records of eternity shall be revealed, it will be seen that our little meeting was not in vain.

They were expected to leave at four o'clock in the morning, and were on hand, as were many of their special friends, to see them off; but the provost guard, which was to go with them to the railroad, was delayed till after the train had gone, consequently they did not get off till five o'clock in the afternoon. To them they were hours long and weary, full of hopes and fears, yet the welcome message came at last, and found them ready. Before they started they gave up all surplus clothing, books, cooking utensils, any thing they had been using,

FILLING UP THE SINKS AT SAVANNAH, GEORGIA.

to their friends, reserving only just enough to get to our lines.

A crowd gathered at the gate, and many slipped the address of "dear ones" into their hands, with the request to "write them a few words, and let them know where and how I am." To them it was a glad hour, and none wished them to be obliged to remain longer.

Amid "Good-by!" "God bless you!" "Hope to meet you the other side of our lines," and a hearty shaking of hands, the fortunate ones passed through the gate and were lost to our sight. We then gave them three hearty parting cheers, and quietly returned to our quarters, sad and somewhat gloomy.

The 5th of August brought us the glorious intelligence of the defeat of Hood and the occupation of Atlanta by our forces. It seemed too good to be true, yet we all hoped it might be. Upon asking the officer of the day of the truth of the rumor, he said "there had been heavy fighting there, and they were afraid they had not been as successful as they had hoped to be." When the news was confirmed, we felt glorious over it for several days.

About this time there was considerable sickness, and the authorities concluded to fill up the open sink we had been using and make us a new one. For this purpose they sent in one day fourteen of their colored people, seven men and seven women, to do this work. They were all barefooted, ragged, and dirty, and to our Northern eyes the women looked sadly out of place. Among them was a boy so white, and his hair was so straight, we had a dispute as to his being a slave, but, upon asking the guard, he told us he was owned there in the city. He could not have been one sixteenth colored, and yet they told us he was a "*slave*"—a "nigger." As I turned away in disgust from the scene, I could but think of the *boasted* morality of the South. They affect great horror at the idea of negro equality; they are very much afraid of the North's embracing the doctrine of miscegenation, and yet here they have the fruit of it right in their midst —no, not *that*, but the fruit of concubinage, practiced from year to year by those who claim to be first in society.

The husband lives in open adultery with his female servants, while his wife encourages him in his crime by using the gold obtained from the sale of the *fruit* of her husband's loins, to procure place and favor in a society that is as corrupt and rotten as herself. But why is this state of things permitted to exist? Does not their pulpit and press denounce it in thunder tones? No, indeed; their press claims that its preservation is essential to the national life, while the pulpit attempts to prove that it is a creature of God—a divine institution. Is it any wonder, then, that we have a war—a war that is to break up and destroy this cursed state of things? May God deal with us justly and mercifully!*

Some ladies called one night to see us, and the officer of the day opened the gate and let them look in upon the hated Yankees. After gazing at us a few moments, one of them remarked "that they did not look as sleek as they did sometimes," which was probably a fact; for some were barefooted, bareheaded, others without pants, more without shirts, and those who had clothes found it difficult to always keep them clean and whole.

The accompanying illustration shows some of the dif-

* Written while in prison.

ficulties we encountered in our attempts to keep clean. Having no extra clothing, when we *did* wash we had to

Washing under Difficulties—Editor on Duty.*

supply the place of clothing as best we could. A common method was to take a blanket and tie it around the waist, making a sort of "petticoat" of it. It was not an uncommon occurrence for the "ladies" to give us a call on washing days (for they were not stated), and would see several of these specimens of Yankee ingenuity *en déshabillé*.

The "*Republican*," one of the morning papers, gave us a specimen of its affection one morning after learning of our tunneling operations. The article was headed

* The above was sketched on the spot without my knowledge or consent, and presented to me by the artist while in Savannah, Georgia.

"The Escaping Yankee Doodles;" and after speaking of the attempt to escape, closed up in the following strain: "*We have hundreds of dogs trained to catch negroes, which are thirsting for blood, and are ready to be put upon trails of escaping Yankees, and we will use them for the benefit of all who attempt to escape; and the best thing the Doodles can do is to remain under the protecting care of Colonel Wayne.*"

Shortly after the same paper treated us to an article which, for pure meanness, has never been excelled even in the *Richmond Examiner* itself.

A Lieutenant Greenwood, 3d Maryland Infantry, died in the hospital. A lady who lived in one part of the hospital building used frequently to come in and see the sick, and minister to their wants. In this way she became quite well acquainted with the lieutenant, and found out he was of the same religious faith as herself. After he died, she bought a lot in the city cemetery, and had him decently buried, paying the expenses of the burial herself.

As soon as Mr. "*Republican*" heard of it, he published the act as an "outrage upon their gallant dead who were buried there; the polluting of the sacred soil with the bodies of those who burn their houses, orphan their children, and ravish their wives, etc.;" claiming "that no such care was shown to their dead in Federal hands," and called upon the city authorities to stop such outrages; but, for the honor of the city be it said, the "*News*" was of a different mind, for it administered a cutting rebuke to the "*Republican*," saying that "all such articles were no credit to the Southern people; that they had *abundant* evidence that their dead were decently buried, and that it was nonsense to spend so much time and ink over so small a matter; that they could afford to be magnanimous and Christian, even if their enemies were not," and thus the matter ended.

Day after day passed, long, wearisome, tedious, bringing us little news, and no prospect of exchange. Sherman had indeed taken Atlanta; Stoneman had made his "*raid*," and been captured, and Grant was thundering before Richmond and Petersburg. Our prison life grew more and more intolerable from day to day, and yet there was no prospect of any thing better in store for us at present, and we could only "while the hours away" in sleep, play, or harrowing thoughts of our situation. *Oh, this turning the mind loose on itself* is what makes prison life so terrible. Could the mind be kept active; had we had books, papers, or had we known what was going on outside of us, we would not have suffered as much as we did. "Oh for a change" said many, and soon it came.

CHAPTER VI.

CHARLESTON, SOUTH CAROLINA.

"Pack up and be ready to *move* to-morrow morning at five o'clock," was an order that came in to us Monday evening, September 12th. "Where now?" inquired we all. "Charleston," said Colonel Wayne. "What for?" said a hundred voices. "I hope for exchange," said Colonel Wayne. "God grant it may be so," said we all, with tremendous cheer, as we separated to make our needed preparation.

The most of the night was spent in cooking our cornmeal and meat, and getting ready to go at the appointed hour. The camp looked very much as camps do after a march. Little fires burning brightly, around which were gathered knots of officers discussing the probabilities of our fate, each hoping that from Charleston we might take our departure to "God's country," to enjoy again the blessings of civilization. We derived much comfort from the fact that some of the officers had been exchanged from there, and possibly we might be among the fortunate ones soon to be *treated* likewise. About this time it had been reported that 600 Rebel officers were in transports off Morris Island; and as that was *our* exact number, *perhaps* they were to be exchanged for us.

Sherman was also pressing on into Georgia, and the Andersonville prisoners were being sent to Charleston and Florence, which made an exchange look very probable.

"Take no government property, not even your cooking utensils," was the order from Colonel Wayne; an order which many of us obeyed to our great inconvenience, as the sequel will show.

We left the yard at 5 15 A.M., the 13th instant, and were marched to the same place where we had left the cars two months before; and, after waiting three quarters of an hour, a train of freight cars was backed down to us, and we were ordered on board, forty being assigned to each car. These cars were old and filthy, and had been used for transporting coal, the bottoms of the cars being covered with about two inches of the dust. I asked one of the Rebel officers for a broom to sweep it out, when he replied, "The Confederacy were not able to furnish brooms to sweep cars for Yankee prisoners;" so into the dirt we had to go, and make the best of it. Many of us left our camp with feelings of sadness, for we had found it the best prison, as to rations and quarters, we had found in Rebeldom; and as we left the city, we felt to thank the authorities for what little they had done for our comfort while among them.

It is one hundred and four miles from Savannah to Charleston. The railroad runs through a low, flat, marshy country, being built much of the way on trestle-work from eight to twelve feet high. The only station of any importance is Pocotaligo, about midway between the two places, and within eleven miles of our lines. Had it been in the night when we passed it, many would have escaped by jumping from the train; but, as it was daylight, they were prevented.

As we neared the city, we could see some of the fortifications on the land side; yet they were empty, and, for the most part, without guns. In crossing the Cooper River, we could see Castle Pinckney in the distance, and, for the first time since we left Richmond, could hear the fire of our own guns. As we entered the city, about 2 30 P.M., the streets were fairly crowded by the negroes, with a slight mixture of the whites. Here we were in the cradle of *Secession*, the city where that *devilish child* was born, and where it had been clothed with the garments of "State Rights," and had gone out to turn the hearts of the people against their father (the United States government).

We left the train, and were marched a mile and a half up "Coming Street," beneath a boiling sun, to the city jail-yard, the grand receptacle for all the Federal prisoners who arrive in Charleston. I think it was the nastiest, dirtiest, filthiest, lousiest place I ever was in. At the time we arrived, they had just removed several hundred of our enlisted men who had come from Andersonville. The ground was literally covered with *lice*. The next morning after my arrival there I killed over fifty on my shirt alone, and my case was not an isolated one.

The yard embraced about an acre. In the north centre of it stands the "city jail." It is built of brick, and consists of two parts. The front is six hundred by one hundred feet, four stories high. The wing is of an octagon shape, extending out toward the centre of the yard, having the same height as the other. A tower forty feet high rises from the centre of the octagon part, and in this they confined their worst criminals. While we were there, the negro soldiers of the 54th and 55th Massachusetts were confined there. Some days these negroes were allowed to come out into the yard, and we had a

JAIL-YARD, CHARLESTON.

very good opportunity of talking with them. We found them *intensely* loyal, only asking that they might have another opportunity to avenge their wrongs while held as prisoners of war. They were intelligent, and the most of them had formerly been free. A few of them had been sent into the country to work, and had never returned, at least so one of their number informed me while talking with him about their treatment. The following song was composed, and often sung by them, for the amusement of the many spectators (inmates of the jail-yard), and was entitled " Parody on ' When this Cruel War is over.' "

I.

When I enlisted in the army
    Then I thought 'twas grand,
Marching thro' the streets of Boston
    Behind a regimental band.
But when at " Wagner" I was captured,
    Then my courage failed;
Now I'm lousy, hungry, naked,
    Here in Charleston jail.

Chorus.

Weeping, sad, and lonely,
    Oh, how bad I feel,
Down in Charleston, South Car'lina,
    Praying for a good square meal.

II.

If Jeff Davis will release me,
    Oh, how glad I'll be!
When I arrive on Morris Island
    Then I shall be free.
Then I'll tell the conscript soldiers
    How they treat us here,
Giving us an old " corn dodger,"
    They call it " prisoners' fare."

III

We are longing, watching, praying,
  But will not repine,
Till Jeff Davis does release us,
  And sends us "in our lines."
Then, with words of kind affection,
  How they'll greet us there !
Wondering how we could live so long
  Upon the "dodger's" fare.

Chorus.

Then we will laugh long and loudly,
  Oh, how glad we'll feel,
When we arrive on Morris Island,
  And eat a good square meal.

They were beautiful singers, and usually between sunset and dark would come to the windows and sing to drive the blues away. One of their favorites seemed to be

"The dearest spot on earth to me
Is home, sweet home !"

And I have seen many a prisoner turn away and wipe his eyes, as it brought up the sweet memories of the past. This, I believe, was the only enjoyment we had in this contemptible "jail-yard."

For quarters, about one third had no shelter at all. Those who had used "A" tents, pitched "flat on the ground." The yard was so small that we were much crowded, and, when it rained, one quarter of it was flooded so we could not use it. When it was pleasant, the sun poured its heat upon us like a fiery furnace. We could get but little fresh air, for the walls were twelve feet high; and when we did, it was a whirling breeze, which raised the dirt and filth from the ground, at times almost suffocating us. In one corner of the yard was a large

WORK-HOUSE, CHARLESTON.

sink, twenty feet square and ten feet deep, for the use of the prisoners in the jail. This had not been emptied for some time, and it was nearly full, constantly emitting an intolerable stench. Complaint was made about it, and they sent in some scavenger carts to clean it out; but oh, it was misery upon misery! for they were so slow about it that, when I left, after nine days' incarceration "in the horrible place," they had not half completed the task.

Some days they would turn out all the deserters, both from our own and the Rebel army—their felons, prostitutes, murderers, thieves (men and women), etc., and thus insult us with the presence of their worst criminals. We were forty-eight hours there before we received any thing to eat, and, when the rations *did* come in, we had neither wood nor utensils with which to cook; and, had it not been for the fact that some of the officers had stolen kettles at Savannah, and kept them hidden on their way out of the prison, we would have been obliged to have eaten our meals *raw*. We made an attack upon the woodwork of the old sink, and got off enough to cook a couple of meals, when they brought in some wood. But at no time while there did they seem to take one particle of pains to make us in the least comfortable; in fact, every thing seemed to be done that would add to our discomfort. At one time there was quite an excitement over some new discoveries, when it was found that two old *cast-iron spittoons* had been found, which served for tolerable good bake-kettles.

The work-house adjoined the yard of the jail, in fact its walls made a portion of the wall on the east side. It was built of brick, and outside presented a very fair appearance. It has towers on each corner, which give it quite an imposing appearance. It once was quite well arranged for its design, yet when the United States officers left it but little of its original shape inside remained. The former master of it lived opposite, but his "occupation was now gone." The following order, picked up within its walls, will show what that was.

"To the Master of the Work-house:

"You will give the negro David a good sound paddling, and send him back by the same guard who accompanies him up. The guard has money to pay the expenses. Please send bill, and oblige

"MILLS, BEACH & CO.

"January 14th, 1856."

Thank God, David is now free, and no guard can accompany him to the work-house for another "paddling."

Some of the men found the plates to the oven, and had broken them up, and were using the doors and pieces of the front for "griddles," upon which they baked their corn meal. A single pump, in an artesian well in the jail-yard, was the only means of getting water, except after a rain, when we could get it out of our old cistern. The well was nearly dry after 2 o'clock P.M. each day, for it was affected by the tide. The water was brackish, and to many a fruitful cause of sickness.

After inflicting upon prisoners this kind of treatment several days, it was the custom of the Rebels to come in and offer *better* quarters to any who would take a parole not to escape or to hold communication with any one outside of the guard in which they might be placed.

We learned that nearly all the officers who had preceded us to Charleston were thus paroled, and were quartered in the Marine and Roper Hospitals.

I gladly availed myself of the opportunity of getting out of the jail-yard, and was sent, with fifty others, to Roper Hospital.

The following is a copy of the parole thus signed:

"Charleston, S. C., C. S. America, September, 1864.

"We, the undersigned, prisoners of war, confined in the city of Charleston, in the Confederate States of America, do pledge our parole, individually, as military men and men of honor, that we will not attempt to pass the lines which shall be established and guarded around our prison-house; nor will we, by letter, word, or sign, hold any intercourse with parties beyond those lines, nor with those who may visit us, without authority. It is understood by us that this parole is voluntary on our part, and given in consideration of privileges secured to us, by lessening the stringency of the guard, of free ingress and egress of the house and appointed grounds during the day, by which we secure a liberty of fresh air and exercise grateful to comfort and health.

"Hereby we admit that this, our parole, binds us in letter and spirit, with no room for doubt or technicality of construction, and its violation will be an act of lasting disgrace. Signed:"

After signing this, we were marched under guard to Roper Hospital, where we found 300 of those who were sent on the first train from Macon. From them we learned that over 70 of the officers escaped on the way down, but the majority of them had been recaptured by *dogs* and *citizens*.

We were glad to meet our old friends, and they, in

turn, greeted us warmly. The place seemed a "paradise," compared to the jail-yard which we had just left. We learned *they* had spent over three weeks in that pen, and been starved even worse than we had, for some days receiving for rations *only an allowance of sorghum and lard.*

Roper Hospital, Charleston.

Roper Hospital was founded by the gentleman whose name it bears, who gave it a munificent donation. The

City Council of Charleston, at two different times, also voted money to complete it. It was designed for a city hospital, and seemed well adapted for that purpose. It stands on a street facing the famous "burnt district" of 1861. It is built of brick, plastered over, and marked; thus giving it the appearance of brown stone. The main building is seventy-eight feet front by sixty feet deep, and four stories high.

On both sides, east and west, are wings, each one hundred feet long by fifty feet deep, and three stories high. On each corner is a tower rising fifteen or twenty feet above the roof, adding beauty as well as strength to the structure. In each wing and on each floor are three large rooms, nearly the size of the wings, which, I conclude, were the rooms containing the beds. The main part of the building has smaller rooms for the dispensary, offices, living rooms, etc. The whole was lighted by a very poor quality of gas, which we were permitted to use till nine o'clock in the evening.

The grounds around the building were quite pleasant, particularly the front yard. It was tastefully laid out, and filled with flowers and shrubbery; and as we were permitted the freedom of the yard, we enjoyed them very much. The back yard was terrible filthy and unhealthy. It used to be policed every day, but they would neglect to carry out the filth, leaving it lying in piles for two or three days at a time, till the very atmosphere became impregnated with the poisonous vapors. But the greatest nuisance was the sink. They allowed the vault to become filled up, and then it ran over, standing in pools in the yard, and no effort was made by them to remedy the evil, and thus it remained while we were there.

It was no wonder we had the yellow fever among us before we left the city. It would have been almost a miracle if we had not.

A well of brackish water supplied us in part, and the balance we drew from two or three old cisterns; and when *they* failed, we went outside under guard to a street pump. The last two weeks we were there we were much troubled for want of water, for the pump to the well gave out, and the cisterns were dry.

The cooking was done in the back yard with such utensils as we could find around the building, or had managed to buy or steal from the Rebels.

Lieutenant Roach, of the 49th New York Volunteers, formerly of Rochester, did us great service. He was a coppersmith, and succeeded in picking up a few old tools, some old stove-pipe and pieces of iron, from which he made several kettles, frying-pans, dishes, etc., for many of the officers. Pieces of old iron were found around the hospital which served for griddles, upon which we baked pancakes. We also built several brick ovens in which we did our bread-baking.

We also found quite a number of old medicine-jars, which were very handy "to have in the house."

Rations were small in quantity, and rather poor in quality. They were issued for ten days at a time, and consisted of flour, three pints; corn meal, two and one third quarts; rice, two quarts; beans, three pints (black, and full of bugs); meat, either four ounces fresh beef, or two ounces of bacon daily, or, in lieu thereof, one gill sorghum.

In addition to our rations, the authorities allowed the market women to come up to the side-walk, that we might purchase from them vegetables, fruit, etc., for our comfort. In addition to this, we also had a sutler inside of the premises. Those who had money managed to live tolerably well, but those who were penniless had to suffer. We could buy a sweet pumpkin for ($5) five dollars; milk, for one dollar and fifty cents per quart; flour, three dollars per pound, and make quite a good pumpkin-pie, as many of the officers did. While here, I think we made more advancement in the culinary art than at any other time while we were in prison. By adding ten dollars' worth of *vegetables* to our daily rations, one could get up quite a good meal. Sweet potatoes were quite plenty, and were purchased more than any thing else by us.

The wood rations did tolerably well, for when we lacked some of the old buildings in the yard would be attacked, and made to supply the deficiency.

THE FIRING UPON THE CITY was continued daily, except when the flag-of-truce boat went down the bay.

The shells usually came over at intervals of thirty minutes, but when a fire broke out they would open three or four *extra* guns, and send them as often as one every five minutes. One Saturday afternoon a fire broke out nearly opposite the work-house, when they commenced shelling it; and so direct was their aim that twice they burst their shells in the midst of the burning buildings. The negroes informed us that it was a common practice of General Gilmore's, and that he had entirely destroyed one of the fire-engines by bursting a shell inside of it, and that the firemen were afraid to go to the fires for fear of being killed by his shells.

From the attic window of the "Roper Hospital" we could look down the bay toward "Morris Island," and could see the flash of our guns in the clear evenings; could trace the course of the shell as it left the mouth of the gun, climbing up, higher, still higher, till it reached the zenith. Then we heard the report of the gun, and would, for the first time, hear the sharp, shrill shriek of the shell cutting its way through the air, and could trace it still farther by its own light, as it gradually descended the other arc of its circle; nearer, and still nearer it came. Now it is right over our heads; it gives out its lightning flash; the danger is past. The report soon follows, and we hear the pieces rattle among the brick walls and wooden tenements beyond us. Had it burst when at its height, its pieces might have struck some of us. They have fallen all around us in the yards where we were, sometimes within five feet of us. Yet, with one exception, during all the time our prisoners were under fire in Charleston, but one man was harmed by them. He was eating his dinner in his room by his table, when a piece of a shell came through the roof, striking his arm, inflicting a flesh wound, smashing up his table, and going on through the floor. May we not say *safely* that "God protected our prisoners while there?"

While here, we received the most mail, and, I think, enjoyed the best mail facilities of any place we had occupied while in prison, except Richmond. Several loads of boxes were also received, in tolerably good condition, much to the joy of those to whom they belonged. The authorities also allowed us to have as many of the morning papers as we chose by paying twenty-five cents for them, which we very gladly did—a privilege we had not enjoyed since we had been in Rebeldom. About the 20th of September, we learned from them that Sherman and Hood were trying to effect terms of an exchange for all the officers who had been captured since the army started in the spring. The 23d, an order came for about 150 to be ready to move in the morning. It was a joyous time for those who were to go, and we all hoped it was only the commencement of a "general exchange" soon to take place; and our expectations were increased by an order received the 29th for all of the naval officers to be sent to Richmond for "exchange." Oh how anxiously we watched the papers to see something that would give us farther hope in the matter, and perhaps would settle the question! But we watched and waited in vain, and soon our feelings sank back into the old state, thus to remain till somebody started a plausible rumor which would arouse them again.

I can not forbear transcribing a few thoughts from my journal, written at this time in my little room in the attic. Whether my predictions have proved true, the public must judge.

"I stand by the little window in the attic of Roper Hospital, and look out upon the 'burnt district' of this city. It is desolation indeed. The bare, broken walls of the ruined houses remain as monuments to the graves of a once thriving business portion of the city. The streets and thoroughfares are deserted, and tall, rank weeds have grown up in their places. As far as I can see, no improvements have taken place since the fire. It seems as though the curse of God was resting on the place to prevent its being rebuilt. It gives me an unpleasant feeling to look upon so much destruction; yet above all this comes the reflection that it is, in fact, but *justice* to this city of sin. It was in this state that the heresy

Burnt District at Charleston.

of secession was born and nursed for years, under the parentage and tuition of J. C. Calhoun. It was in this city that the open act of secession was first determined upon and carried out. It was from this state that the infamous

Bully Brooks received his testimonials of approbation for his murderous attempt to crush free speech. It was in this harbor, and by an inhabitant of this city, that our 'dear old flag' was *first* insulted, and our brave Anderson and his men compelled to leave a post of honor they had sworn to defend and protect for their government. Here they make their (not empty) boast that they are the leaders of this rebellious movement. Is it *wrong*, then, that the streets of this city should be deserted—that her thoroughfares should be waste places? Could God be *just* on earth, and suffer her to remain in all her pride and strength? *This* is the cup, O Charleston, that thou hadst mixed for our New York, Boston, Philadelphia. How glad are we to see thee drinking the same! Yet, if God be just, thou hast only *tasted* yet. Fire and sword are yet in reserve for thee, and they will *surely* come. From every battle-field of our fair land comes up the blood of our slain heroes, crying to heaven for vengeance. As thou hast been *foremost* in bringing about this awful sacrifice, so thou must drink the *deepest* of the bitter cup. Go on, then, in thy mad career. God's time is not yet.

"'Live while ye may—
Enjoy *short* pleasures,
For *long* woes are to succeed.'

"Thy press and people may talk of independence—another victory, and the work is done—in time the delusion will vanish, and the truth will appear. Learn a lesson while ye may, or it will be said of you, as of Jerusalem, 'If thou hadst known, even thou, at least in this thy day, the things which belong unto thy peace; but now they are hid from thine eyes.'"

The following beautiful poem was written by Professor

J. Ogden, the author of "The Fourth of July at Macon, Georgia."

CHARLESTON, SOUTH CAROLINA.

I.

Oh, thou doomed city of the evil seed,*
   Long nursed by baneful passion's heated breath!
Now bursts the germ, and lo, the evil deed
   Invites the sword of war, the stroke of death!
Suns smile on thee, and yet thou smilest not;
Thy fame, thy fashion are alike forgot.
Consumption festers in thy inmost heart;
The shirt of Nessus fouls thy secret part.

II.

Lo, in thy streets—thy boast in other days—
   Grim silence sits, and rancorous weeds arise!
No joyous mirth, nor hymns of grateful praise,
   Greet human ears nor court the upper skies;
But deadly pallor, and a fearful looking for
The hand of vengeance and the sword of war.
Thy prayer is answered, and around, above,
The wrath of God and man doth hourly move.

III.

Thy foes are in thy heart, and lie unseen;
   They drink thy life-blood and thy substance up;
And though in pride thou usest to sit a queen,
   Justice at last commends the bitter cup.
The blood of slaves upon thy skirts is found;
Their tears have soaked this sacrilegious ground.
The chains that manacled their ebon arms
Now clank about thine own in dread alarms.

IV.

Thy sanctuaries are forsaken now;
   Dark mould and moss cling to thy fretted towers;
Deep rents and seams, where straggling lichens grow,
   And no sweet voice of prayer at vestal hours;

---

* The doctrine of State Rights, as taught by John C. Calhoun.

But voice of screaming shot and bursting shell,
Thy deep damnation and thy doom foretell.
The fire has left a swamp of broken walls,
Where night-hags revel in thy ruined halls.

v.

Oh, vain thy boast, proud city, desolate!
    Thy curses rest upon thy guilty head!
In folly's madness, thou didst desecrate
    Thy sacred vows, to holy Union wed.
And now behold the fruit of this thy sin:
Thy courts without o'errun, defiled within;
Gross darkness broods upon thy holy place;
Forsaken *all*, thy pride in deep disgrace.

vi.

Wail, city of the proud palmetto-tree!
    Thy figs and vines shall bloom for thee no more!
Thou scorn'dst the hand of God, that made thee free,
    In driving freemen from their native shore.
Thy rivers still seek peacefully the sea,
Yet bear no wealth on them, no joy for thee.
Thy isles look out and bask beneath the sun,
But silence reigns—*their Sabbath is begun!*

vii.

Blood! BLOOD is on thy skirts, oh city doomed!
    The cry of vengeance hath begirt thee round;
Here, where the citron and the orange bloomed,
    God's curse rests on the half-forsaken ground!
Thy treason, passion-nursed, is overgrown—
Thy cup of wrath is full, is overflown.
Repent, for God can yet a remnant save,
But traitors and their deeds shall find the grave!

Hospital, Charleston, S. C., Sept. 25th, 1864.

CHAPTER VII.

AT COLUMBIA, SOUTH CAROLINA—CAMP SORGHUM.*

"BE ready to move to Columbia, the capital, in an hour," said Captain Mobly to us the morning of the 5th of October, while we were all busily engaged in getting breakfast. It was not altogether unexpected; for the "*Mercury*," several days before, had spoken of the provost marshal being sent to Columbia to prepare a *good place* for the "prisoners." The reason of this move the Rebels did not condescend to inform us, but we supposed the principal one was, to remove us from under the fire of General Gilmore's guns. Perhaps the breaking out of the yellow fever among us had something to do with it. All the officials told us we should be much better off in Columbia than Charleston; the old story of improvement, often told, less often realized.

We "packed up" and waited in the front yard till eight, when the gates were opened, and we marched into the road or street, with guards on either side. Just before we left, the Irish and negro washerwomen came flocking to the fence with the bundles of clothes that had been given them to wash, many of them only the night before. They had been put into the wash-tub, only to be wrung out and returned to their owners, wet and still unwashed. Quite a number were as unfortunate as your

---

* So named, because that was the principal ration we received while there.

humble servant, who sent out his only whole and best shirt to be washed, anxiously waiting its return, that he might indulge in the luxury of a *clean* one. Vain hope! No shirt returned to him, and he was obliged to go to the capital of the chivalrous State of South Carolina with only the *remnant* of a six dollar sutler's piece of flannel by that name.

Having been moved several times before, we had learned wisdom thereby; and hence we determined to leave nothing that would add to our comfort in a new camp that we could possibly carry. As we stood in the street, we formed the most motley-looking crowd I have ever seen. Boxes packed with remnants of dishes, and rags tied up with an old piece of rope, a stick thrust through, and the whole borne on the shoulders of two. Chairs, pails, satchels, packs of blankets and brooms, old arch doors, griddles, benches, pieces of boards, kettles, pans and cups, were all taken along with us. Dressed as we were, blue, gray, red, white, and, in fact, a mixture of many colors, we looked more like the inmates of some county poorhouse or insane asylum than United States military officers.

As we passed the Marine Hospital we were joined by 100 more. We soon entered upon King Street, the "Broadway" of Charleston, and as we passed along up its now deserted walks we could see some of the fruits of secession. Tall grass and rank weeds were growing untrodden in its midst and alongside its walks. Block after block we passed that was *entirely* closed; many, with only one door opened, revealing scantily-filled shelves and empty show-cases. This was the retribution that South Carolina was to visit upon Northern cities during the war. Truly, "they that dig a pit shall fall therein."

We could also see the marks of our shells upon the houses and business places, showing plainly the fact that the shelling of the city was not in vain. Several of the officers managed to escape, on our march through the city, by dodging into the alleys; and in one case a Rebel sergeant came and took one out, marched him off with all the show of authority, and that night deserted with him to Morris Island—a plan previously agreed upon. *

We marched with very little regularity, filling the street from side to side, straggling as much as possible, to facilitate the escape of those who were trying to get off. The citizens, and especially the negroes, who thronged the walks, treated us with kindness and courtesy, bestowing what favors they could upon us, without the knowledge and interference of the guard. Bread, tobacco, pipes, water, and, in some cases, whisky was handed out to us. One jolly good fellow, a German, fell in company with some others of his nation, who pushed through the guard, and walked with him from near the hospital to the railroad train, about two miles. They very graciously treated him so often to the contents of a mysterious black bottle, that by the time he reached the dépôt he was "gloriously drunk," as well as his companions, which fact the guard discovering, drove them all off at the point of the bayonet, our prisoner among the rest, for he had on a suit of Rebel gray.

When we reached the cars we were nearly exhausted, for the day was intensely hot. Embarked again in boxcars, but were situated very comfortably, for we were not very much crowded. Just before we started, General

Gilmore sent over his compliments in the shape of a thirty-pound shell, which struck in a field near us without bursting. We gave it three hearty cheers. The whistle blowed, and on we went toward Columbia. Passed through a very poor section of country, and arrived at Branchville at 6 P.M.; prepared to rest as best we could, and finally arrived at Columbia at 1 A.M. Were kept in the cars until daylight, when we disembarked, and found a train, both before and behind us, loaded with officers. Thus we were all together again as we were at Macon. Soon after we disembarked, a Captain Semple, in whose charge we now were, rode into our midst, and gave orders that all the baggage should be made ready to be transported in wagons to camp. "Bully for Columbia," said we; "may this state of things continue for many days." For once, we began to hope we had changed for the better. Our baggage loaded, we sat down to wait for orders. No breakfast, and nothing to eat. Ten, eleven, twelve, one, and two o'clock came and passed, and still we were there. The hot sun poured down upon us; we had no shade. Some of the officers got uneasy, and began to explore. Near us they found a cellar filled with bacon, but they could not reach it. Found a long pole, drove a nail into the end for a hook, and went fishing. Met with decided success, judging from the bacon that I saw in the hands of the officers; but, alas! the game was discovered, and the issue of bacon from that time was *stopped*.

At four o'clock an order came for us to move, but it was only to the other side of the dépôt, to get into a yard for safer keeping. An attempt was made to purchase bread, and, in part, succeeded. By sending little boys after it, we could get it for fifty cents a loaf; but as soon as it came to the knowledge of Captain Semple, he ordered it stopped, and appointed a sutler, who soon came down with a load, and asked seventy-five cents. This started a proposition to "raid" him, which so frightened the poor fellow that he sold for any thing the prisoners were inclined to pay; but it was a dear job for us, for when they got us in their power again we had to atone for our temerity.

A guard was placed around us, and, without any thing to eat or promise of any, we were told we would remain there all night, and perhaps longer. We had no wood. Many had no rations, no money, and were very hungry. *Wait* was the word, and must be the act. A few, who had a little meal, made an attack on the fence, got a little wood, and made mush. About five o'clock it began to rain, a regular South Carolina shower, and continued until about eleven that evening. Not one of us had a particle of shelter, and were consequently drenched to the skin. The night turned cold, and, without fires, it was any thing but agreeable. But it was no use to repine; so, in the midst of the rain, a number of us collected together at the point nearest the dépôt, and sung, lustily, "Rally round the Flag," "The Star-spangled Banner," "Red, White, and Blue," and other patriotic pieces, for the benefit of a crowd of our "secesh" friends, who had gathered in the building opposite to look upon "the hated Yankee prisoners." For once, at least, Columbia had loyal men and patriotic singing in her midst.

As the rain continued, the ground was flooded, till, in some places, it was ankle deep. Sleep and rest were out of the question, as we were obliged to walk to keep warm.

CAPTURE OF THE FUGITIVES.

Morning dawned at last, revealing two hideous-looking cannon that had been planted near us during the night. Had the rebels wished to use them upon us they would have been of little service, for, as we scattered, their own people would be in as great danger as the prisoners.

While waiting here, a Lieutenant Parker was brought in, who had escaped from the train on its way from Charleston to Columbia. He had been recaptured, with others, by the "blood-hounds." He was badly torn by them, and was so weak he could scarcely stand up. He was taken to the hospital that night, where he died the next day from his wounds—*a sacrifice to Southern chivalry.*

While we were thus waiting, Captain Semple came among us, and asked us to take a "parole" not to escape, same as we had in Charleston, representing that he had a fine camp for us about two miles from the city; that we should have the largest freedom that could possibly be allowed; should be supplied with good comfortable tents for shelter; should have enlisted men to do our cooking for us; should be supplied with any thing and every thing they could possibly furnish for our comfort; that mails, money, and boxes should be delivered up to us without delay; a sutler appointed who should be limited in his prices, that we might not be imposed upon; in short, it should be very little like a prison, but much like a soldier's camp.

When asked if all these things should be ours now, he answered that they had not got the things quite ready, but they would have them in a few days.

"We wait till we see the advantages of a parole before we take it," said we *all.*

About eight o'clock we were marched out on the Augusta Road, across the Saluda River, about two miles from the city, on the top of a hill overlooking the valley. Around an old worn-out corn-field, partially covered with second-growth pines, had been cut a space for a guard-line. Here were posted their lines of sentinels, and into this we were turned to make ourselves as comfortable as we could. This was the *good place* that had been provided for us, and not to escape from which, we were asked to give our parole of honor.

The beauties of our situation can be summed up in a few words. They turned us out, like so many cattle, into an old worn-out field containing about half a dozen little pine-trees six inches in diameter, without a foot of board, or a piece of canvas for shelter; without a spade, an ax, a shovel, a cooking utensil, or any thing to make or keep ourselves comfortable. The wood, water, and sink were all outside of the guard-line the first two weeks we were there. If a man wanted to get something to eat, and wished a pail of water, he could go and stand by the guard-line opposite the place, and when his turn came out of 1200, could go and get his bucket filled. If he wanted wood, he could go and stand at another place, and, taking his turn, go out, break off some twigs and brush, come in and cook his little pot of mush, provided he could borrow something to cook it in. If he would attend the calls of nature, no matter how pressing, he must wait his turn. It was not an uncommon sight to see 100 standing in line at each of the places named, waiting their turn.

As soon as we were on the spot, Captain Semple came to the senior officer of the prisoners, Colonel Huey, 8th

Pennsylvania Cavalry, and informed him that he had one hundred wall-tents in the city, which he would send up *at once* for the use of the prisoners, and that he had telegraphed to Charleston for a sufficiency to cover all the officers, and that "they would do the best they could for us." This last was a stereotyped phrase which we heard from every Rebel official with whom we had to do. Although we should have known better, we concluded to wait a few days before we tried to build much of a house. A week passed, and seeing no prospect of being furnished with the promised tents, and feeling the need of some kind of shelter, made, as best we could of the pine brush, *shanties*, which, though uncomfortable, seemed better than to lie on the open ground.

About this time we had a cold storm of two weeks duration, raining nearly every day. We were almost entirely destitute of blankets or overcoats. Our other clothing was poor, and very thin, consisting of a pair of pants, often nothing but cotton at that, perhaps made from an old commissary meal-sack; a ragged shirt, or *none at all*, and a coat with the lining torn out, buttons sold off, and patched with many colors; a pair of boots or shoes, mended with straps, strings, cloth, any thing; if we had socks, they were patched from top to toe with various-colored cloth. Through all of this the wind would sweep with a vengeance that kept us shivering from morning till night, and from night till morning. Our little brush houses were no protection from the storm; our clothing was little better; we had little wood, and could get but a small quantity, and that of secondgrowth green pine; we were camped on the top of a hill, where the wind had a fair sweep at us, and, taking all of these things together, we were about as uncomfortable as we could be.

The ladies at home, "God bless them," did us a kindness which we shall never forget. Through the Sanitary Commission, they sent us several boxes of goods, originally designed, no doubt, for a hospital, yet none the less acceptable. Upon opening the boxes, we found shirts, drawers, towels, pocket-handkerchiefs, a few hospital gowns, bed-sacks, and several quilts. These were judiciously divided among us, giving to each one a towel, a handkerchief, and either a shirt or a pair of drawers, *but not both*, else some one would have to go without. Although not a tithe of what we needed to make us comfortable, yet they did us much good.

Soon after this the Christian Commission sent us a valuable donation in the shape of a box of reading matter, books, papers, pamphlets, etc. As soon as word was given that they were for distribution, they did not last five minutes. All wished to get something that would help to pass a lonely hour.

After about four weeks, the hope of being supplied with tents, or any kind of shelter, died out of our hearts, and we set about building ourselves some kind of winter-quarters, for it was evident we were to stay there till spring. The Rebels seemed to have come to the same conclusion, and, to enable us to build houses for ourselves, brought in for 1200 men *eight axes and ten shovels*. To facilitate matters also, a *kind-hearted sutler* sold us axes for the moderate price of forty-five dollars each, and a helve for five dollars. Those who had money bought private axes, those who had none had to wait their turn for one that the Rebels furnished, or depend on borrowing. That we might get at the timber, the commandant allowed a certain number to be paroled each day. Their names were written on a piece of paper, handed to the officer of the day, who instructed the guard to pass them in and out at their pleasure till night. This worked very well for those paroled, but some of the shrewd Yankees saw too good an opportunity to escape; watching their chances, they would go to a guard who was passing out the paroled men, and go out with them; or, if stopped, *convince* him he had been out before. Passing out, he forgot to return, and thus the game went on for several days, when it was detected. Then the order was changed, and all the paroled men must pass through at a given point. Then some of the paroled men who wished to escape would go to the officer of the day, take up their parole, come inside, put on a haversack well filled, pass out again by the sentinel who had been passing him before, and who was ignorant of the fact of his surrendering his parole. That trick was finally discovered, and then the paroled men were not allowed to come in till night, after being once paroled, but would bring their timber to the "guard-line" and throw it over, when it would be taken up by comrades inside and carried to their tent. If one wished to run away, he would watch his opportunity when the guard was not looking, and change off with a paroled man, and he in turn would slip over the guard-line when there was a crowd. Finally, there were so many escaping that the paroling was stopped altogether, and we could only get wood and building-timber at the stated time, when the guard was arranged for that purpose in the following manner, viz.:

Two reliefs of the guard, usually about 80 men, were

deployed around a piece of wood each day for a couple of hours, and we were allowed to get all the wood we could during that time. Some days we could get *much*, some days but little. This time was usually seized upon to "demoralize" the guard, *i. e.*, find one alone, and strike a bargain to let you run his beat at night for a consideration, or, better, let you stray past him *now* while in the woods. In many cases it succeeded. Generally fifty dollars, in Confederate money, would buy the best of them. A bargain was usually made for a party of five or six, and the guard with whom you traded was sure to bribe the ones each side of him. Sometimes an arrangement would be made by which they were to shoot into the air after the officers had succeeded in crossing the line, thus allaying any suspicion that might arise in case they should be caught in the act. A few, determined and reckless, attempted to run the guard without any negotiation. Many escaped that way; but three or four were wounded, and one was killed outright.

Many, very many more would have attempted to escape, had they possessed clothing and shoes fit to travel in. A frequent dodge was to go and play what was called "the hospital game." The members of the hospital were on parole, and were permitted to come in and out just when they chose. Almost every day they came in to buy bread at the sutler's, which they would exhibit to the guard as a kind of pass, and thus be permitted to return. Soon one, who had "escape on the brain," would go to the sutler, buy half a dozen loaves of bread, put on his overcoat, get a cane, limp up to the guard-line, show his bread, pass out, hobble over to the hospital, stay around till dark; suddenly get well, take to the woods, and bid good-by to prison, till recaptured, at least. This succeeded very well, till one day it was overdone and discovered, after about thirty had escaped.

While we were trying to build our quarters, it was quite amusing to attempt to go through camp. The space was very much crowded, and no regularity in laying it out. Each one built his cabin just where he could find a place. There was only one way by which you could go straight through the camp, and that was by an old road. Houses would go down and up again the same day. Whole sections would disappear, and be rebuilt in different shape. If you would find a friend, go where he *did* live, and you would find him *gone, house and all*. It was much like a city. We had our friends and few acquaintances, and beyond this knew nothing of those who were our near neighbors. Occasionally we would have a fire, and a call for certain "engines;" but "tear down" was our only remedy at such times. Wood was so scarce we could not indulge in the luxury of a bonfire very often.

Hauling Wood, Camp Sorghum.

The labor of building any thing like a comfortable cabin was very great, as we had so few tools, and had to bring the timber so far, sometimes nearly half a mile. About one half had quarters, when we were removed to the city.

A few days after our arrival quite an excitement was raised over the discovery of a few grains of gold in a little run near the creek. Old Californians turned out *en masse*, but, after washing the sand and gravel for a few hours, gave it up as a hoax. Our anxiety to find the *yellow* banished the *blues*, for one day at least.

As the papers had informed us of the nomination of Abraham Lincoln for a second term to the Presidency, upon consultation of the senior officers from the several states, it was determined to hold an election, and, if possible, send the returns through to our government. That they might get through in time, it was proposed, and agreed upon, to hold it on the 17th of October, which was accordingly done. Ballot-boxes were *improvised*, from a starch-box sent from home with "goodies" in it, to the whole hat of a "fresh fish," and a list posted up, appointing the senior officer belonging to the regiment of each state as the judge of election. The day passed off quietly, considering all things. A bulletin-board was erected at head-quarters, and dispatches received from different sections were posted for the information of the public. The following are some of them:

"New York, October 17th, 11 A.M.

"New York is going *all right* up to this hour."

"October 17th, 12 M.

"Highly Important from Kansas!!

"The Border Ruffians attacked the polls and drove

the Free State men away, killing three (3) and wounding six (6). Afterward the Free State men assembled, and succeeded in dispersing the Ruffians, and the state has gone Republican by a large majority ! ! !"

"Trenton, N. J., October 17th, 1864, 12 M.
"Special to the 'Bulletin.'

"It is rumored that, at a meeting of the citizens of the state, it was decided that, unless McClellan was elected President, the state would furnish no more 'apple whisky for the Congress of the United States.'"

"It is believed that the above is a false rumor, gotten up by the Black Republicans.—*Ed. Bulletin.*"

The following is the official report of the election, compiled by Captain Piggott, 8th Pennsylvania Cavalry, and kindly furnished me by Lieutenant Phelps, same regiment. It is taken from the official record now in my possession.

States.	For Lincoln.	For Johnson.	For McClellan.	For Pendleton.	Lincoln's Majority.	Johnson's Majority.	McClellan's Majority.	Pendleton's Majority.
1. Maine	25	25	0	0	25	25	0	0
2. New Hampshire	7	7	0	0	7	7	0	0
3. Vermont	29	29	1	1	28	28	0	0
4. Rhode Island	13	13	0	0	13	13	0	0
5. Connecticut	34	35	3	0	31	35	0	0
6. Massachusetts	43	44	5	2	38	42	0	0
7. New York	171	173	29	29	142	144	0	0
8. New Jersey	25	23	6	3	19	20	0	0
9. Pennsylvania	187	187	35	26	152	161	0	0
10. Delaware	3	2	0	0	3	2	0	0
11. Maryland	21	21	2	1	19	20	0	0
12. West Virginia	19	19	1	1	18	18	0	0
13. Ohio	142	144	15	12	127	132	0	0
14. Indiana	72	72	11	8	61	64	0	0
15. Illinois	79	80	8	7	71	73	0	0
16. Michigan	40	36	10	8	30	28	0	0
17. Wisconsin	19	19	1	0	18	19	0	0
18. Minnesota	5	5	0	0	5	5	0	0
19. Iowa	36	36	0	0	36	36	0	0
20. Missouri	10	10	0	0	10	10	0	0
21. Kansas	2	2	0	0	2	2	0	0
22. Kentucky	13	15	16	14	0	1	3	0
23. Tennessee	26	31	0	0	26	31	0	0
24. Alabama	1	1	0	0	1	1	0	0
25. Florida	1	1	0	0	1	1	0	0
26. California	1	1	0	0	1	1	0	0
Total	1024	1031	143	112	884	919	3	0

No. of officers in the prison on the day of the election..... 1382.
" Votes cast for President..................... 1167.
"   "   Vice-President.............. 1143.
Scattering Votes.. 5.

When the result of the election was announced it was greeted with hearty cheers, and Captain Semple said he would have it published in the city papers, but I did not hear of its being done, and I think it was not. For a few weeks they permitted us to buy the newspapers, and we took some comfort from reading the news. It made us feel as though we were not entirely buried out of the world after all. It was through this source we first learned of the re-election of President Lincoln, much to the joy of our hearts, as readers can judge from the vote we gave him.

About the latter part of this month Captain Semple was superseded in command of the prisoners by Lieutenant Colonel Means; but he, being soon placed in command of the post at Columbia, a Major Griswold, a renegade Marylander, who fled south with Winder at the commencement of the war, to assist in destroying our government, was placed in command of the prison. I think he was one of the most unprincipled men we had over us while prisoners. His character will be best illustrated by some of the following incidents.

At the time when the "escape fever" ran high, and many of the officers were leaving, he remarked, in the presence of a crowd of prisoners, "I should be very sorry to be obliged to open my artillery on the camp, *but, unless this running away is stopped, I shall certainly do it.*" On the morning of the 1st of December a cold-blooded murder was committed by a man named Williams, of Williams's Battalion, 3d South Carolina Reserves. I think he lived at Newberry C. H.

As we had been much crowded for room, in building our camp, many of the cabins were placed very near the dead line. On the west side, near the north corner, was one made under ground. The corner of it was about three feet from the dead line. Around this was a path along which the officers had been accustomed to pass without molestation from the guard. On this morning the wood-guard had been thrown out to the one below, opposite this point, and officers were passing in and out at pleasure. It was not uncommon for an officer to be allowed to cross diagonally the dead line to reach the wood-guard. Lieutenant Turbane, of the 66th New York Volunteers, came from his quarters near the centre of the camp, with an ax in his hand, to go out after wood. He started to go down this path, when the guard halted him and ordered him back. Without parleying a word, he turned around to retrace his steps, when Williams shot him in the back, the ball passing completely through him, into the tent in front of him. He staggered forward a few steps, fell, and died within ten minutes, without speaking a word. Those who saw the whole transaction testify he was fully six feet inside the dead line; that the sentinel must have known his purpose in going down that way. There was not the least cause to suspect him of attempting to escape. The morning was bright and clear, and it was then about ten o'clock. He had threatened to shoot several before that morning.

What did Major Griswold do about it? The officer of the day relieved the guard, yet without taking away his arms or accoutrements. He sauntered along up to headquarters, staid around there a while, *and in the afternoon was sent back on guard again, and posted on the front line.* As might be expected, we were very much incensed at such treatment, and some threats of violence toward the murderer were indulged in, in case he should come into camp. Knowledge of this came to Major Griswold, *and, the next morning, he sent that same* MURDERER *into camp, accompanied by a body-guard, to drive out the officers to roll-call.* As a military act, this was one of the meanest, most contemptible insults that could be offered us.

On the 22d of October they murdered Lieutenant

Young, 4th Pennsylvania Cavalry. He was sitting in his chair, in the evening of that day, chatting gayly with his companions around his little fire. His term of service had expired the day before, and he was telling his messmates of his plans for the future, when "bang" went a sentinel's gun, and he fell over into the arms of a comrade. He was shot directly under the right shoulder, his back being toward the guard-line. Of course a rush was made to the spot, when the guard threatened *to shoot again* if the crowd did not disperse. The lieutenant spoke a few words concerning his wound, groaned a few times, and was gone. "What will we do?" "Can we stand this?" were questions asked by many. Yet all felt that nothing could be done, and we must take every thing as patiently as we could.

The authorities furnished a plain coffin, and the next day permitted several of the officers to attend his burial, among them Lieutenant ———, formerly a minister, who made a prayer at the grave, and on the following Sabbath preached a funeral sermon from 2 Cor., v., 1. The circumstance left a gloom upon the entire camp. In this connection, I would speak of the deaths of Captain Wennick, 19th Pennsylvania Cavalry, and Lieutenant Spofford, of an Illinois regiment, who both died of yellow fever a few days after our arrival at Columbia, supposed to have been contracted before they left Charleston. Lieutenant Spofford was an old prisoner. Captured at Chickamauga, he spent the winter in Libby; and, but a few days before, I had been talking with him of the future. He spoke of a wife and child whom he had not seen for nearly three years. They were waiting for him in his Western home. He talked of the comforts that awaited him on his return from the war. But, alas, wife and child await in vain! And yet not they alone. Over 30,000 mothers, wives, sisters, fathers, wait in vain for the return of their murdered treasures from Belle Isle, Andersonville, Florence, Salisbury, and other prisons of the South.

As I am in a mournful strain, I will mention one other tragical event, which took place on the 8th of December.

Just at daylight that morning two strangers were discovered, closely locked, going through the camp, evidently with the intent of spying out the secret by which so many of the officers succeeded in making their escape. They had well-nigh succeeded, when the attention of some of the prisoners was called to their mysterious actions. It was decided they must not be allowed to leave camp with the knowledge they possessed, for it would prevent the escape of others. "They must be killed at once."

Bring an ax. It was brought, and the deed was done.

But now how to *hide* the deed was the question. An old well answered the purpose, and into this the bodies were thrown, and hastily covered with earth. Roll-call followed soon after, when a search was made by the guard for our two *friends*. After an hour spent in vain, they formed a skirmish-line across the camp, drove us all between the dead-line and the guard-line, and searched again for the missing members of the "chivalric society."

One of the guards testified positively to seeing them inside camp just after daylight, but could tell nothing farther.

As the party came near the well, they discovered some fresh earth on the outside, and, upon closer examination, found that all was not right inside of the well. One of the party descended to a little excavation in the side of it, and, after a few minutes' work, brought to light the missing — DOGS, dead *blood-hounds* — two of a pack that had been brought there on purpose to catch Yankees, and were put around the camp every morning to discover if any "Yankees" had made fresh tracks for liberty during the night.

As the dogs were dragged out by the guard, their resurrection was greeted with tremendous applause, groans, howls, barks, and some even plead that they might be left to make soup for dinner, as we had then been without an issue of meat since we left Charleston. But the authorities were relentless, and we had to go without our "dog soup." Still, we had one consolation, there were two less dogs in South Carolina that we knew of.

In the afternoon of that day Captain M—— came to the guard-line with a list of officers in his hand, and began to call for them. Visions of prison walls and dungeons rose up before those called for, and it was with difficulty some of them could be persuaded to go out. Soon, however, it was found they were "*special*" exchanges, and then the aspect of the matter changed somewhat.

All of the sick, all of the nurses were included, besides about eighty others. Several names were called of officers who had escaped, and, when it could be done without detection, another took their place, signing the name of the absent to the parole rather than his own.

One of those who had been paroled played a very contemptible, mean trick upon an officer who had thus signed the name of a brother officer from his own regiment. He

G

had already signed the parole, had also been called out with the party to go, and every thing was "all right," when this officer stepped up to Major Griswold and informed him of the facts in the case. It did not better the condition of *any one at all*, for the officer who reported the case was already paroled; nobody would have taken the place of the escaped officer. The exchanged party was just one less than it would have been had the case not been reported, yet no one was benefited by it.

The party left the next day about three o'clock. It was a terrible cold, windy time to us who remained, yet pleasant, I suppose, to those who left. Those who were among the fortunate, and chanced to have better clothes than comrades who were to stay, very generously made a change, leaving the *best*, and *all* they possibly could. I do not think a blanket was taken by a single individual away from the camp. We gave them three hearty cheers as they passed out of sight. Quite a number of letters were sent out by those who remained, informing their friends of their true condition. Others simply gave addresses of friends, that those who went out might write for them as soon as inside of our lines. "This," said the Rebels, "is the beginning of a general exchange, and none of you will be here much longer." We derived some hope from it, yet many were faithless till the war was over.

An amusing and *profitable* incident transpired in camp a little while before this. Our artist has represented it as "drawing meat ration."

A *black boar*, somewhat wild, came out of the woods near us, and by some means crossed the guard-line and entered camp. No sooner was he over the dead line

Drawing Meat Ration.

than several officers made for him, with visions of ham before their eyes. Porky made the best time he could, running toward the centre of the camp. The crowd of chasers increased, and Porky put on more steam. Clubs, stones, sticks, and hands were all brought into requisition to stop him, though for a while unsuccessful. But, alas! as Porky was born to be eaten, his short race was soon run, and he "*died nobly*" to satisfy the appetites of Yankee vandals.

As a consequence, there was much commotion in camp during the chase, which the Rebels seeing, and taking the alarm, turned out their regiment of guards, manned their artillery, and prepared to quell the insurrection at once. But, as soon as the cause of the excitement was known, they broke ranks in disgust, over which we had a most hearty laugh. It was not an uncommon occurrence for them to turn out the whole guard of infantry and artillery over the accidental discharge of a gun, or even loud hallooing in camp would effect the same thing, much to our satisfaction.

At this time about one third of the officers had succeeded, by hard work and indomitable energy, in building places that in part protected them from the inclemency of the season. It was now cold, and although we were in the "sunny South," yet the ground would freeze nights hard enough to bear a horse. Those who had still to live in their brush houses suffered very much from the cold.

Shanties, Columbia.

A few boxes had been received from home in tolerably good condition, and some were indulging in the luxury of good clean new clothes, and also of sugar, coffee, and some other delicacies. The last we received was in November, and the day the officers left a mail was received, among which were letters addressed to several of the officers, stating that our government had revoked the order allowing boxes to be sent through the lines to prisoners, etc.

"What could it mean?" inquired each one of his neighbor. It means "exchange," said the more hopeful. "It must mean that," said the sanguine. "Our government don't care for us any more," said the despondent. "They have used us all they can, and now they leave us to die, like old worn-out mules, and it looks by this order as though they would prevent us from enjoying again even the comforts our friends would send us. "Wait and see, before you condemn," said faithful patriotism. And we did wait; oh, how long it seemed.

After we began to make ourselves a little comfortable, we were favored with the following order from General Hardee, dated

"Head-quarters, Department of South Carolina, Georgia, and Florida. Charleston, S. C., November 14, 1864.

"COLONEL,—The Lieutenant General directs that you report to these head-quarters the name of every man who escapes from your custody. Also, that you notify the Federal officers that they *must* give their parole not to attempt to escape, or else they will be confined in a *pen* in the same manner that the privates now are.

"Very respectfully, your obedient servant,
"Signed,   R. C. GILCHRIST, A.A.A.G.
"To Lieutenant Colonel Means, Commanding Federal Prisoners, Columbia, South Carolina."

CHAPTER VIII.

COLUMBIA, SOUTH CAROLINA—"ASYLUM PRISON."

TRUE to their promise "that, if we did not stop escaping, they would put us in a *pen*, as the enlisted men were," the 11th of December, a cold, cheerless, and windy day, an order came for us to be ready to move the following day to the city.

The morning of the 12th found us all very busy packing up, preparing to move. With unprecedented liberality, they furnished some wagons to transport our baggage, and several expresses came up, which were hired at exorbitant rates, and used to transport baggage also. But little was left in camp, for the wagons were piled high as they could carry with poles, pieces of rails, slabs split from trees, any thing and every thing that could minister to our comfort.

To us it seemed rather hard to be turned out from even as poor quarters as we then had, in midwinter, and obliged to commence again to make ourselves comfortable. But there was no help for us, and we were *obliged* to submit. Before we left, however, we had one of the grandest sights we had seen for a long time, viz., a "camp on fire." About one half of the houses were built of pine brush, and were quite dry. These were nearly all set on fire, and they did, indeed, look beautiful. There had been an express order from Major Griswold not to burn them, but the incendiaries got among them, and away they went.

After the wagons were loaded, they were formed in column, and the officers formed also near the "dead line," preparatory to their march through the capital of South Carolina. We reached the city in safety, the prisoners following the train.

Probably one of the most noticeable features of this train, and that which was the cause of the most remarks, was a "cart" belonging to Colonel Thorp, 1st New York Dragoons — our commissary. Himself and Lieutenant Roach, one of his messmates, made it with an axe, auger, and case-knife. It contained the household goods of his mess, and was drawn by himself, Major Penfield, 5th New York Cavalry, Adjutant Goodrich, 85th New York, Lieutenant Pitt, 85th New York, Lieutenant Bradley, 85th New York, and Lieutenant Abbott, 1st New York Dragoons; said by the prisoners to have made a magnificent (mule) team.

We were marched through the principal street of the city, yet, compared with Northern cities, it had the appearance of a Sabbath. Men, women, and children looked out upon us as we passed, indulging in coarse, vulgar jest at our expense, that occasionally met our ears. When near the centre of the city, some one discovered Captain Tabb, of Macon notoriety. His name was called out, and, as he was recognized, was greeted with groans and hisses by the entire column. One man asked us who were drawing the cart "if we were not Sherman's wagon-train," and we answered him, "We thought South Carolina would see Sherman's train as soon as it wished to."

We reached the Insane Asylum yard about 3 P.M., and after some delay were sent inside. There we found for our accommodation two small buildings to be used as hospitals, and a *shell* of another, twenty-four feet square, with a part of a roof on. But it was of no use to repine or grumble. We must make the best of our situation by improving upon it all we could.

The yard contained about two acres, surrounded by a brick wall on three sides ten feet high and two feet thick. The fourth side was a board fence, which separated us from the asylum. In the other yard were planted two pieces of artillery, and port-holes were cut through the board fence to allow the muzzles to come through in case of action.

Instead of a platform for sentries to walk on, as at Macon, they had sentry-boxes outside of the wall. The water arrangements were very good, consisting of six large troughs placed in a line, supplied by a hydrant which kept them full all the time. Three of them we used for washing purposes, while in the other three the water was kept clean for cooking purposes. The water was always abundant, and of good quality.

QUARTERS.

I can not say as much of our quarters in the new camp. As before stated, we found a shell of a building twenty-four feet square, standing in the northwest corner of the yard. This was a model of the kind of houses we were all to have *at once*. They would furnish the lumber, timber, nails, tools, etc., if we would do the work for ourselves. "Give us the materials, and we will make the houses," said we all. Each building was to contain

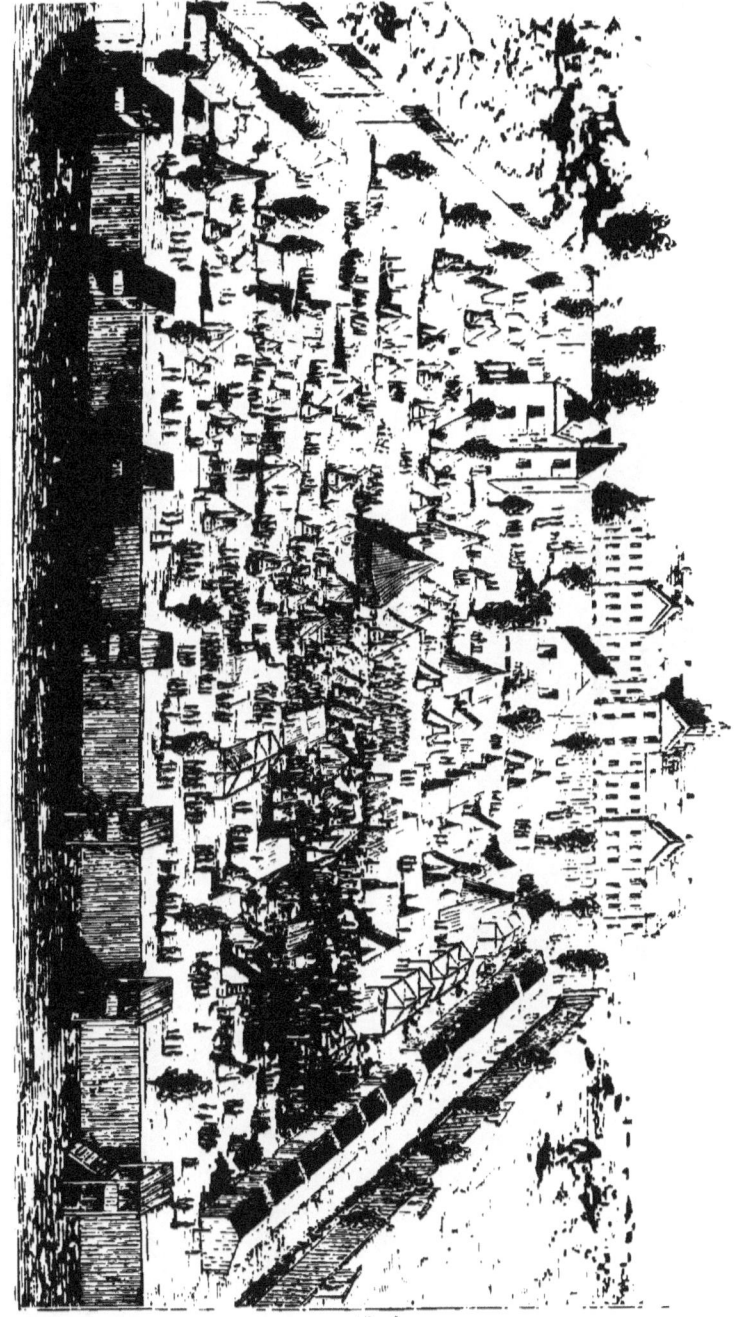
ASYLUM CAMP, COLUMBIA, SOUTH CAROLINA.

thirty-six men, to be divided into two rooms, having a double fireplace and chimney in the centre. At the close of the third day, all of the frames were up for the thirty-two buildings necessary for our comfort, and three of them covered. Many more would have been done, could we have had the materials as promised. The next morning Major Griswold informed us the government had impressed all the locomotives and cars, and they could get no more lumber till they could haul it from the country, sixteen miles. I think we got two loads in that way, when the necessity of fortifying Columbia became apparent, and all the teams were impressed for that purpose. About once or twice a week, after that, we would get a load or two of lumber, so that, when we left Columbia, instead of having thirty-two buildings we had thirteen.

To remedy this in part, they sent in some old tents and pieces of tents, which were used to the best advantage possible, and, by digging holes in the ground, crawling under the buildings, and making clay houses, nearly all had some place they called "quarters." Yet many, very many of them were no better than the open air, for they were poor protection against the storm and cold. The weather at this time was cold and freezing, our clothing was growing thinner and thinner, and it was not an unusual thing to find officers walking at all times of the night to keep warm.

The WOOD ration was very small indeed, averaging a piece about as large and as long as your arm from the elbow for one man. It was totally insufficient for cooking purposes, to say nothing of an attempt to keep warm by the fire. That was a luxury to be enjoyed hereafter. There was a wood screen before the sink;

Drawing Wood, Asylum Camp, South Carolina.

yet this was all torn down and burned up; every chip and stick was picked up, and carefully preserved for future use. There was much suffering all this time for want of fuel both to cook with and keep warm. Days that we received it at all, it was usually divided at night by the commissaries. Generally a lively time during its division.

RATIONS.

I did not say any thing about rations in the previous chapter, for they were uniform while in Columbia. In the first place, they stopped the *meat*, and *we were one hundred and thirty-three days in the city of Columbia, South Carolina, without a particle of any thing of the meat kind being issued to us.* In lieu thereof we received daily one gill of sorghum,* also one pint of coarse corn meal, *often*

---

* Sorghum was made from the Chinese sugar-cane, and that that we

ground cob and all; two table-spoonfuls of salt for five days, two table-spoonfuls of rice for five days, and this was ALL for *one hundred and thirty-three consecutive days.* To atone in part for not giving us meat, they proposed, upon our arrival at Columbia, to give us flour. The first issue was tolerably fair, and consisted of about a pint to a man for five days. The second looked like plaster, and was as black as buckwheat flour or rye, and looked very much like the sweepings of some mill; even this failed, and they gave us an issue of "shorts" from the tail-end of the bolt, and then they gave us "bran," and that ended the flour issue. Some of the officers suggested to the Rebel commissary the propriety of bringing us in some cutting-boxes and *straw,* and that would save farther issues of bread-stuff at all to us, but the suggestion was not acted upon.

To add to our troubles, they neglected to issue us any cooking utensils, although they often promised to do so. Had we not smuggled them through from other places, and bought others, we would have been compelled to have eaten our corn-meal raw.

Here, as in other places, although much more so, we were obliged to borrow and lend. The following "bill of fare" was an average of the day's meals at this place. Breakfast, hot mush and sorghum, or corn-meal cakes and sorghum; dinner and supper together, cold mush and sorghum, or corn-meal cakes, with a little rice in them, once in five days, with sorghum; dessert, pone and sorghum (if you could borrow a skillet to bake in).

Thus it went on day after day. The most of the cook-

got was usually black, sour, bitter, and very filthy. It gave the most of us the diarrhœa.

Sutler's Establishment.

ing had to be done *at once* for the day, for want of wood. Those who had money, or could get it, of course fared better, being able to buy a little meat, sweet potatoes, flour, beans, pepper, etc. The following was the

LIST OF PRICES IN ASYLUM PRISON.

Sweet potatoes, per bushel.	$35 00	Sheeting, coarse article, yd.	$10 00
Wheat bread, 6 oz. loaves..	1 50	Thread, black linen, lb......	150 00
Fresh Beef, lb.................	4 00	Combs, common, each......	5 00
Pork or Bacon, lb............	7 00	Tooth-brushes, each..........	10 00
Flour, lb........................	3 50	Lead pencils, each............	3 00
Butter, lb.......................	20 00	Playing cards, per pack.....	35 00
Lard, lb.	15 00	Socks, cotton, very scarce...	14 00
Tea, lb.	120 00	Shoes, English army, pair...	100 00
Sugar, brown, lb..............	18 00	Pepper, black, lb..............	35 00
Coffee, not in market.		Nutmegs, each.................	2 50
Salt, lb...........................	2 00	Soda, lb.	15 00
Candles, lb.....................	20 00	Chickens, pair, small.. 10 to	20 00
Mutton, very scarce, lb......	5 00	Rebel axes, each...............	45 00
Sole Leather, lb...............	45 00	Ink, you furnish bottle.......	1 00
Eggs, per doz..................	10 00	Steel pens, each...............	25
Smoking Tobacco, lb........	10 00	Pumpkins, sweet.......... 5 to 8	00
Paper, foolscap, per ream. .	225 00	Peanuts, pint...................	2 00
Envelopes, each...............	25		

Other things were in like proportion. No doubt many will say " that prices in Confederate money are not much higher than the same articles would cost in greenbacks with us;" but you must remember at what price we procured the value of the money sent us. The following plans were the principal ones adopted by the officers to get it.

MONEY SENT FROM FRIENDS.

The letter containing the money was first passed into the hands of the Rebel quartermaster, opened, the money and letter taken out, the amount it contained indorsed on the envelope, and that would be sent in to you, and your name posted on the bulletin-board, with the amount in the quartermaster's hands set opposite your name.

But you did not draw the money, or any part of it, from the quartermaster, but would give him an order to convert your money in his hands into Confederate money at government rates.* You could not draw even *this* from him, but you would be obliged to give another order for the quartermaster to pay over to the sutler the Confederate money belonging to you, and he (the sutler), in turn, would give you a due-bill on himself, upon which you might trade at the prices above named.

It will be very plain to any one that this plan was only one of swindling—a plan for the quartermaster and sutler to trade off their worthless currency for gold and greenbacks. I do not know the part General Winder played in this game, but judge it considerable, from the fact that the quartermaster first proposed to pay us our gold and silver, and convert the greenbacks only, as there was a law against trading in them; but as soon as General Winder arrived, he ordered that we should not receive a dollar of United States or Confederate money. They claimed that it was necessary to prevent their guards from being bribed, and thus allowing us to escape — a point which certainly was very well for them to guard, as there was much danger from it.

BILLS OF EXCHANGE.

Another method of raising the wind was to nego-

---

* The government rates were always much lower than the same kind of currency was selling in the city. The following are about the rates paid while we were in prison:

	Gov.	Elsewhere.		Gov.	Elsewhere.
Gold...............	33	47	Greenbacks........	3½	10
"	57	60	"	5	20
Silver...............	27	35			
"	50	55			

tiate bills of exchange. The one wishing money would draw up a legal bill in *duplicate*, sign both, and indorse across one end of each the following "*falsehood*" — "This money was loaned to me while a prisoner for my own personal use, as a favor. I therefore desire it paid." An old gentleman by the name of Potter, from Charleston, formerly from Rhode Island, followed us to Columbia on purpose to buy these bills, to accommodate the officers while in trouble, as they were his friends, and he *had always been a Union man*, and, in consideration of this fact, he proposed to give us *two dollars* in Confederate currency for one dollar in greenbacks, or *six dollars* in Confederate currency *for one in gold*, while at the *same time* greenbacks were worth fifteen and twenty for one, and gold was worth *and selling* at fifty for one. There was *Unionism* with a vengeance for you. All of this business had to be done on the sly — Potter leaving his currency with one of the officers, who transacted the business for him. He at one trip sold over $250,000 of his worthless stuff for *gold*, or its equivalent in greenbacks, at these rates. These bills were then sent North (*how*, I never found out), were presented and paid. We were thus enabled to get a little money to buy something to eat to keep ourselves from starving. Watches, knives, jewelry, boots, hats, buttons, any thing that would sell, was parted with to obtain money for this purpose.

It was no excuse for them to say they did not have it for us; they *did* have it, and every day they could bring in to us and sell at rates one third higher than their market. Every five days we would buy *more* than the amount of our rations for that time, thus proving conclusively that the rations were not *one half* that we needed to keep us in health, saying nothing of comfort.

The following estimate was handed me by Captain Cook, who was in the sutler's shop at the time. Read it, and then remember we ate all of this in *addition* to our rations, and then judge what those did who could not buy.

Estimate of Provisions sold every five Days in Asylum Prison, Columbia, South Carolina.

Sweet Potatoes	35 bushels.
Bread	4000 loaves.
Beef, fresh	3450 lbs.
Pork	1200 lbs.

Is it any wonder our enlisted men starved to death on the Rebel government rations? This is the reason *why* the officers did not look as bad as the men when they came out of prison.

MAIL.

During the summer we got very little mail till we arrived at Charleston. There it was more *regular;* several times we got quite a quantity at Columbia. The usual method of distribution was for the adjutant to mount a box, stump, steps, or any thing he could find, and call off the names, throw the letters into the crowd, and they would be passed from one to the other till it reached the right one. The call for "letters" would bring out the majority of the officers. How anxious have been the hearts of us all, while standing with the multitude waiting for our names to be called, that we might each hear a word from " wife," " mother," " sister," "brother," " home," and yet *how many* times have we turned away,

DELIVERING THE NAIL

after an hour's waiting, without receiving the coveted epistle. Often we used to write. Large mails were taken out and *destroyed*, as we learned afterward by some of the officers of Sherman's army, who left us at Charleston to be exchanged. They were taken to Macon, and not permitted to go farther. They testify to having seen a dry-goods box of letters, written by the officers while in Macon to friends at home, lying open as waste paper. Several picked them over, and took out their own letters and destroyed them. The postage stamps had been all taken off, and there they were left. At Columbia they told us they sent them as fast as they could read them, but they could get very few who could read letters, and that delayed them somewhat — a fact which will account in part for the failure of friends to hear from their husbands, sons, brothers, while in prison. As paper and writing material were so high, it was not much encouragement to try to write home after these facts became known.

AMUSEMENTS.

The principal amusement here was furnished by a "band" and "glee-club." The band was composed of Lieutenant Chandler, first violin; Lieutenant Manning, second violin; Lieutenant Rockwell, flute; Major Pratt, bass viol. The instruments were bought while we were in Charleston, and were furnished by contribution, costing some $800 Confederate money. Pleasant evenings they would assemble on the stoop of the hospital, and discourse sweet music to us for hours at a time. Quite often gentlemen and ladies from the city would come up to listen, and see the Yankees.

The "glee-club" was a splendid affair, composed of Major Isett, of a Wisconsin regiment, Captain Patterson, 3d West Virginia Cavalry, Lieut ——, and Lieutenant —— (names forgotten). 'Twas by them "Sherman's March to the Sea" was first sung, bringing down the house with tremendous applause.

MEETINGS.

Dr. Palmer,* formerly of New Orleans, came in and preached two very good sermons for us to large and attentive audiences, and another minister from the city came in once. We had a Bible-class every day at 12 M., which was well attended, and very interesting and profitable. Had prayer-meetings on Sabbath evening, and also on Thursday evening. While here, Lieutenant Henderson, 14th and 15th Illinois Battalion, died, and, upon a petition being sent to Major Griswold for permission for several of his friends to go out with his body, and bestow upon him the rites of a Christian burial, he refused it on the ground "*that* it was too far to the grave for us to walk, and we could not go." Another specimen of Southern chivalry. Matters at this time seemed to be growing worse and worse. Many of the officers were getting sick, the rations were notoriously small and poor, our clothing was about all gone, and there was no immediate prospect of exchange. We learned also that New York and Philadelphia had each fitted out a vessel, loaded them with provisions, and sent them to the Rebels at Savannah and other places, but

---

* The same who prayed at the commencement of the war that the "yellow fever might destroy our men faster than the bullets." It is said he has since repented.—*Ed.*

we United States officers and soldiers in Rebeldom—*we could be passed by*, and not even have the privilege of receiving any thing from our friends at home. Surely we thought things had come to a strange pass, and a committee was appointed to address a letter to President Lincoln upon the subject, asking that something might be done for us. True, we had heard that each government was to supply its own prisoners with necessaries, but we could not learn that any thing was being done for us. The following letter was written by Colonel Thorp, chairman of the committee, and indorsed by all who heard it read or saw it. It was the intention to send it through the lines by some officer who escaped, but I think it never reached our government.

"Asylum Prison, Columbia, South Carolina,
January 25th, 1865.

"To his Excellency ABRAHAM LINCOLN,
President of the United States:

"SIR,—Having been requested by the Federal officers now confined in prison at Columbia, South Carolina, to communicate with our government in relation to their condition and circumstances, I have the honor to address you as follows. That the treatment which Federal officers in prison have received at the hands of the Confederate authorities is well understood at Washington is generally presumed and believed.

"It has been one hundred and twenty (120) days since the Confederate authorities have issued us a ration of meat of any kind; and their long-continued barbarity in this respect, practiced upon Federal officers held as prisoners, has become intolerable and merciless in the extreme.

"Therefore, possessing as we do, and ever shall, let whatever be our fate, a deathless love and devotion for our common cause and country, the law of preservation imperatively demands that we most respectfully ask and pray your excellency to send, through such channels and by such means as may be most expedient for our government, a sufficient supply of shoes, blankets, clothing, meat, and bread, to protect twelve hundred (1200) officers, many of whom are without sufficient shelter, and entirely destitute of shoes and blankets, from the bleak winter winds, and relieve them from a gnawing hunger more insufferable than a preying virus.

"The stern but wise policy which seems to dictate a longer continuance in prison furnishes a subject for no complaint, and all are willing to await deliverance until those who administer the laws for millions of freemen shall decide it consistent with the exigencies of the service, and compatible with the interests of our government.

"I have the honor to be, very respectfully, your obedient servant."

CHANGE.

Not money, but a change of officers who had charge inside of the prison. One day the drum beat at three o'clock, an unusual hour, and we went out to roll-call, and found we had a new adjutant and inspector, a Dutch-Frenchman. He had been a prisoner in our hands a while, having been captured at Gettysburg. Before we broke ranks he made us the following laconic speech:

"Shentlemens, I comes to take command of you. I've been in Fort Delaware fifteen months. Your peoples teach me how to behave myself. I spects more of you than brivates. I does for you all I can. You treats me like shentlemen, I treats you like shentlemen. Break ranks—march."

We greeted this with a tremendous cheer, each hoping new lords would bring new laws that would better our condition; but, alas! they were false hopes, for, after about a week's duty, he got "gloriously drunk," quarreled with the surgeon, was arrested and taken to jail, and that was the last we heard of him.

About this time a disease broke out in camp known as

EXCHANGE ON THE BRAIN.

It was contagious, and was just as certain to affect a prisoner as measles are children. All must have it, not once or twice only, but it is liable to return at *any* time with greater or less fury. The premonitory symptoms are a slight remembrance of home, thoughts of greenbacks, visions of turkeys, ham and eggs, beefsteak, vegetables, wheat bread, comfortable quarters, and civilized society. If no remedies are applied, in a few days you will find the disease in its second stage. The sufferer will talk about going home (sometime), being tired of sorghum and corn meal, and freely expressing his opinion thereon; and, if accustomed to use strong English, will indulge in a few denunciatory adjectives.

If the disease continues its course uninterrupted, you will soon find the patient advanced to the third stage, from which it usually becomes chronic. He will now rave somewhat about his situation and the course of the government upon the question of exchange, threatening to leave the service the first opportunity; regretting deep-

H

ly that he was ever captured, or (in some cases) ever entered the service; bitterly denouncing the Rebels and all that pertains to them; saying strong, harsh things against the government, Secretary of War, General Butler; till, finally, the fire exhausts itself, and the patient goes off and takes a nap, after which he feels better.

We had many discussions over this subject *pro* and *con*. It was urged there was no principle involved; if there had been, how came so many "special exchanges" to take place? More or less of them were constantly occurring, and if the government could exchange forty or fifty, could it not *all?* Did the *negro* question stop it? Had not our government a sufficient number of Rebel prisoners, so that they could afford to exchange all our white soldiers, and then have a sufficient number of Rebels left as hostages for our colored soldiers? Has the government forgotten us? If not, why prevent our friends ministering to our necessities? Have our services ceased to be as valuable to our government as before we were captured? Must we remain idle here, while our brethren in arms are finishing the rebellion? We entered the fight boldly, with burning, patriotic hearts; and the inside view of the rebellion, as seen through prison bars, has not quenched that fire, although it may have smothered a little of it in the hearts of some. Oh how much we desired to join our brave comrades who were distinguishing themselves on so many bloody fields that will be remembered in history! But no, we must remain in *masterly inactivity;* must *die* almost for want of something to do. A thousand times over would we have preferred the toils, hardships, and exposures of the campaign, to the dull, monotonous life in Rebel prisons.

TUNNELING AGAIN.

About the middle of January, one morning, we were surprised by the officer of the day bringing in a guard, and, proceeding directly to one of the tents on the northeast side of the camp, drove out the inmates, and commenced searching for a "tunnel," and was rewarded by discovering a splendid one *nearly completed.* Two or three nights more, and it would have been ready for use. Hopes were again blasted, for we were ordered to remove the tent to another part of the camp, and thus the hard labor of many nights was unceremoniously destroyed.

Before night a paper was posted on the hospital, reading something like the following, viz.:

"NOTICE!

"General Winder directs that I inform the Federal prisoners under my command that, unless the tunneling is stopped, he will cause all the buildings, tents, lumber, boards, and shade-trees to be removed from the yard.

"I would also say that I shall use force for force if any attempt is made to injure any prisoner suspected of reporting tunneling at these head-quarters.

"(Signed), —— GRISWOLD,
"Major Commanding Federal Prisoners."

The reason of inserting the last clause was the suspicion in camp that one of the prisoners had reported the tunnel to the Rebel authorities, and there was talk of lynching him on the spot. He was not seen after we left Columbia, I believe.

This threat of Winder's was only the signal for tunneling to commence; for, at the time we were hurried away so unceremoniously, nearly a dozen were in progress, a part of them nearly completed, which would let out two persons each minute. They were not discovered till after we left, and, as Winder was gone, I suppose the buildings were left standing.

DEATH OF WINDER.

The 8th of February we first heard of Winder's death, which caused great joy through all the prison camps—joy that he could no longer torture Union prisoners.

He was directly and the immediate cause of all the unnecessary suffering among us. He was the commissary general of prisoners, and he had it in his power to say what they should have to eat, where and what kind of quarters they should occupy, and what they should have to minister to their comfort. In all the prisons, so far as I have been able to learn, there was great rejoicing over his death. There was one other noticeable feature in his administration. As he was a renegade Baltimorean, he selected, as prison officials, Marylanders of his own stamp—men who had left their own state, and run into others to help destroy the government.

The following story concerning the cause of Winder's death obtained much circulation among the prisoners. I do not vouch for the truth of the statement, only the story.

When General Winder was first placed in command of the Federal prisoners, he made an arrangement with his Satanic Majesty that he (*Winder*) should have unlimited power to torment Union prisoners while the war lasted;

and, farther, that there should be no "general exchange" while he lived; that when an exchange *did* take place, his work was done, and his master might come and claim him.

Certain it is exchange *has* taken place, and Winder is —gone.

AN INCIDENT.

Quite an amusing incident transpired while here in this yard one morning, showing how men with high notions get taken down sometimes by being made prisoners of war.

An officer from Sherman's army, well uniformed, and apparently accustomed to good fare and the conveniences of life, came into the prison one morning soon after daylight. As he looked upon the ragged, half-naked, and hungry specimens of humanity before him, he remarked, "He wouldn't live *so;* he would show prisoners how they ought to live." After looking about a while, he found his way to the senior officers' quarters, where the following conversation took place.

Capt. Colonel, I am a prisoner, just arrived, and have come up to see you, and find out what I must do.

Col. Very well, sir; I shall be happy to do any thing for you that I can.

Capt. Well, I must have a place to live, and I suppose the first thing I want is a tent.

Col. I don't think you will be able to get one, for there are a good many officers here before you who have not been able to get a particle of shelter as yet. If there were any tents to issue, *they* would have the first claim.

Capt. But where shall I stay?

Col. Any where you please, sir.

Capt. Where shall I sleep nights?

Col. In any place you can find unoccupied. Perhaps you can find room under one of those hospitals. They will keep the dew off a little.

Capt. But I have no blankets. How will I get along in that case?

Col. The best way you can, sir.

Capt. Don't you think they (the Rebels) will give me a pair?

Col. I don't think they will. I have never known of their doing any such thing.

Capt. Well, I am hungry; what shall I do for rations?

Col. They will issue you some in a couple of days.

Capt. (*Somewhat astonished*). What will I do till then?

Col. Oh, we will divide with you, as we always do with fresh fish.

Capt. Will they give me any thing to draw my rations in?

Col. I don't think they will. I have never known of their doing any such thing.

Capt. What will I do, then, for something to put them in?

Col. Tear up your red shirt, drawers, coat-sleeve linings—any thing you have in the cloth line about you; or, if you prefer, you can keep your clothes, and go without rations.

Capt. Will I get cooking utensils?

Col. I don't think you will. The Rebels are not in the habit of giving us such things.

Capt. What will *I do*, then?

Col. Borrow of any body you can. There are a few cooking utensils in camp, and, *when not in use*, you can borrow them without difficulty.

Capt. (*Turning away in disgust*). Well, I think such kind of treatment is rather rough for civilized beings, any way.

Col. That's about the conclusion we have all come to, and congratulate you on learning your lesson so quick.

CHAPTER IX.

"HOMEWARD BOUND."

The month of February was full of rumors to us. Upon every breeze was borne tidings of an "exchange" soon to take place. We had heard of the meeting of the Peace Commissioners in Hampton Roads, and of its failure on the part of the Rebels to gain any advantage over our government. Major Griswold told us that the failure had only strengthened the bond of union that held the South to its work of resistance; that they were to reorganize a campaign for ten years upon an entirely new basis; that they were to put 300,000 negro troops in the field against us, and they would yet *break the power of the United States government, and be independent.*

He farther told us that the terms of a general exchange had been agreed upon, and we would all be home within a month. Putting these things with the report of the debate in our Congress upon the exchange question, the statement that "Mr. Wilson had been informed by the Secretary of War that all obstacles had been removed to an exchange of prisoners, we began to take some hope. To add to our exchange stock, the Rebel adjutant general brought in shortly after a slip clipped from one of their papers, stating that "Captain Hatch, who accompanied the Peace Commissioners to General Grant's headquarters, was notified by General

Grant himself that a general exchange of prisoners would take place with as little delay as possible."

As might be expected, there was much excitement in camp over these statements, which so well agreed. "*Is it true?*" was asked hundreds of times.

Our hopes were still farther heightened on the 13th of February, when an order came for 600 to be ready to move to Charlotte, North Carolina, with the assurance that we would remain there but a few days, and then be sent on to Richmond. We also learned from the faithful negro* that Sherman was approaching Columbia, and it was unsafe to keep us longer there. "The old story," said we, as we packed up, meanwhile making our arrangements to escape from the train on its way to Charlotte.

We left the Asylum Prison-yard the 14th of February, bag and baggage, making about the appearance we usually did when we moved. Soon after we reached the cars it began to rain, turned cold, the rain became sleet, making the trip decidedly uncomfortable. We were stowed in box-cars, as usual, forty together. Many of the guards, who attempted to ride outside by order of Major Griswold, nearly perished, and were finally obliged to come inside. The cars were old and rickety, and during the night two of them broke down and had to be abandoned. Once the train broke, leaving six of the cars on the track, while the locomotive ran off to the station, five miles distant, before the accident was discovered by the engineer. It

* This same negro brought in all the papers we had while in Asylum Prison. A few days before we left he was caught with one in the toe of his shoe. They gave him one hundred lashes, and threatened to kill him if he repeated the act. When he told of it he said, while the fire flashed from his eyes, "Dey may kill dis nigger, but dey can't make him hate de Yankees."

was nearly time for an up express. We had out no tail lights, or any thing to show we were in the way, and it was only by threatening to leave the train *en masse* that we could persuade them to build a fire on the track to warn trains of danger. Fortunately, the "runaway" came back in time to take us out of the way before any accidents happened.

As the night was so bad, many who had determined to escape were deterred. Such a storm I have seldom seen. It was almost impossible to live out in the woods, as one escaping would be obliged to. Yet some braved it, the majority only to be recaptured after several days and nights of starvation and travel.

We arrived at Charlotte, North Carolina, at four o'clock on the afternoon of the 15th, and, disembarking in the mud and water, marched three quarters of a mile to a little pine grove, which was called by some "Camp Necessity," by others "Camp Bacon," for here we received the first meat we had had in over one hundred and thirty days. It was also denominated "Camp Exchange," but it received that title after we were inside our lines.

Here we had a few old "A" tents for shelter, otherwise there was not the least convenience or preparation for our comfort. But we had been so long used to abuse we were not much disappointed, and proceeded to make ourselves as comfortable as we could. The ground was soft and wet, and the water we drank was obtained from an old goose-pond. We had been there but a little while when Captain Stewart (in whose charge we now were, and he was a gentleman) informed us that we would not stay there long, for he had just received a communication from Colonel Hoke, commandant of the post, stating that he had received a dispatch from Richmond saying that the terms of a "general exchange" had been agreed upon, and it would commence in a few days, and, to clinch it, he (Colonel Hoke) said he believed it to be true. "Another move, and less guards," said the "old fish," and turned away with disgust, while some of the "freshest" invested quite largely.

During the day following Colonel Hoke himself rode down to our camp, and had an interview with our senior officer, Colonel Shedd, 30th Illinois, in which he reiterated all he had written to Captain Stewart. Another thing that added weight to all this was the fact that the Rebel guard that surrounded us was totally inefficient and terribly demoralized, yet no effort was made to increase its efficiency or punish the delinquents. Officers could and did escape both day and night while we were there. This fact alone kept many back who would have escaped had the guards been kept more strict. Nor were these facts hidden from the Rebel authorities, for Colonel Hoke sent down a request "that Colonel Shedd would ask the officers not to straggle up town, as they had a very strong police guard, and some of them might get into trouble. We were joined here by those left at Columbia, so that we were all together again.

On Sunday the 19th, an order came for 200 to leave at 5 P.M., which they did in good spirits, arriving the next morning at Greensboro'. 200 others left the next morning, passed the first detachment at Greensboro', and went on toward Raleigh, the capital of the state. Passed it in the night, and arrived at Goldsboro' the next morning at four o'clock. We at once disembarked, and built some little fires as best we could, and waited for morning, to see what would "turn up." Soon it came, and with it a train of 700 of our starved prisoners from Florence and Salisbury. They had been sent forward to Wilmington for exchange, but General Foster, who was conducting the campaign there, had had no orders from General Grant to receive prisoners at that point, and hence he refused to entertain the flag of truce the Rebels sent out to him, for it was likely to interfere in his capture of Wilmington. Hence they were obliged to come back to Goldsboro' again, and await farther orders.

I wish it were in my power to portray on this page the scene of suffering that met us as those men attempted to get off the train. They had ridden all night in open flat cars, without a particle of shelter or fire. It was in February, and a bitter cold, damp night, and, scantily clothed as they were, they had suffered beyond account. Three had died during the night, and were still on the train. Not one of them had a whole garment on, while nearly all were destitute of shirts or coats. A ragged or patched pair of pants, and a piece of an old blanket, constituted the wardrobe of the majority. Their faces were blackened by the pitch-pine smoke from the fires over which they had cooked their rations, while traces of soap and water were lost altogether. Hair and beard in their natural state. Yet all of this was nothing compared to their diseased, starving condition. In short, no words can describe their appearance. The sunken eye, the gaping mouth, the filthy skin, the clothes and head alive with vermin, the repelling bony contour, all conspired to lead to the conclusion that they were the victims of starvation, cruelty, and exposure to a degree unparalleled in the history of humanity. Many of them were unable to walk, or stand even, and would fall upon their knees as soon as they touched the ground. They informed us they had had nothing to eat for twenty-four hours, and were suffering from both hunger and thirst. We gathered every thing we had with us that was eatable or wearable, and attempted to take it to them, when the guards presented their bayonets to us, with orders to have no communication with them whatever. Doubling clothes and rations into one bundle, we pitched them over the guards' heads, and oh! such a sight! Never were dogs more ravenous for a bone than were those poor boys for something to eat and wear. Mother—perhaps it was thy only boy, thy pride and stay; wife—perhaps thy husband was among those on his knees scrambling, with all his little remaining strength, to get a morsel of corn bread; sister—thy brother was one of those, brave and true, a martyr for his country. These were the sons, husbands, brothers, that these "chivalric" Southrons (God save the mark!) would return to us, "wrecks only of their former selves." As a specimen, I pulled off an old hospital gown, and threw it to one poor fellow who had neither coat, vest, nor shirt. As it struck his bare back, he turned around and picked it up. "Put it on," said I. He looked at me with a demented stare, when I repeated the command. He hugged it to his naked breast, and was moving off, when I called to him again to "put it on." He seemed to realize for a moment that it was something to wear, when he made one or two feeble efforts to get his arms through one of the sleeves; but his mind seemed to wander again, and, hugging it as before, he marched off. Nor was this an isolated case.

They soon marched them off out of our sight, and the commandant of the post issued an order that none of the citizens should visit them, or minister in any way to their comfort. *Three others died* in attempting to go two hundred rods, while more than twenty were obliged to fall out from exhaustion; and these they told us were the *well* ones. Is it any wonder that, as we stood and looked at these brave men who had thus suffered for their country, we swore by Him who is just we would not leave the service till the rebellion was *crushed?*

As they were marching off, Lieutenant Powell, of South Carolina, who had them in charge, turned to several of us officers and remarked, "They have generally been well treated and well fed, but for a few days past they have had rather a hard time of it."

Well fed and well treated! He *lied,* and he knew it. The proof of it was too plain to need contradiction. Every soldier present was a living witness to the falsehood. Their blackened faces, that had not seen soap since they had been in the Rebel states, answered against it. The sunken cheeks, glassy, protruding eyes, and idiotic stare denied the assertion. Every feature, limb, organ, and muscle, as well as every garment, were patent proofs to the *willful lie* he had uttered.

Orders were finally received, and at eight o'clock we left for Greensboro' and Richmond, to go through the lines on the James River; but, on arriving at Raleigh again, we were sent by a down train, containing Captain Hatch, who was on his way to Wilmington with a special order from General Grant to General Foster to receive us at that point, or one near there that might be agreed upon. We were ordered to remain at Raleigh till he could be heard from, which it was expected would take two or three days.

We remained on the train till daylight, when we discovered a large proportion of those we had left at Charlotte bivouacked on the bank near us, and during the day the rest of them arrived. We found that about half of those left at Charlotte had been paroled preparatory to exchange, and this day and part of the following was spent in making out our papers.

INCIDENT.

While waiting here, one of the officers, who was not feeling well, noticing a fine house near by, walked up there to see if he could get a little milk to tempt his appetite. Entering the house, he very politely asked the lady for some milk, stating he was not well, and he wished it for his supper.

Lady. We have nothing for Yankees, for they are our enemies, overrunning our country, killing our people, and destroying our property.

Officer. (*Taking out a slip of paper*). Will you please give me your name?

Lady. No, sir.

Officer. Well, it is of but little matter. I shall be back here in a few days, and shall remember the place.

As he turned to leave he discovered a colored servant in the room, and, turning to her, asked her mistress's name.

Lady. Don't you tell him. If you do I will kill you!

The officer then walked out, but as he was passing out of the gate he met a Rebel officer, who tauntingly said to him, "You didn't get much in there, did you?"

Officer. All right, sir. Matters may change somewhat in time. And he related what had passed between the woman and himself, and then returned to camp.

Next morning, soon after daylight, what was his surprise at receiving a nice pitcher of milk from this same lady, with her compliments, and the apology that "the milk had been all used up when he called yesterday."

Query. Didn't she come? etc. * * *

A DIABOLICAL PLOT.

At 3 P.M. we were ordered to Camp Holmes, an old Rebel conscript camp two miles from the city. Two trains of cars were sent down, loaded, and went up "all right." Two hundred of us still remained, when one of the trains of platform cars came back to take us up. We started, and just as we were leaving the city, passing round a curve on an embankment fifty feet high, we ran through an *open switch!* How it came open, or who opened it, are questions unanswered.* The engine, tender, and two cars ran off the track; the engine plowed in the bank, tipped up on its side, and *stopped when it lacked only a foot of running down the bank.* Had the ground been a little harder, a little narrower, or the train running a trifle faster, nothing would have saved us from sure and certain death—*how* many, God alone can tell. Fortunately, but two or three were hurt, and they not seriously, simply sprained ankles from jumping.

We were then obliged to walk to camp, and found it,

---

* The developments of the Conspiracy trial give us good reason to believe it was a plan to destroy as many as they could of us, of which the starvation process was a part. If they would *starve* men, would they hesitate to *murder* them by wholesale?

as we had expected, dirty, lousy, filthy, and inconvenient. While here we had plenty of "skirmishing" to do, a duty that was as necessary, *daily*, as it was to eat. To a "fresh

Skirmishing.

fish" it seemed rather indelicate, but he soon became as bold as any. No class was exempt, neither was any place. Libby, Macon, Charleston, cars—all were infested with these vermin. A good story is told of General Dow while in Libby. An officer, discovering the general with his shirt off, looking it carefully over, accosted him with, "General, are you lousy?"

"No; but my shirt is!" was the prompt reply.

We remained here till Monday afternoon, when a train came up and took 300, and at 9 P.M. 570 more of us got on and into eight box-cars, while the balance came on the next day. At this time, I believe, there were no complaints about being crowded or of poor accommodations.

At 11 30 we found ourselves again at Goldsboro', and we camped one and a half miles from the city, on the Weldon Road, with the promise that we should go on at eight o'clock. However, as we expected, we staid till the next day at 5 P.M. There was also a camp of enlisted men about a mile from us, and they were suffering all it was possible for them to suffer and live. Many of them *did not live.* Some of the "ladies," God bless them, loyal women of North Carolina, heard of the sufferings of these poor men, and, regardless of the "order" of the commandant of the post, *visited* them, ministering to their wants as best they could. Some of them came eight miles on foot, through the mud and wet. And one old lady and her two daughters (a Mrs. Scott, of Wilson County, Black Creek District, North Carolina) came in an ox-cart, twenty miles, to do what they could. I was able to obtain only the names of the following. There were others; let them be remembered by every patriot, for they were liable to arrest at the time they were there. Mary Ann Peacock, Goldsboro', North Carolina; Mary Starling, Mary A. Worrel, Rachel Worrel, Hepsey Jackson, Martha Sicer, Pikeville, North Carolina. It may be truly said of them, as of one of old, "They have done what they could."

While here we received a magnificent donation of a wagon-load of provisions from Snow Hill, North Carolina. Before it was unloaded, all said, "Send it to the enlisted men," and there it went, with a contribution of $470 from the officers with it. I would also mention that several gentlemen at Raleigh remembered us kindly in the shape of provisions, and prominent among them was Governor Holden.

PASSING THE LINE FOR EXCHANGE.

We left Goldsboro' at 6 P.M., crowded, piled, jammed on the train, inside and out, and, amid songs and cheers, started for Wilmington, which was now in our possession. Rode all night, and daylight found us standing on the track, three miles from Northeast Bridge, fourteen miles from Wilmington. This place, we found, was the outpost picket-line of the Rebels. At eight o'clock down came Colonel Hatch (late captain) on a special train, with a white flag flying from his engine. As he ran on to a switch, we backed up and passed him, giving him one of our good loyal Union songs. He then took the lead, and we followed. All this certainly looked like exchange. As we neared the bridge our expectations began to rise, and each one was looking ahead to catch a sight, as soon as possible, of something that was not "Rebel." "Three cheers for Colonel Mulford and the boys in blue," said one, and we gave them with a will. As the train came to a stand, all seemed impressed with the idea that we must be silent, or the spell would be broken. We now disembarked, and, forming in line, were counted through the ranks of our soldiers (the escort about twenty), they presenting arms to us.

No doubt it would have been an interesting sight to our friends (it was to us) to see us march through, ragged, destitute, hungry, lean, and gaunt, yet feeling well, I assure you.

As soon as one passed the line of the soldiers he would start on a "double-quick" down the road, swinging his piece of a hat (if he had one), and cheer most lustily. About a quarter of a mile out they stopped us, to form for marching. Here the scene that took place beggars description. We laughed, cried, hurraed, hugged, kissed, rolled in the sand, and — rejoiced generally. Many declared it was the happiest day of their lives. Up to this point we had transported all our baggage, and now you could see it "high in air," or lying around promiscuously; ration-bags of corn meal, pots, pails, pans, kettles, pieces of old blankets—all went, and glad were we to leave them, too. This was the first time we had seen *plenty* of corn meal since captured. We also cheered for General Grant, Sherman, Lincoln, Johnson, and General Exchange, all voting that the latter personage was the "biggest general" of the whole.

After a little delay, which was necessary to count all through, we started for Cape Fear River, where our forces were encamped. A mile and a half brought us, for the first time, in sight of our flag. As soon as the head of the column came in sight of it, it began to cheer, which ran down its whole length.

The 6th Connecticut was encamped on the bank of the river, and at the end of the pontoon bridge they had erected a bower of evergreens. In the centre of the arch was a card, surrounded by a beautiful wreath of evergreens, on which was printed

"WELCOME, BROTHERS."

From the centre of this arch were flung out the national colors, while their band played

"Hail to the chief who in triumph advances."

Cheer followed cheer, and shout followed shout, till we reached the river. This we crossed in silence, and passed the flags with uncovered heads—many in tears, while not a few stepped out of the ranks and kissed the sacred emblem of freedom — a blessed privilege they had not enjoyed for many long months.

As we reached the top of the hill, we found the whole division turned out with side-arms to meet us, and they gave us a hearty welcome. We were marched to a pine grove, where we were served with hard bread, cold boiled fresh beef, and coffee. Our friends can judge what we did with it, for it was a full meal, the *first* for a long time. Dinner, or rather breakfast over, for we had been twenty-four hours without food, we sang songs in the exuberance of our joy, patriotic, national, and comic, and those of us who were able started to march to Wilmington — nine miles; and such marching! We made it in less than three hours, for each one walked as though he feared to be behind, lest he should be "gobbled" by some stray Rebel. As we arrived at Wilmington we were taken to a "retreat," supplied with supper, and allowed the freedom of the city. The next day we embarked on board a steamer for Annapolis, which place we reached after five days and a *comfortable* amount of sea-sickness. Here we were promptly met by officers who did all they could for us, prominent among whom was our old friend Uncle Sam. If we had ever supposed he had forgotten us in our imprisonment, these fears were dispelled upon our arrival here. We quickly obtained new outfits, and, after a few days, received a "leave of absence" for thirty days to visit our friends.

I trust we were not ungrateful to Him who had so safely brought us through all our troubles, and it is our earnest wish that, whatever else may befall us, He will spare us a return to Rebel prisons.

CHAPTER X.

AT ANDERSONVILLE.

It is from no unfair motives that I am induced to make the following statement of what I saw and experienced while a prisoner in the hands of the Rebels during the spring, summer, and autumn of 1864. I have tried to give a truthful account of some of the cruelties and sufferings which our poor boys were called to endure in filthy, loathsome Southern prisons and hospitals. It seems to me there can be no reason for any one to make a false report of the miseries we received at the hands of our heartless captors and brutal prison-keepers. To tell the truth of them is all that is needed to convince any reasonable man of their barbarities, and fiendish attempt to deprive our soldiers, whom the fortune of war had thrown into their power, of every comfort and enjoyment of life.

But to my narrative. I was captured April 2d, 1864, at Plymouth, North Carolina. It is to the credit of the Rebel soldiers whose good fortune it was to capture our command, stationed there to hold and defend the place, that we were treated with considerable courtesy and kindness while in their power.

To my knowledge, no outrages were committed upon any of our white troops, though I believe the small negro force with us fared very hard.

Our men were allowed to retain their blankets and

overcoats, and all little articles of value which they might have upon their persons. Many of the men had about them large sums of money, which they were allowed to keep.

From Plymouth a long and wearisome march was made to Tarboro', a very pretty town, situated on the Neuse, a few miles from Goldsboro'. By the time we arrived there the men were much fagged and worn out. The last day of the march we were without rations, and suffered a great deal from hunger and weariness. Soon after reaching our camping ground, near the town, rations were issued to us. There were a few "cow pease," or beans more properly, some corn meal, a small piece of bacon, and a very meagre allowance of salt, for each man. Some old iron kettles, tins, etc., were provided for us to cook our food in, and a small quantity of wood furnished, and we managed to prepare a repast which was very palatable to our well whetted appetites. A system of trading was immediately commenced, which was carried on for a while very briskly, but was finally prohibited by the Rebel authorities.

Our men would barter away their watches, rings, gold pens, pen-holders, pocket-knives, coat-buttons, etc., for "Confederate pone cakes," hard bread, and bacon, from the Rebels. The most exorbitant prices were demanded by both parties, our men, however, generally getting the best bargain. We had remained at Tarboro' but a few days when orders were received to remove all the Union prisoners who could travel to Andersonville, Georgia, immediately. We had already suffered much, both from hunger and exposure. Many were sick and feeble; all were anxious to leave, and we felt much re-

I

lief at hearing that preparations had been made to remove us to a pleasanter and more fruitful portion of the Confederacy. We were informed that Camp Sumter, the prison to which we were going, occupied a delightful locality, and also that our food there would be more wholesome and plenteous than that which we had yet received. Their fair accounts and pleasing stories but increased our anxiety to be off, and it was with no little pleasure that, on the morning of April 29th, we bade adieu to the gloomy field into which we had been turned as so many brutes, and marched with quite joyous hearts to the dépôt in town. Here we were confined, and crowded by forties into small and loathsome box-cars. Besides our own enormous numbers, six Rebel guards were stationed in each "carriage," a name which I heard applied by a foppish young officer to the miserable concern aboard which we were literally packed. Of course the Rebels occupied the door, and we nearly suffocated.

Under such circumstances, many of the boys, less sanguine and hopeful than others, began to express doubts concerning the stories which we had heard, and intimated that they were all mere fabrications to deceive us, and make it an easier matter to convey us to Camp Sumter.

Without doubt such was the case. It is certain that they made the utmost efforts to get us through to the stockade at Andersonville under as small a guard as possible. We arrived in Charleston on Sunday morning, May 1st. To our great surprise, we found that some of the inhabitants of the city were friendly to us. They distributed tobacco and cigars among the men, and some secretly brought them food.

Months afterward, some of our suffering, dying boys

found inestimable friends in the Sisters of Charity who abode in the city.

Leaving Charleston at an early hour in the afternoon, we were hurried on at quite a rapid rate toward Savannah, Georgia. About six o'clock in the evening it commenced storming very hard, and, being on platform cars, we were thoroughly drenched with rain.

At about nine o'clock we changed cars a short distance from Savannah, for Macon, at which place we arrived the following day, a little past noon.

I was much pleased with Macon. It is a handsome city, and pleasantly situated on the Ocmulgee River—a stream of some importance. It contained a number of fine residences, several churches, two or three large iron foundries, and a car-factory, I believe. Trees, flowers, and gardens presented an appearance not unlike that of early summer at home. Almost every thing there was looking pleasant and beautiful, and I felt very sad at leaving, knowing, as I then did, something of the true character of our future abode. Late in the afternoon of May 2d we left Macon on our way to Andersonville, at which place we arrived some time in the evening.

Soon after our arrival there we were marched into an open field near by, where we remained during the night.

It being very cold, large fires had been made by the Rebel soldiers for our comfort. For this little act of kindness we indeed felt very grateful to them. The next morning, May 3d, a sinister-looking little foreigner came down to us, and, with considerable bluster and many oaths, began to form us into "detachments" containing 270 men each. These "detachments" were subdivided into "messes" of ninety each, and placed under the control of a sergeant, whose duty it was to attend "roll-call," drawing rations, etc.

At length, every thing being ready, we were escorted into the prison under a strong guard.

It is impossible to describe our feelings at this time. Every where around us were men in the most abject wretchedness and misery. Immediately on our arrival among them they began to gather around us, and in a very touching manner related the sad story of their sufferings and wrongs. We could only *sympathize* with them. Beyond that we could do nothing. We knew full well that the same cruelties which they had experienced were in store for us. The prospect before us was dark indeed. In the afternoon of the day on which I entered the prison I ventured out some distance into the camp. Every where was the most unmistakable evidence of intense suffering and destitution. Hundreds of the men were without shelter, and but very few had any comfortable clothing.

The supply of wood was very small, scarcely enough to cook with, and the poor fellows were obliged to lie, night after night, week after week, on the cold, damp ground, without even a fire to warm themselves by.

The Rebels may claim that there was some cause for not issuing a sufficient quantity of food to our prisoners at Andersonville, but for not granting us wood enough to keep us warm and to cook with there can be no apology. On three sides of the prison there was an immense woodland, from which all the wood that we needed could have been provided with very little difficulty. The same holds true in regard to shelter. I am persuaded that it was an act of premeditated inhumanity on the part of our enemies not to give us shelter. It would have required but a few weeks' time and a few scores of hands to have built barracks for our comfortless boys there which would have been the means of saving hundreds of precious lives. If the Rebels would have granted us even the rough, unhewn logs, and axes to work with, we would have built them ourselves.

The camp at this time was in a most loathsome condition. It then covered an area of about fifteen acres, and was inclosed by a high stockade, built of pine logs, hewn and closely joined together. Upward of twenty feet from the stockade was the fatal "dead line," beyond which any poor fellow passing was almost certain to be fired upon by some of the ever-watchful sentries.

In the centre of the camp, and extending entirely around it, was a broad ravine, which toward the beginning of summer became one of the filthiest places imaginable, and was one of the chief causes of the vast amount of sickness which existed during the months of July and August following. About this time, May 10th, the average rate of mortality daily was upward of fifteen. It afterward rose as high as seventy-five and one hundred.

Sunday, May 15th, a wretched cripple, who had the reputation about camp of being a very dangerous fellow, willing, for a double ration, to inform the Rebels of all plans made for escape which he might discover or accidentally hear of, was mortally wounded by a Rebel sentinel while on duty. For some unknown reason, the miserable man purposely passed beyond the dead line. The guard ordered him to go back; he refused to do so, and used some insulting language in reply. The sentry then fired upon him. He fell, horribly wounded, and lived only about two hours.

Sunday, May 22, a little incident of some note occurred in camp, to the great satisfaction of the well-disposed.

It must be confessed that great demoralization prevailed among the prisoners. Quarrels and fights were of frequent occurrence.

But the worst of all were the murderous deeds perpetrated by a desperate set of fellows, who had banded themselves together for the purpose of robbing the defenseless among them. From the sick and powerless they would steal blankets and pails for cooking in; and if a man was known to possess money, he was in danger of being deprived of it all, and possibly of his life besides. This morning one of the heartless scoundrels had been caught in the act of stealing from some one of his companions, and met with summary punishment. A part of his head and beard were shaven, and he was then exposed to the view of any who might wish to see him. After this he was turned over to the commandant of the prison, who immediately released him, but promised the men that in the future they might inflict what punishment they should deem proper on all whom they should catch engaged in robbing their comrades. The prime cause of all this demoralization among the men was the treatment they received at the hands of the Rebels. Had the Confederate authorities provided food in sufficient quantities for our men, and furnished other necessary comforts, it is altogether possible that no such deeds would have been committed in the camp; certainly they would have been very rare.

Toward the close of May our rations were "cut down"

fearfully. Starvation really began to stare us in the face. There were but few who were not suffering the pangs of hunger continually. Our daily allowance was only about half of a small loaf of corn bread, about four ounces of bacon, and a little "mush" made of Indian meal partially cooked in water.

A portion of the camp drew raw rations, and fared somewhat better than those whose food was prepared before issued to them. Our food, when cooked outside, was always prepared in the most careless and indifferent manner. It not unfrequently occurred that even the meagre supply of bread which we did receive was sent into us half cooked, and, when in this condition, it would become during the night totally unfit to eat.

About the close of summer cooked beans were issued to us. These were always in a most disgusting state, and could have been eaten only by starving men. There was always a copious supply of gravel, pods, and, what was still worse, bugs, in each man's allowance of this miserable farce.

June 3d a large number of wounded men were received at the camp, many of them in very destitute circumstances.

But few, if any of them, were admitted to the hospital, though a large number had severe and painful wounds. Their sufferings became intense, almost unendurable. Without shelter during the day, they suffered indescribably from scorching, burning heat, and at night perhaps not less so from the cold. Many died. It could not be otherwise. Who but the merciless enemies of our country can be held accountable for this fiendish sacrifice of valuable lives?

The morning of June 9th a very unjust order was promulgated throughout camp. We had been permitted to send, nearly every day, a small squad of men from some of the detachments, under Rebel guards, into the woods near by, to procure some fuel for the camp, but it was now decided that no more should be allowed to go forward until they would solemnly pledge themselves not to attempt to escape while outside the stockade for that purpose; and if, after having given their pledge, they should violate it, the detachment to which they belonged should receive rations only every alternate day until the time that those who had escaped should be recaptured. To go without wood was impossible; to submit was the only way by which we could obtain it, and consequently we were under the necessity of yielding to the base demand.

Sunday morning, June 19th, one of our men, unfortunately getting beyond the dead line, was fired upon by a guard. He was missed, but the ball wounded two others, one severely.

On the 21st another man was shot while merely reaching beyond the dead line for a small piece of wood which he needed.

Toward the close of June sickness and death began to prevail in camp to an alarming extent. The men died by scores daily. But few were admitted to the hospital, and even when received there it was not until life was nearly extinct. The old prisoners who had been incarcerated for months at Belle Island were falling away with fearful rapidity. Nearly all of those still living could see nothing before them but a slow, torturing death from a most painful disease, which had been caused by a want of proper food and constant exposure. None can fully realize the intense agony, the horrid suspense and wretchedness felt by these unfortunate men, but those who have had a like experience. Indeed, their sufferings were beyond description. Only a few could receive medical treatment, and that scarcely worth mentioning, while in every part of camp were as brave and loyal soldiers as any that had ever taken up arms in defense of freedom, suffering and dying in a manner that might have shocked even the rude sensibilities of an American savage.

It seemed that, the more bitter our anguish became, the more delighted were our fiendish keepers. Not satisfied with the cruelties inflicted upon us, they even carried their animosities beyond this life, and declined to give a Christian burial to our dead. I will not now longer dwell upon this subject. It is too painful to contemplate.

July 13th, one of the men, in attempting to procure some clean water to drink, passed a little beyond the dead line, and was fired upon by two of the guards almost simultaneously. Both balls missed him, but took effect upon two other men, killing one of them immediately.

About the middle of July I was fortunate enough to make the acquaintance of a most excellent young man from Philadelphia, a member of the 7th Pennsylvania R. C. Volunteers, Joseph Egalf by name, who was actively engaged in caring for our neglected wounded men. From morning till night he went about dressing their wounds and ministering to their wants, and was unremitting in his efforts to benefit and comfort them. All in suffering had his sympathy and compassion, and his aid, so far as it was in his power to render assistance. What finally became of him I do not know, but, should he be living, it is hoped something may be done to reward him handsomely for his many acts of love and kindness toward our poor boys who were with him at Andersonville.

I find the following written in my diary under date of July 25th: "While walking in camp this morning, I observed several poor fellows lying upon the ground, without shelter, blanket, coat, or even blouse—merely shirt and pants to protect them from the bitter cold of the past night." There are a great many in camp in the same condition, and hundreds who are without shelter, blanket, and overcoat.

To some it may seem incredible that it should be very cold during the night at this season of the year, but such was indeed the case.

It may be asked, What became of the prisoners' clothing? I answer that, except in a few instances, it was stolen by the Rebels. Many a poor fellow can remember how unceremoniously he was stripped of almost every thing of value in his possession in an hour after his capture. Resistance was useless. To resist was to expose one's self to certain death. If a bare command would not bring a man out of his new boots, or induce him to give up his coat, a loaded pistol pointed at his head would.

July 27th, another of our men was shot. He received a horrible wound in the head, and was carried out of camp in a dying condition.

August 4th, still another was shot, receiving a severe wound through the body. August 6th, another cold-blooded murder was committed.

One of the men, passing a little too near the stockade,

was shot dead by a guard on duty. It had become dangerous to pass at the regular crossing. The sentinels seemed to be more vigilant than ever before in watching for opportunities to shoot down our poor unarmed men. No one was safe. No warning was given to a thoughtless intruder. The first thing one would know of his terrible condition after passing the fatal line was a quick, sharp report, a groan, and all was over—another murder committed. About the middle of August the rate of mortality was about eight per day. Diarrhœa and scurvy were the chief scourges of the camp. The fearful work of death was visible every where around us. I have frequently seen as many as thirty dead men lying in a row at the prison gate to be carried out for burial.

It was sad, indescribably so, to see these brave men dying so far from home and its hallowed associations. No fond parents near to speak words of comfort and tenderness. None able to minister to their temporal necessities—none who could alleviate their sufferings. Alone they must writhe in the agonies of death—*alone* to die. It was under such circumstances of darkness and misery that the shining truths of Christianity shone out before men in their unsurpassed glory and heavenly beauty. Many a freed, joyous spirit went from that foul, loathsome prison to immortal life and happiness.

Thus far only some of the *physical* sufferings consequent to our imprisonment have been briefly mentioned; it is now time to refer, for a few moments, to the intense *mental* trials and afflictions which we prisoners experienced.

In my diary, under date of August 24th, I find the following: "I believe the loss of health, exposure to privation, and physical suffering consequent upon the manner of life in which we are now compelled to live, are not the saddest effects of our present captivity. But that which is the more lamentable is the mental debility which, under the present state of things, we must necessarily experience." Again, "The finer feelings—that which makes more lovely—as social being, love, affection, friendship, kindness, and courtesy, are being constantly deadened—rooted out from the heart, leaving it in a most woeful condition." Scarcely an hour in which anxiety about distant friends, suspense in regard to the future, and frequent despair, were not felt. It seems to me that the mind must have been in a state of trouble and anxiety nearly all the time its frail tenement was suffering from confinement and disease. It was almost impossible to procure reading matter. Some of the soldiers had Bibles and Testaments, which were eagerly sought after and read by many of the men.

It was with great difficulty one could think very attentively about other subjects than home and release from imprisonment. A topic for conversation might be introduced among a squad of men; perhaps they might talk about it for a few moments, but it would soon be dropped, and home, friends, and possibility or probability of exchange would come up for discussion. Men—brave men, indeed—became gloomy and despondent. Light faded from the once brilliant, fiery eye; the color disappeared from the manly countenance; manhood seemed to forget itself—the entire man was speedily drifting toward a fearful ruin. Hope had nearly vanished. The mind was laboring under intense agony.

To some the burden was too much, and they have never recovered from its baneful effects. Others have nearly recovered, but the scars remain.

September 7th, the removal of the prisoners from Camp Sumter to other portions of the Confederacy was commanded. We were induced by the Rebel authorities to believe that this unexpected movement was for a general exchange. With this belief our men could be sent away with only a small force guarding them, which was a consideration of no little importance with the Rebels just at that time.

Suddenly stricken down with a violent attack of the scurvy, I was unable to leave with my detachment, and was left with the sick in camp. After suffering several days, I managed to get out with the first squad of sick which left for Florence, South Carolina.

I was quite weak and feeble when I arrived at Florence, but a change of climate and diet rapidly improved my condition, and in a few days I was able to walk about without crutches. Soon afterward I was detailed as hospital steward and paroled.

From that time till my release, November 30th, my treatment was much better than it had been while I was at Camp Sumter; but in regard to that received by the thousands of poor fellows in the prison, there was but little apparent change. They suffered from cold and hunger perhaps more than while at Andersonville.

Sickness and death prevailed in every section of the camp. A few weeks before my release, measures were taken to build barracks for the sick. A bakery was also established, and a small loaf of wheat bread issued to the patients daily. The surgeons in charge seemed to do as well as possible with the small resources and means which they possessed. Indeed they were very kind to us, and manifested considerable interest in our welfare. Some supplies from the United States Sanitary Commission were received, and distributed with great care among the destitute and needy. So far as I was able to discern —and I had many opportunities to observe for myself, being privileged to go in and out of the prison at any hour during the day—I found that the Rebel authorities acted honestly, though perhaps not wisely in all cases, in regard to distributing the blankets, shoes, pants, and underclothing to our men, which had been provided for them by the Sanitary Commission.

I will here close my accounts of the sufferings of our friends. So far as I am concerned personally, I can forgive our bitter foes the cruelties which they have inflicted upon me. I do not desire revenge. That is farthest from my heart. God will punish them for their evil deeds. They have already suffered terribly. I feel that all should now try to do whatever they can to narrow the breach which exists between them and ourselves. I have always been glad our government so nobly declined to resort to retaliation. We can not afford to be cruel. It is our highest honor to reward good for evil.

The magnanimity of our people is beyond question, and our enemies must acknowledge it. Our arms have conquered their proud hosts; our kindness must now subdue the enmity of their hearts. We must be neither too lenient nor too severe. To the *leaders* who precipitated us into four years of bloodshed and war, the severest punishment which the law can give; but to the poor misguided masses, that clemency which only a noble people are capable of exercising.

CHAPTER XI.

AMONG THE NEGROES.

WE crossed the Saluda River in the morning, and lay in the woods till after dark. We then started out to find the road which led to Greenville. Crossing an old field, and while passing a gate, we heard some one call out "Who's dar?" Supposing it to be a negro, we halted, and sent one of our party to see who it might be. It was an old negro woman about fifty years of age. As the officer approached her, she said,

"Ah! I knows who yous is; yous Yankees 'scape from prison. I seed two ob your men two days ago; dey staid at my house all night. I feed um, and dey went on dere way in de way you're all gwine."

"But why," said the officers, "do you feed the Yankees?"

"Because dey doing so much for us: we knows dat you is 'bout all de friends we hab long time ago — dat you is gwine to make us free. I lib in dat old house yonder, and takes care of my old mudder, who's now 'bout hundred year old. You see I am not fit for de field no more, so I lib dar, and take care of her now. She told me, while I was a little gal, 'bout dat—how dat we warnt always gwine to be slaves; dat de Lord would deliver us as he deliber de Mosesites in the wilderness grate while ago, and when dis war commenced we tink de time is come. It come bery slow, gentl'men, but den we knows it's comin'."

Officer. Can you give us something to eat?

Negro. I wish I could go and bake you som bread, but I goes to meet my old man down to de riber.

Officer. Very well; can you direct us to the Greenville Road?

Negro. Yes, dat big road up dar; turn to de lef; go careful; make no noise.

Leaving the old lady, we marched on about three miles, when we were suddenly accosted by a good ebony gentleman from the side of the road. It was an old negro man about forty, who was going to spend the Sabbath with his wife, who was owned on a plantation some miles distant from his place of servitude. It will be remembered that slaves were permitted to spend the Sabbath with their families. We halted, and commenced conversation with him as follows:

Officer. To whom do you belong?

Negro. Massa G—— H——, sah.

Officer. Is he a good master, and how does he treat you?

Negro. Well, he did treat us bery well before de war, but since dat some of de boys rund away, and he treat us bery badly!

Officer. And have you ever heard of the Yankees?

Negro. Yes, we heard great deal 'bout dem people. Massa G—— tell us great many bad tings 'bout dem, but den we can't tell 'bout dat, after all.

Officer. Did you ever see any of them?

Negro. Widout you is some; yous look like um.

Officer. If we should tell you that we were Yankees,

would you believe it, and could you give us something to eat?

Negro. Ob corse, I'd b'lieve you, and I will do all I can for you. If you will go wid me, I will get some tatoes, bread, and meat.

He then went back with us three miles, and, after secreting us in the thicket, went away, saying, "I return in an hour; when I come I cough to let you know it's me; if any body come and don't cough, keep bery still; dat ain't *me!*"

In about an hour we heard a violent coughing in the wood, like one in the last stage of consumption. Presently our sable friend made his appearance with two large loaves of bread, several pounds of bacon, some sweet potatoes, and salt, all of which were very acceptable, as we had been forty-eight hours without food. He told us if we could wait another hour he would get more bread and potatoes. We waited until the cough again announced his return, bearing three loaves more of bread and some potatoes. He then went two miles with us on our way. When we again reached the road, before he left us, I asked him if he knew what the Yankees were doing for *them?*

"Oh yes," said he, "we knows all 'bout dat. You is de frens ob de black people. Massa Lincum make us free by de proclamashun."

Officer. Who told you that Mr. Lincoln had made you free?

Negro. Jane, de cook, what teaches massa's children to read, tell us 'bout it.

Officer. Who is thiis Massa Lincoln of whom you speak?

Negro. He am de Bresident ob de United States, whats been 'lected by de people; but de Rebs refuse de noledge ob it, and make Jeff Davis bresident.

Officer. Don't you think Jeff Davis a better president than Lincoln?

Negro. (Shaking his head, and exposing his ivory.) Better nor Lincum, whats been 'lected by de people; whats 'titled to de posishum; whats de black people's frend; whats made us all free? Yah! yah! can't tell dese children any ting 'bout dat—dey knows all 'bout it.

Officer. You know Lincoln is putting a great many of your boys into the army, and getting them killed. You don't think Jeff would do that, do you?

Negro. Whats de better, to be killed in de field wid de bullet, fitin' for liberty, or wid de whip, pickin' de cotton for notin'? For my part, I tink de army is de best, and if I was free, I'd be dar myself.

Officer. Well, Frank, you must wait your time, and I hope it is not far distant, when you will be a free man.

Negro. If I neber is free myself, I hopes to make de children free.

Officer. You have children, then?

Negro. Seven; and I wants dem all free and edecated like de white folks.

Officer. Do you think your children could learn to read?

Negro. Why, ob corse dey can. Why, dar's Jane, what cooks at de house, she can read better dan missus herself, and den she teaches de white children to read. And den dar is a kullurd preacher ober dar, why he can jest git rite up and read a hymn jest as good as any man you eber heard. Now you see if Jane can read. Why, ob corse she ain't quite so black as I be, but den her muder was jest as black a niggah as you eber see."

By this time we arrived at the corner of the road, and, when about to leave, the old man extended his brawny hand, saying, "I lebe you here, hoping dat all de black people you meet will be kind to you, and dat you will hab a safe jorney to your frens." Never did I more fully appreciate any blessings which heaven bestowed on me than those we received at the hands of old Frank, and never did I feel more like saying God bless them, and may the good work go on until their entire race shall enjoy the blessings of freedom.

After leaving the old man we marched until about two o'clock in the morning, when we met another negro in the road, with a large bundle of something under his arm. We stopped him, and asked him what he had. He refused to tell for some time; but on learning, however, that we were Yankees, he unrolled his bundle, and exposed several fine fat chickens, saying, "I got dese for a Sunday dinner; but de Yankees are frends to us, we frends to dem; now, dem's my words—take um."

We paid the boy for his chickens, and charged him to say nothing of meeting us, and we went on our way rejoicing. To justify himself in taking the chickens, he said he had had no meat given to him for forty days, and that he had lived exclusively on sorghum, sweet potatoes, and rice.

Another instance will suffice to illustrate the point which I desire to make. Several days after the above transpired, our rations again getting short, we thought it expedient to speak to another negro in order to get some. As we halted one morning in a piece of woods (it will be remembered that we traveled exclusively at night, to avoid detection) to seek protection for the day, we discovered some negro men in an old field about half a mile distant, engaged in plowing. We at once determined to avail ourselves of the opportunity, and I was designated to go and speak to them, and see if they could do any thing for us. Creeping down to the edge of the field, I secreted myself in the bushes until they had passed several times round, so as to satisfy myself that no white man was with them. Seeing they were all of the sable hue, I rapped on the fence with my cane and halted them, whereupon one exclaimed, "Gor A'mighty, how comes you dar? Who is ye?␣␣Whar you come from?" I cautioned them to make no noise, and told them I wished to talk with one of them, while the others (five in number) could go on about their work. They appointed a spokesman to talk with me, and the others went up to the mules, and on they went. The following conversation then passed between us.

Officer. What kind of a man are you?

Negro. Up and down, sah.

Officer. What is your name?

Negro. My name Phil.

Officer. To whom do you belong?

Negro. To Lieutenant A——, sah.

Officer. Ah! your master is an officer, then?

Negro. Yes, sah. He's been down to de Charleston on duty, sah. We all been down dar, banking up 'gainst de Yankees.

Officer. On the fortifications I suppose you mean?

Negro. Yes, sah?

Officer. Did you hear the Yankee shells, then?

Negro. Hear um! We gets to feel some ob dem. Some ob our boys killed dar; and some ob massa's company.

Officer. Well, now, Phil, did you ever see a Yankee?

Negro. No, sah?

Officer. I suppose you think they are very bad people; and if you should see one, you would tell your master, and have him arrested?

Negro. No, sah, I no does dat. De Yankees is de frends ob de black people.

Officer. How do you know the Yankees are your friends?

Negro. Oh, we hear massa talkin' 'bout it. He call um d—d abolitionis; we knows wat dat means.

Officer. What do you understand by an *abolitionist?*

Negro. Means de—de year ob jubilee am comin', when all de black people gwine to be free.

Officer. Well, Phil, that is a very good definition; but who told you that you were to be made free?

Negro. Oh, we gets it.

Officer. Well, if I should tell you that I was a Yankee, would you believe it?

Negro. I tinks you be, already.

Officer. You think right. Do you think you could do any thing for me?

Negro. Do any thing? What you wants done? I can do ebery ting.

Officer. I want something to eat; can you get it for me, and how many do you think you could feed?

Negro. (Somewhat excited.) I could feed an *army* ob you.

Officer. You are just the boy we have been looking for.

And now, if you will promise me upon your honor that you will not expose us, and come with me, I will introduce you to my comrades.

Negro. I neber tells. (Turning to his comrades.) Boys, keep de mules agwine.

I then, accompanied by the negro, crept cautiously back to where my comrades, four in number, were awaiting me, and introduced them to my friend Phil. The reader can better imagine the scene which followed than I can describe it. There was a poor ignorant slave, who, notwithstanding the many dreams of liberty which had often passed before his mind, was listening with breathless anxiety to what his new friends had to say. The conversation was about as follows:

Negro. Is you gwine to make us all free? We tink you is.

Officer. Certainly, P——; the President has proclaimed you all free, and we have already liberated about one million of your people.

Negro. You ain't gwine to sell us to Cuba, is you? Massa says you is; we don't b'lieve it's so.

Officer. No, Phil, we are not going to sell a man of you. We are going to make *men* of you — send your children to school, and teach you to read. How would you like that?

Negro. Larn us to read! Gor A'mighty, we can larn it.

Officer. Well, Phil, we will tell you more about this some other time. Do you think this a safe place for us to-day?

Negro. Yes; if you keeps bery still, it's all right. I comes here to-night when I gets through my work, brings you to a better place, and gibs you all de provisions you wants. Now you keeps still, and I comes all right."

So saying, he bounded away, and well-nigh forgot himself in singing

"De kingdom am a comin',
And de year ob jubilee,"

when one of our party called to him, "*Still*, Phil, *still.*" He turned around, made a low bow, saying, "Oh yes, sah, I forgot," and was soon out of sight.

The "*whoa, whoa, whoa*" soon announced the fact that our friend was with his mule; and then we lay down to rest and wait. True to his promise, as night came on, our friend Phil came back to us, accompanied by his brother, saying, "Well, you all here yet? We no forgets you, and you no discobered by any white man."

Officer. No, Phil, we knew you were *all right;* but who is this you have with you?

Negro. Dat's my bruder—he's all right too. What *I* is, *he* am; no fears ob him. Come, let's be gwine.

So saying, he led the way, and we followed for about a mile, when we came to an old school-house, and, taking two pairs of our old shoes, which had been badly worn by the march, promised to get them mended, and return to us in two hours "with provisions enough to last us a week."

We now went into the school-house to wait and watch during the two long hours. Slowly the time passed off, and some of the party began to fear something had happened to Phil, when the signal "rap" announced his return to us; but, on opening the door, found—*not* Phil, but another old negro, who, being anxious to talk with a "live Yankee," had arranged with Phil to come and bring us some provisions, and thus obtain the coveted interview.

He informed us that the shoes would be ready at ten o'clock, and, at the same time, holding out a large tin server, exclaimed, "Come still; dis ain't Phil, dis is B——; but I is all right. I brings you what we calls a meat pie; you calls it what you wants to; and dis ain't all we's gwine to gib you: de oder boys be here soon wid de shoes and pervishuns."

The old man informed us that he was the oldest hand on the plantation; that he had had five children, three of whom had been sold off the place; "but now," said he, "we tinks de time's comin' when we has better days; when we ain't gwine to be sold any more; when we gits pay for work jest like oder folks, and sends de chil'ren to school, and de wimens works in de house, and de men in de field. Does you tink dat time eber *will* come, massa?"

Officer. Yes, B——; when this war is over there will probably be no more slavery, and then you will be free to work for whom you like.

Negro. Dat's what we tinks; but massa tells us dat we is gwine to be sold to Cuba, whar dey works great deal harder dan dey do here. We don't mind de work, but den we gets notin' for it—dat's de trouble; but here comes de oder boys wid de shoes.

The younger negroes then came in, and, in addition to the shoes, brought us a pair of stockings, several loaves of bread, a basket of sweet potatoes, and a nice quantity of baked meat. As it was then late (10 P.M.), there was little time to be lost in words. Packing up again, we left the old house, and, accompanied by Phil, started to find our direct road again. As we were walking along, Phil startled us with the question, "Massa, does you tinks you will be able to find de way to Tennessee? Mighty long way dar, and bery crooked road; and now, massa, I tinks you better take a guide wid you, to show you de way, and I wants to go wid you. I knows all de way from heah to Knoxville, and I wants to be free once before I dies."

Officer. No, Phil, your time has not come yet, and although we would gladly help you to your freedom, yet we are only prisoners of war, and liable to be caught any hour, and should you be found with us, it would be the signal for an indiscriminate hanging of the whole of us. Wait patiently a little while longer, and your time of deliverance will certainly come.

Phil now bade us an affectionate "Good-by, God bless yous!" and turned back, while we went on our way rejoicing. We traveled very hard that night, laid by the next day as usual, and started out the next; but, after traveling six miles, I was forced to tarry behind, while the others pushed on. My long imprisonment unfitted me for such hard work, while the scantiness of the fare had reduced my strength so much that I was unable to travel with the rest of the party. I lay in the woods till daylight; but, finding myself prostrated with a raging fever, accompanied by rheumatism, it was impossible for me to proceed. To stay there was to die. I could only find a house and give myself up, which I did that forenoon. As I expected, I was sent back to prison, then to the hospital, where for five weeks I paid the penalty

K

of an attempt to be a free man in a run of fever. But, thanks to a merciful Providence, life was spared, and I was with the happy ones who were paroled and came through the lines on the 1st of March, 1865, having been in Rebel prisons twenty months.

CHAPTER XII.

IN SEARCH OF LIBERTY.

"Camp Federal Prisoners, Columbia, South Carolina, January 12, 1865.

"FRIEND ABBOTT,—I have the honor of transmitting to you the following brief account of the escape, adventures, and final recapture of our party, and hope it may be of some interest to your readers. On the 28th of November last, Captain Hays, 95th New York Volunteer Infantry, Captain Mooney, 16th New York Volunteer Cavalry, and myself, started on a tour of adventure through Rebeldom, with the hope of finally reaching our lines. We had provided ourselves with a few bunches of matches, several loaves of bread, a little salt, coffee, and tea, which had been sent us from home; these, with a small tin cup, a tin pail, and a blanket for each of us, constituted our supply and baggage train. At about two o'clock in the afternoon I was successful in passing the guard, and, after remaining in the wood a short distance from camp a couple of hours, was joined by the other members of the party, who had also, by several strategical movements, just been able to make good their escape. Our haversacks and blankets were safely smuggled through the line by the wood squad. All being in readiness, we hastened to put a safe distance between us and camp, and to find the direct road leading to Lexington Court-house before it was too dark. We had to move very cautiously, as we were hardly beyond sight of the guard, and still very near their quarters; however, we were successful. The sun was just sinking out of sight as we reached the wood, and found a thicket of small pines in which we secreted ourselves until dark. After impatiently remaining here a few hours we resumed our journey, marching in Indian file, Captain Hays taking the lead. He had just returned the day before from a similar expedition, having been recaptured after an absence of three weeks. We found his experience to be of inestimable value to us throughout the journey. We had no more than reached the road before we came in rather unpleasant proximity to an old man with a horse and wagon. He had stopped in the road to adjust his load, and the darkness was so great, we had come close upon him before either party was aware of the presence of the other. We did not stop to excuse our sudden appearance, but quickly moved on, much in doubt which had been thrown in the greatest fright; he, fearing from our stealthy movements and queer appearance that we might be highwaymen, or we, for fear he might recognize us as escaped prisoners, and report the direction we were taking. A short distance farther on we were obliged to flank a house well lighted up, standing near the road, in which, from the numerous voices we could hear, we thought a large party had gathered. While we were passing around through the wood for this purpose, a small squad of cavalrymen passed us, from whose conversation we were enabled to learn that we had taken the direct road to Lexington, of which we had been in considerable doubt; also, that we might expect to meet more of their number at any time. In fact, we had not gone over two miles farther when we met another party of them, from whom we were only able to save ourselves by making a rapid flight into a thick wood where they could not follow with their horses. They therefore gave up the pursuit and passed on, leaving us to get out of the bushes and briers as best we could. We had moved with the greatest possible caution, but the sand was so deep in the road we were unable to hear them till they rode up very near us. When we got within some three miles of Lexington there were numerous fires by the road, which we concluded must have been built by soldiers in bivouac for the night, who were on their way to Hamburgh. Thinking it rather dangerous to attempt passing them, we went into camp, although it wanted several hours of morning. This conclusion was the more readily accepted by Captain Mooney and myself, for we found traveling very tiresome after our long imprisonment on scanty rations of corn meal and sorghum; so, in a large wood some distance from the road, we spread our blankets and lay down to rest until morning, with hearts truly thankful that we had made even this short distance without being arrested and returned to a Confederate prison — the most loathsome and detestably-conducted place for the accommodation of human beings known in America. At daylight we moved a little farther back into the wood, and one of the party started off in search of water, but was compelled to return before he could find any on account of a hunter, who, with gun and dogs, was scournig the wood in which we lay for game. This hunter not only prevented our getting water, but greatly disturbed the quiet of our minds, keeping us on the move from place to place until the middle of the afternoon, when, greatly to our relief, the barking of the dogs died away in the distance, and we were again at liberty to get water and cook our coffee preparatory to the evening march. The experience of this day taught us we had made a great mistake in the selection of our camp. It was far away from water, and in heavy hardwood timber, in which, at this season of the year, plenty of game was to be found, and therefore almost certain to be visited by hunters. Afterward we were particular in this respect, and generally very fortunate in finding thickets of pine near good water.

"Early in the evening we resumed our march, and by nine o'clock had successfully flanked Lexington Courthouse, and were on the road leading to Wise's Ferry, where we proposed to cross the river before morning. After traveling a few miles the cloudy darkness broke away, and we discovered, through our limited knowledge of the position of the stars, that we were going in the wrong direction. We had kept too much to the right, and the course we were now pursuing would take us back to Columbia. We had now evidently traveled several miles out of our way, and were considerably perplexed to find out our exact position; but, as there was a house a short distance ahead, we concluded that one of the party should go there in search of a negro guide. Captain Hays undertook this service, the remaining two moving forward to within easy supporting distance, in case any alarm should be raised at the house. The skill, caution, and success with which he accomplished it proved that his previous experience of three weeks had made him proficient in the art. Our new guide was the first negro, and, indeed, the first person we had spoken to since our escape. He was a tall, intelligent, fine-looking young negro, or rather mulatto, for his regular features and peculiar tinge of complexion indicated that other than negro blood flowed in his veins. On being asked if he knew who we were, he quickly replied, 'You are Yankees. I knew that as soon as I heard this man (pointing to Captain Hays) whistle in the yard; and then his voice does not sound like our people's, and he has just such blue clothes as I have heard *you uns wear*. Master tells us you are very bad men, and would sell us to Cuba if you could catch us, but we don't believe him;' and, with a knowing toss of the head, 'we blacks here know more'n they think on.' He was very ready and willing to give us all the information he could, which was much more than we expected. He told us we were only a few miles from the plantation of a gentleman who (we had been informed before leaving camp) was a good Union man. He said this man was very good to his servants, and he had heard that he was opposed to fighting the Yankees. We did not let him know that we suspected him to be a Union man, for fear we might implicate him, but told him we thought we could get provisions of the negroes on his plantation, and engaged him to conduct us there. Soon after we had started with our guide he advised us to stop and see an old colored man who had just returned that evening from Columbia, who would probably have a late newspaper, which he was in the habit of getting whenever he could, and reading the news to his fellow-servants who were not so fortunate as to possess that acquirement. He thought this old man was a powerful 'telligent nigger—knew all about the country, the news, the war, and almost every thing else. We had not been permitted to see the papers for some time before leaving camp, and could not well pass this old man without giving him a call, especially as he gave promise of proving to be really an intelligent contraband; so call we did, and were well paid for our trouble. He not only gave us a 'New South Carolinian' he had that day purchased of a newsboy in the city, but repeated all the rumors, general news, surmises of the neighborhood in regard to the late movements of General Sherman in Georgia which he had overheard in conversation between the white folks when he happened to be present. His recitation was nearly as interesting as his newspaper, and, I presume, contained quite as reliable information, for he told us he had heard the Yankees had beaten the Rebels very severely in Georgia, and that is an item of news seldom allowed to appear in the columns of Confederate newspapers. We found this old man possessed a good intellect and some judgment, as well as excellent memory, which, with his having taught himself to read, made him indeed an exception among his fellow-slaves. He said it took him a powerful long time, but, with a little assistance received from white children, he had picked up his knowledge of reading by his own hard study. While we were talking with him, his wife, or the old 'oman, as he called her, had with great hospitality prepared for us a supper of hot hoe-cakes, roasted sweet potatoes, cold roasted opossum, and fresh milk, of which we partook with grateful hearts and a good relish. Having thanked the old man for his information, and his sable companion for her wholesome viands, we took leave of them, and followed our guide, who conducted us several miles across the country, the most part through a heavy pine forest, and, where no path or road was visible to us, he kept as straight forward as if he had been traveling a well-beaten path. The negroes appear to be perfectly familiar with every stump and tree in the woods in their neighborhood. No matter how dense the forest, or how close the thicket through which we were obliged to travel, we always found our negro guides able to pilot us through them without losing their way. In a very short time we arrived at the residence of the Union planter. Not wishing, however, to disturb him in the night, we passed on to one of his negro cabins, where a good fire was soon kindled for our benefit, before which, lying on the floor wrapped in our blankets, we were soon in the peaceful enjoyment of welcomed sleep. Just before daylight on the morning of the 30th we were awakened by one of the colored men, who said he had been watching over us all the time we were sleeping for fear something might occur whereby we would be detected and returned to prison. He showed us a fine pine thicket in which we could conceal ourselves during the day, and to which he soon brought us a good breakfast. He told us he would let his master know we were there, and knew he would be pleased to have an interview with us if we desired. We had not intended to let any of the servants know we thought their master was a Union man, or that we intended to call on him, for fear it might be found out by his neighbors in the future to his injury, until this man told us his master had kept twelve escaped Yankee officers at his house only the Sunday before, and had given him permission to go with them a short distance as guide; therefore we concluded to have him inform his master of our wish to have an interview with him. The negroes had given us all the information we required, but we were desirous of seeing and conversing with a man who, notwithstanding his having been born and educated, and now living in South Carolina, the hot-bed of secession, still retained his love for the government formed by Washington and his patriotic associates. In a short time the servant came back, saying his master would come out to us in the afternoon, which he did, and also sent us out a large supply of provisions. He remained with us several hours, and gave us much interesting information about the Union men of the South, also the names of a number who lived in that part of the state, with permission to inform them, in case we should make them a call, that he had named them to us as such. He said he had been opposed to secession from the first, and thought it equally unjust and impolitic in the South to attempt the destruction of so good and liberal a government, and the dismemberment of so powerful and prosperous a nation. He believed they had made themselves responsible for all the misery and suffering occasioned by this cruel and bloody war by firing the first gun on Fort Sumter. In respect to slavery, he had always regarded it as a local institution, over which the state, while a member of the Federal Union, had entire jurisdiction, but had always considered it an institution which had ever been injurious both to the moral, social, and political prosperity of the South, and had, therefore, been in favor of a gradual emancipation, believing *that* method would be much the best for both master and slave. Like most Southern men, he thought the slaves would not be capable of supporting themselves when first liberated, and that so many set free in one community at one time would create great disorder and suffering. On learning that we intended to cross the river, he gave us some very valuable information in regard to the probable direction that would be taken by a party who were going over the next day, with their bloodhounds, to hunt for a notorious deserter who had long escaped the clutches of the enrolling officers, and frequently baffled the pursuit of their dogs. He also tendered us the services of one of his servants to take us across the river and conduct us to the main road on the other side. He promised to give the servant the necessary instruction, and told us we might put implicit confidence in him, as he was a very faithful man; then, with many wishes for the safety and success of our journey, he took leave of us. After his departure other members of his family visited us, and brought additional supplies, so that we were fearful we would be obliged to postpone our departure, or abandon part of our provisions for want of transportation, as our haversacks and all our pockets were already greatly overloaded.

"Soon after dark we set out for the river with the servant, whose services we had gladly accepted from our Union friend. As soon as we reached it, torches were lighted and preparations made for crossing. We could not help remarking the peculiarity of our situation, and the many interesting features it presented. Here, on the banks of the Saluda, were three Federal officers, fugitives from Confederate imprisonment; one held on high a blazing pitch-pine torch, which cast far its fitful light out on the rippling waters of the river as they went swiftly gliding by, and revealed their guide, a large, masculine, well-built negro slave, who had succeeded in finding a boat, and now, with sleeves rolled up, stood bending forward, a foot on each gunwale, attempting to bail out the water with which it was filled, using for the purpose a short paddle with which he afterward propelled the boat, while the smoke he puffed from the comical short pipe he held firmly in his teeth went dancing gayly about his head. We could but remark, and rejoice over the great change made in the laws of our government and the sentiments of the people since the commencement of this war. Had this same scene occurred before the war on the banks of the Ohio, or even the St. Lawrence, and the condition of the parties so changed that this slave, who was now risking *his* life to secure *our* escape, had been the fugitive fleeing from Southern slavery, and we were aiding or in any way abetting him in that flight, the laws of our country and the sentiments of a large class of the people would have held us guilty of a high misdemeanor; while now neither the law nor public opinion of our country require Northern freemen to become slave-catchers for their Southern neighbors, and those who would then have been punished for assisting the fugitive in his escape are now allowed to fight for his freedom.

"Our guide having succeeded in clearing his boat, which we discovered to be nothing more than a small, rude, flat-bottom, with neither seats nor oars, paddled it out of the little bay so as to cross above the shoals, and then pulled it to the shore and we went on board, seating ourselves as best we could, and were soon landed safely on the opposite bank. Pursuing our course several miles through swamps and woods, we came to the main road leading from Columbia to Newberry Courthouse. Not needing the services of our guide any farther, he returned, and we kept forward until nearly daylight, when we went into camp. On the morning of December 2d we were not a little surprised at seeing a man rise up suddenly by the road and come out to meet us. He proved, however, to be Lieutenant Fowler, one of Major Wanzer's party, who escaped from camp about the same time we did. He had concealed himself on discovering the approach of our party, but as soon as we came up he recognized and came out to meet us. The remainder of the party were concealed a short distance from there, and he was out after provisions, which he had previously engaged of the negroes, and the blowing of a horn now informed him that they were cooked and ready for use. On his telling us that plenty of food could be procured for us also, we halted and went into camp. The next night we did not start until a late hour, in order to allow the other party sufficient time to get several miles ahead of us, so that on the morning of the 3d we had only reached Jalapa, a distance of nine miles, as the thick darkness seen just before day was fast giving place to the early light of morning. We left the road, and crossed over through the fields some distance to a large barn, where one of the party remained to await the early arrival of the negro servants, who the nearly exhausted state of our haversacks warned us it was time to consult. The negroes soon came, and he was successful in making himself known to one of them, who agreed to furnish us with provisions some time during the day. While they were talking, the negro recognized his master's voice at the barn, and told him to conceal himself immediately; he succeeded in doing so, and in gaining the rear of an old, unoccupied house in which the other two had taken refuge, when we all made a rapid flight for the woods, and were not tardy in placing a long distance between us, and thought our successful escape well rewarded us for the loss of a good breakfast—therefore patiently endured the many loud complainings of an unappeased appetite.

"The morning of the 4th of December found us comfortably stowed away in a shuck barn on the plantation of Mr. Little. Our colored friends had supplied us with all necessary food and information, and at daylight had concealed us in the barn. We had made a long march during the night, and had a delightful rest during most of the day, although the perfect quiet of our minds was several times greatly disturbed by the sudden appearance of Mr. Little at the barn. We kept perfectly quiet, not moving or rustling even a single corn-husk that concealed us, hardly daring to breathe for fear we would make known our place of concealment, and he passed by, little suspecting the pile before him was any thing else than it appeared, a pile of husks. Several times during the day the servants smuggled provisions out to us, and at night provided a large supply for the journey. They informed us that, some miles ahead, the people, on learning of the escape of several Federal officers from Columbia, had established a picket on the road; and the negroes, hearing of it through their masters, had formed a counter-picket on the road below them, so as to apprise the officers and conduct them around the picket kept by their masters. The negroes said they thought it their duty to do all they could for the Yankees, since Massa Lincum and the Yankees were doing so much for them, and thought they could watch as many nights as their masters. We were safely conducted around the pickets, and on the morning of the 5th camped in a wood a short distance from Young's Store.

"We resumed our journey early on the night of the 5th, but had not traveled many miles before we heard the heavy and loud talking of an approaching party. We quickly concealed ourselves among the bushes by the side of the road, and were much surprised, as they passed by, to learn from their conversation that part of their number were some of our fellow-officers, who had just been recaptured, and the remainder were their escort. The negroes soon after informed us that four officers had been recaptured through the ignorance of a half-witted negro to whom they had applied for provisions. On traveling a short distance farther we suddenly came up to a solitary horseman, who, on meeting and discovering who we were, attempted to halt us; but, seeing that we paid no particular regard to his urgent invitation to stop, rode off, and a couple of hours later we were not surprised at hearing several horsemen rapidly riding up in our rear. However, as we expected to be pursued, we kept a good look-out, and had no great trouble in shunning them, and soon after went into camp. The next night we concluded not to travel, as the negroes told us this party had informed the whole neighborhood that we were somewhere in their midst. We would not trust ourselves in a building, but laid out in the woods, although we had a cold, drenching rain-storm during nearly the whole day and night.

"On the morning of December the 8th we arrived in the neighborhood of Greenville Court-house, and stopped at a negro cabin near the town, where, on account of a very severe storm of snow and sleet, we remained until the evening of the 11th. For our purpose this place was very favorable. The cabin was some distance from the dwelling of the planter, and was only occupied by one person, he an aged colored man, who, with a hospitality that would cause many of us more intelligent and fortunate whites to blush, welcomed our arrival, and freely shared with us his small allowance of meat and corn meal. He said his wife had been sold, and taken away some thirty or forty miles, and their children had been taken away so far they had lost all traces of them. We found him engaged braiding a basket for a Christmas present to his wife. One would think, from the cheerful manner he chanted a lively negro air, as he nimbly wove the braid, that he was as happy as any young lover in anticipation of visiting his lady love. His cabin was very open and uncomfortable, affording but little shelter from the piercing storm of wind and sleet that raged without; but, rolled in our blankets and stretched out on the floor, with a good hickory fire burning in the capacious fireplace at our feet, we were able to pass the night quite comfortably. During the day we laid secreted among the corn-husks in a small barn not far from the cabin. At night the neighboring negroes would bring us provisions, and an old colored man, who appeared to be the particular friend of our host, would bring us a hot dinner each day—excellent dinners they were, too. At this we were not a little surprised, until he told us his master was off to the war, and his old woman was cook for their master, so he could get whatever food he wished, and do about as he pleased. The Southern slave, though honest in most respects, especially with his fellow-slaves, will have whatever he desires, if his master's kitchen, cellar, or hen-roost contains it, and he is able to extract it therefrom. Nor is he any more scrupulous about his labor. With no interest to stimulate him to action, he nods over his hoe, and sleeps away the day at the plow, whenever the vigilant eye of the overseer will permit. But at night he is to be found up at almost all hours, at work for himself or visiting with his companions. They are not watched so closely now as they were before the war. Then, if found by the patrol away from their plantation without a written pass from their master, they would be arrested and whipped. But now, the negroes say, 'the Yankees are giving the Southern whites something to do besides standing over them with the whip.' We were much amused hearing the negroes give their views of the war. They have some very peculiar opinions about it, but in general are well informed, at least much better than we expected to find them. They had received horrible descriptions of the climate and people of Cuba, and had been told by their masters, 'the Yankees, if they could catch them or entice them away, would sell them to the State of Cuba as slaves.' They did not exactly believe it, but I noticed they were very desirous of knowing all about it.

"On the evening of the 9th our party was happily augmented by the arrival of Lieutenant Murphy, 97th New York Volunteers, and Captain Pennypacker, 14th Pennsylvania Cavalry, who, uniting their fortunes with ours, continued to move with us until we were finally recaptured. When we went to our hiding-place among the corn-husks on the morning of the 10th, our surprise can hardly be imagined at finding it already occupied. Major Wanzer and his party of four other officers had been directed here by the negroes, and had arrived just before day and concealed themselves in the barn. We surprised and awakened them by throwing our blankets up in their midst on the loft. They could not conjecture what or who was about to appear to them until we climbed up the side, and they saw us, with heads peering above the beams, looking down in amazement on them; then they recognized and sprang forward to meet and greet us, all laughing heartily over our mutually happy surprise. After flanking the town of Greenville on the evening of the 11th, we kept a little north of a westerly course. The snow in the roads had nearly all been worn away during the day, but it was very rough and hard. The night was bitter cold, so that, on going into camp the next morning, we found ourselves nearly exhausted with cold, hunger, and fatigue. After working long and diligently with the wet wood we had gathered from under the snow, we succeeded in kindling a fire, around which we were soon lying asleep. The evening of the 14th we arrived in the neighborhood of Wallhollow, where we were supplied with provisions by a white woman. One of our party went to her dwelling, supposing it to be a negro cabin. It was a small log-cabin, similar to those occupied by the negroes. On learning that her husband was a conscript, and also a prisoner at the North, he made himself known, and she gave us all the aid in her power. She had a large family of small children, who depended on her labor for support. Her husband being a conscript, she received none of the benefits of the relief committee. If he had volunteered, she would have been able to purchase provisions at government prices, which generally were but a trifle in comparison to the market prices; she would also have received other needful assistance from that institution. We had to give her money, and she was obliged to go out and purchase meal before she could furnish our supper. An old negro brought us a large piece of fresh pork, which, with the widow's hoe-cake, made us an excellent repast. Here we were again joined by Captain Pierce, 3d New York Cavalry, and Lieutenant Fowler, — New Jersey Infantry, of Major Wanzer's party. The major and the other two of his party had been captured a short distance back, and they had now come up to join us. This addition increased our number to seven.

"On the evening of the 15th we were safely conducted around the town by a colored man, who had been procured for that purpose by the white woman with whom we stopped. We had the name of a Union man in the town, but he happened to be absent on business, and we were not able to wait for him. On our return through this town we found a strong Union element in it. When we had marched about four miles from the village we came to the foot of the mountains. The first range is called by the negroes Stump-house Mountain. Up these we now commenced to wind our way. From the time we struck into the mountains until we were recaptured near Hiwassa, Town County, Georgia, we had traveled over forty-five miles in nearly a westerly direction through them, and were told by the citizens we would have had to travel over twenty-five miles farther before we would have been entirely through them. During the night of the 16th we were obliged to ford the Tugalo River. It is the principal fork of the Savannah, and forms the boundary between South Carolina and Georgia. Its waters were a little above waist deep, and were very cold and rapid, so that the crossing was both dangerous and unpleasant, especially as the night was dark, and we had our clothing, haversacks, etc., to carry on our sholuders high out of the water. The crossing, however, was made without accident. That same night we were obliged to cross two other large streams, one of them as many as seven times. Occasionally we would find a log to walk on, but generally were obliged to cross by fording. When we had reached the summit of the Blue Ridge, we all seated ourselves, lighted our pipes, and enjoyed a good, quiet, and peaceful smoke. This was the greatest feast we could afford, for our haversack contained but a little piece of broiled goose, the remnant of the evening's meal. The people in that section were generally very poor, and owned no negroes. We missed the assistance of the slaves very much. Large numbers of wild turkeys, foxes, and squirrels, together with some bears and deer, are to be found here, and occasionally an Indian family, still living among these mountains, secure from the steady advance of civilization. We had no trouble in finding among the ravines good places of concealment, where we could keep a fire all day. Often during the day we would leave our hiding-place and stealthily ascend the nearest mountain peak, from which we could look forth and enjoy the delightful and magnificent scenery which on every side lay spread out before us. But these fine scenes would not appease our craving appetites. We suffered greatly for the want of food. We tried to procure provisions at a great many cabins, but were unable to get even a little corn meal, although we offered to pay for it. Some would tell us they lived a long way from the mill, and had only enough for their breakfast. Others would say they had neither flour nor meal of any kind; that the roads were so bad they had not been to mill, and were obliged to depend on what game they could bring down in the woods.

"On the night of the 18th the whole party, except Lieutenant Fowler, were recaptured near Hiwassa, Georgia, by the neglect of one of the party not keeping watch outside a house to which two of the others had gone for food. We were recaptured at the house of Captain John Cornby by himself and his neighbors, whom he had sent his children out to call in for that purpose. Both he and his family treated us kindly, giving us a good supper and breakfast. At nine o'clock the next morning we were started back through the mountains over the same road we had come. When we arrived at Clayton we were delivered to Captain Singleton, who also treated us kindly, keeping us a day and a night at his own dwelling, trusting to our word of honor not to attempt an escape. This we preferred doing to being locked up in a county jail. Although the captain himself was a gentleman, the escort he gave us were neither gentlemen nor soldiers. By their fiendish treatment of us, they forfeited all right to be regarded as either. We were not over ten miles from the captain's residence, when they not very politely invited us to exchange our clothing for theirs, also to give up the several other articles we had about our persons. On our objecting to this arrangement, they informed us they would shoot us if we did not comply with their request. This they had threatened several times, and were as often refused, when they conducted us to some very large and deep holes, dug by a mining company in search of copper, into which they told us they would throw us after having shot us, as they had threatened. These caves were up in the mountains, far from any human habitation, and we could tell by their manner that they had decided on what to do with us, and that this was the last time they intended to make peaceful offers to us; so we concluded to part with the articles they desired. After this we had no great trouble with them. However, they watched us closely, giving us no chance to escape. Captain Hays succeeded in jumping through a small window, and getting a short distance from a house where we stopped over night, but their pursuit of him was so vigorous that he was obliged to give himself up to them again. On our arrival at Wallhollow we were treated kindly by both soldiers and citizens. The surgeon of the post requested the provost marshal, to whom we had been delivered, to allow us to stay with him at his hospital. His request was granted, and we had an excellent supper and breakfast, and clean floor to sleep on, with plenty of wood to keep the fire burning through the night. At this place we took the cars for Anderson, where we arrived on the evening of the 24th, and remained in the jail until the morning of the 26th, when we again went aboard of the cars, and arrived late in the evening at Columbia. Here we remained over night in jail, and on the morning of the 27th were taken up to camp, after an absence of four weeks and one day.

"I have the honor, lieutenant, to remain your humble servant, Major ———."

CHAPTER XIII.

"IN THE HOSPITAL" AT CHARLESTON, SOUTH CAROLINA.

"My name is A. F. Tipton, of the 8th Iowa Cavalry. I was taken sick at the work-house, and sent to the hospital August 25th, 1864, at Rikersville, four miles from the central part of the city of Charleston. My disease was chronic diarrhœa. I had a tolerably good bed, not over and above clean. I was there till the 9th of October, and my sheets were changed but *once*, and that was a sample of the sheet-changing. They pretended to clean the hospital once a week, but it was oftener two. The rations were most miserable, and consisted of corn bread, rice, grits,* and occasionally a little beef. The bread was made of water and meal, half baked. The rice and grits were never well cooked, and always so badly smoked that a sick man could hardly eat them at all. Many were almost starved for want of good wholesome food. Dr. Todd, the surgeon in charge, said it was impossible to get comforts for us, for the authorities *would not* permit them. The hospital was an old German fair garden, and contained four wards. The average number of deaths in each ward was from six to ten every twenty-four hours. They usually did not bring men there till they were almost dead. I have seen them bring in our soldiers, and, after washing and putting them to bed,

---

* *Grits* are cracked corn, or what some people call "*samp.*"

leave them till morning. It was not an uncommon thing to find five or six of them *dead in their beds* at daylight. Sometimes they would be almost black from yellow fever before they would remove them to the hospital. One man, belonging to the 8th New York Cavalry, said a Rebel officer kicked him while attempting to get on the cars because he did not move faster, and at the time he was too weak to do more. The doctor said his death was caused by the kick. Many more would have died but for the kindness of the 'Sisters of Charity,' who visited us occasionally, and, in part, supplied our wants. The hospital steward, Sanders, was a perfect brute. He called us d—d Yankees, and said the more of us they killed in the hospital the fewer there would be to shoot after we were exchanged. At one time the 'Sisters of Charity' came with a few delicacies for us. The steward asked them why they did not take them to their (Rebel) hospital. They replied that their men had friends to care for them, while these had none, and many of them were depending for life upon some extra help. He went into a rage, and ordered them off, not permitting them to do any thing for us, and threatened to confiscate all they had if they came there again."

CHAPTER XIV.

AN ADVENTURE.

Thrilling Adventures of Lieutenant Francis Murphy, Company " G," 97th Regiment New York Volunteers, who escaped from Prison at Columbia, South Carolina, November 28th, 1864, in company with Captains Pennypacker and Ottinger, as related by himself.

"WE left camp on the night of the 28th of November, and went directly south until we struck the Augusta and Columbia turnpike, one mile from camp. We then turned westward in the direction of Lexington Courthouse. On traveling about three miles we were somewhat surprised at seeing a camp-fire in front of us on the road-side. After reconnoitring the place closely, we discovered it to be a wagon-camp. The men were at supper. After carefully flanking it, we got on the road again, and continued our journey with caution. After traveling some four miles farther, we heard a great noise in front of us. Our hearts beat quick; could not think what it was; still we went on, and at last discovered it to be a negro singing-school. Some fifty negroes were there learning to sing. From the noise they made, we thought all the men and hounds in South Carolina were after us; but, after satisfying ourselves of what it was, we went on a little farther, and halted to get some water. All of a sudden two cavalrymen rode up. We had just

L

time to drop down in the water. The horses saw us and were frightened, but the riders, supposing it the fault of the horses, whipped them severely and went on, to our great satisfaction. After that we went on without interruption, passing through Lexington Court-house, and at daylight found ourselves four miles west of the court-house, where we hid ourselves in a swamp for the day.

"November 29th. After resting all day, to-night we set out again, and after traveling about four miles came on another camp-fire. We examined it carefully, saw the horses around, so flanked it, and got on the road again. Some half a mile in advance of the camp we heard hounds and men in the woods to the south of us, but, supposing them to be negroes, we went on; were soon halted by two men — one a major, the other a captain, who were in ambuscade. They were in charge of the camp we just passed, and belonged to the hunting party. They were detailed to collect the government 'tax in kind;' told us that all those camps we passed were camps of 'tax-wagons' that were collecting government tax, and bringing it to Columbia. After questioning us as to who we were, and from where we came, said they must return with us to headquarters at Columbia. They then took us to their camp one half mile back. Seeing we were prisoners again, we thought we might make the best of it, so entered freely into conversation on different subjects, and passed the night quite pleasantly. We told them of our long imprisonment, and of all we had suffered while in prison. They sympathized with us much, and said they were sorry to hear it; wished the war would soon end, etc., to all of which we agreed. As luck would have it, our captors proved to be gentlemen.

They treated us kindly, and after breakfast very generously set us at liberty. They gave us valuable information, and wished we might get home safely.

"November 30th. We again resumed our journey, and, after traveling about four miles, ran almost on to a hunting-party, who seemed to occupy the road right in front of us; so, lest we might fall into the hands of the Philistines, we concluded to flank the hunting-party, but in doing so we lost our course, and next morning found ourselves as far from the place of destination as when we started; however, we lay down to sleep, as it was not yet quite daylight. I had fallen fast asleep, and was dreaming of home and friends, feeling happy in my imaginations, when I was suddenly aroused by a wild yell. To my great surprise, I saw a man with a fowling-piece in his hand, with a blazing fire on his back, and a large dog at his feet. While I was meditating as to whether this was real or imaginary, he advanced toward me to within ten paces, and gave another prodigious yell, looking, as I thought, right at me. Oh! what a spectacle to see in the midst of the wild woods, and just awakened from sleep. My very heart almost jumped out of my mouth. In a moment he changed his direction, and went off without seeing us. I afterward learned that this was the custom of hunting the coon at night in South Carolina. Shortly afterward the sun made his appearance, proclaiming day, which allayed all our fears, and we went to rest for the day. Toward sundown I made a reconnoissance, and discovered where we were from a negro who was plowing. He gave me some rations, and directions as to how to get to the right road.

"At night, December 1st, we again set out at an early

hour; struck the Augusta and Columbia pike some four miles from where we spent the day. After following the pike several miles, we called at the plantation of Mr. ——, where the negroes gave us all the information we required. They took us to another plantation, where we found seven more of our officers, who were at supper with the negroes. After supper we all started to cross the Saluda River at different ferries. When we came to the place where we were to part, we halted and took farewell of each other, not liking to travel together, as we considered it safer to travel in squads of two or three. After parting with our fellow-officers, my companions and I went together, but the night being dark, no stars to guide us, we lost our way, and, after traveling all night, found ourselves six miles below the ferry where we intended to cross. Tired, disheartened, and sore-footed, we hid ourselves for the day. After sleeping till near sundown I made another reconnoissance, and found out by a guide-board where we were.

"December 2d. At night we started, and before we reached the road differed as to the direction to take; so my two companions went one way and I another, all aiming to cross the river at the same ferry. As I came to four corners of road, I was at a loss to know which way to go, so resolved to try and see a negro at the first house I came to, in order to get the proper information. I soon saw a large house, with a number of negro huts all around; but there were two large dogs in the yard that disputed my entrance in such a manner that I could not enter the yard without alarming the white inhabitants. At last I saw one hut in the most remote part of the yard, and there I concluded to go; but, in order to baffle the vigilance of the dogs, I went around to the back of the hut, so as to go in the back way. Just as I was crossing the fence a rail broke, and the occupant of the hut, being a negress, who was there spinning, saw me and got frightened. I, seeing her terror, rushed toward her in order to quell her alarm, but I only added to her fright. She made for the planter's house, screeching all the way, until she aroused all the inmates of the place. I, of course, took for the woods with all possible speed, pursued by dogs and men, but I soon outdistanced them, and reached the high road in safety, where I found a guide-board which gave me the direction I was looking for. In two hours after I reached the long-looked-for ferry in safety, and in a short time after was joined by my two companions whom I left in the woods in the forepart of the night. We remained there until the next night.

"December 3d. Took the road leading to Newberry Court-house, where we arrived at daylight the next morning. Not liking to go through the town, we flanked it to the left, crossed Bush River, and hid ourselves in the woods for the day. Here, I regret to say, we parted with Captain Ottinger, he not being able to go any farther on account of pain in his limbs.

"Next night, December 4th, Captain Pennypacker and myself set out for Lawrenceville Court-house, thirty-six miles from Newberry. After traveling till near daylight, as we were very hungry, we kept looking out to see if any negroes were about, so as to get some breakfast, as they are the only ones from whom we can obtain food, or to whom we dare apply. Near daylight we came to a plantation where there were some twenty negro huts, and in one of them we saw a light. I resolved to try and get breakfast. I went carefully to the door of the hut, and was about to knock, when I heard a woman say 'breakfast's ready.' I started at the sound of the voice, knowing it was no negro voice, went carefully round to the window, and looked in, and saw it was a white man's house—overseer's—a very unusual thing for a white man to live in a negro hut. I left as soon as possible, and hurried on two miles farther, when I saw another light, and also saw a negro man carrying a torch; so I went up and made myself known, stating that I wanted some breakfast. He said that he could not get me any thing to eat then, but he would be plowing that day in a certain field, and would give me something there; so on we went, and concealed ourselves in the woods close by where the negro was to be plowing, and went to sleep. Late in the afternoon we awoke, and Captain Pennypacker started for the field where the negro was plowing to get some rations. In a few minutes I saw him returning on the double-quick. He stated that he ran against the overseer, and that he supposed he was after help to capture us; so we started on the run, running some four miles, outdistancing our pursuers, when we rested until night.

"December 5th. We again took the road to Lawrenceville Court-house. After marching some six miles we met two negroes, who brought us thirty dollars' worth of rations, which we did justice to in the way of eating. After supper we continued our journey, and passed safely through Lawrenceville Court-house at about 3 o'clock A.M., without even the bark of a dog, and secreted ourselves for the day in a wood four miles west of the town, on the Greenville Road.

"December 6th. At an early hour we took the Greenville pike, and, after traveling some distance, lost the direct road, were tracked and pursued by dogs and men, run down a hill, and crossed a deep creek by a mill, and had to give up our journey for that day on account of rain.

"Next day, December 7th, we were encircled by roads, and, not knowing which way to take, I resolved to try and find a negro and get some information. At about 2 o'clock P.M. I heard some one chopping. Supposing it to be a negro man, I went to see, and, after going some ways in the direction of the sound, discovered it to be a white man. My horror was great lest he might see me, and, retreating carefully, I trampled on a rotten limb, which attracted the attention of two hounds of his that were not far from me. They made a tremendous noise, and took after me. I ran at the top of my speed, pursued by the man and his dogs. Finding it impossible to get off, I jumped into an old water-course, and kept the dogs at bay with my club until their owner came up. He called off the dogs, and questioned me as to who I was and where I was going. I told him that I belonged at Columbia, which was true, and that I was going home; that, seeing persimmon-trees in the wood, I was after some, when his dogs saw and made for me. This explanation seemed to satisfy him, and I started off; but he bid me hold on, and come and have supper with him. Fearing some treachery might be intended, I declined, saying I was in too much of a hurry, and went on. As I went off he looked after me, and I could see that he was examining my boots and uniform. Of course he knew he could not capture me without help.

Every man in the Confederacy is a soldier authorized to arrest any suspicious persons. As soon as I could I found my companion. We changed our direction, and went off on the run through the woods, guided by the sun. After going about two miles, we could hear the hounds on our track, as though we were hares or foxes; however, we went on some two miles farther, when the hounds and horsemen came in sight at about a mile distant. We thought we were gone certain, but thoughts of home and friends kept up our drooping spirits, and we run on the best we could. As we descended into a valley the cry of the hounds warned us of their near approach, and we could hear the voices of the horsemen distinctly encouraging them on. At this moment we saw two young ladies passing in a foot-path that came through the woods. After they passed we took their track in the opposite direction, thereby confounding the scent of the hounds, and once more we escaped.

"After getting rid of our pursuers we halted until dark, got over our fright, and then took the road again. We had a severe march through mud and rain, and in the morning found ourselves fourteen miles from Greenville, when we concealed ourselves in a swamp near by, to remain for the day.

"December 8th. At night we started for Greenville. We traveled about eight miles, and, getting very hungry, I went into a negro hut. I told them who I was; that I was making my escape from prison, and that I wanted some supper. They said I could have any thing they had in the house, and that they were so happy to have it in their power to help me some; so the females went to cooking, while all the men gathered around me to learn what Mr. Lincoln intended to do with them. I told them that he intended to set them all free. At hearing that, they fell down on their knees and offered a fervent prayer to the Great Giver of all for their speedy deliverance. They wanted to know if Mr. Lincoln would be re-elected. I told them that he was elected for four years more, and then they cheered. At this time supper was announced, and a splendid supper it was. We ate heartily, and got some provisions to carry away. One of the men gave us valuable information; told us of the militia, and where they were posted; also told us how to flank Greenville safely; so, after bidding our benefactors an affectionate farewell, we departed, I leaving some United States money as a recompense for their kindness. After we came to the cross-roads where we were to flank Greenville it commenced snowing. We then rested until sundown, when we again set out, and made a good night's march of twenty-two miles, being then fourteen miles from Greenville. We passed the next day hidden in the woods, and at night set out for Greenville. About two miles out we were crossing a creek, when we were overtaken by a mounted cavalryman. He bid us good-night, and passed on; but as soon as he left we took a different road, fearing that we might be pursued. At midnight we went to a negro hut, and the inmates got us a good meal, and gave us some eatables to carry with us. They told us where the Rebels had their pickets posted, and told us how to flank the village; so we left our dark friends and started, observing the instructions they gave us, and flanked the town on our left. It commenced storming and blowing so furiously that we were compelled to give up our march and seek shelter in an old barn that was half filled with straw. Here we found three of our officers, viz., Major Young, 76th New York, Captain Mooney, 16th New York Cavalry, and Captain Hays, 95th New York. We all stopped here until the night of the 11th, when we continued our journey for Pickens Court-house. We traveled twenty miles that night on a rough road, with hummocks frozen hard, until the blood ran out of my feet. But the thought of home was every thing to us, and we kept on until morning, then slept on the snow all day without fire.

"December 12th. We came within two miles of Pickens Court-house, a distance of fourteen miles. I came near givig up on account of blisters on my feet and heels.

"December 13th. We resumed our march until we came to Pickens Court-house. We were informed previously that there was a railroad running from there to Walhallia, a distance of twelve miles; but there was no such road there. We went all around the village, hoping to find the railroad, until all the dogs in the place were after us. At last we took the pike, and started for Wallhollow; but, after a few hours' march, lost our way, owing to the darkness of the night, and, after traveling all night, found ourselves in the morning but about six miles from Pickens Court-house.

"December 14th. After traveling all night we reached Wallhollow, found a Union house, told them who we were, got a good supper, and there rested all night and next day, in order to get some rations cooked.

"On the night of the 15th we started for Clayton, Georgia, guided around the village by a negro. We flanked the town to the right, and struck the pike road about one mile from town. We crossed Stump-house Mountain and tunnel that night, flanking wagon-camps every few miles.

"December 16th. The weather was very cold and freezing. After traveling about four miles, we came to the Tugalo River. This river is about eight rods wide, and has no bridge across it. Here we had to strip off, tie our clothes on our shoulders, and ford it in the cold night. Several times I thought the current would sweep me off, but we resolved to brave all danger for the sake of liberty, and we reached the other side in safety, dried ourselves the best we could, put on our clothes, and went on. To our sorrow, we had to cross four streams in the same way that night. At daylight we were within three miles of Clayton, but, being tired and foot-sore, rested for the day.

"December 17th. At night we started in the rain and mud, traveled through small creeks and mud-holes all night, passing through Clayton at midnight; took the Hiwassa Road, and, after several miles' travel, daylight stayed our march until night.

"At dark on the 18th we commenced to cross the terminus of the Blue Ridge Mountains. We tried to get some food, but could not; so we marched on through rain and mud, every mile or two had to cross a creek or brook without a bridge, and at daylight we stopped for the day on the top of the Blue Ridge Mountains without food.

"December 19th. We took the road again, and traveled all night; got into the Hiwassa valley, within five miles of Hiwassa village, but failed to get food. Hunger now became so intense that we could hardly stand it longer, and we resolved this night to obtain food, no matter how great the risk might be.

"December 20th. At night we went to a farm-house in order to obtain some rations and supper. Three of us went in to buy for the rest, while the others watched on the outside, lest they should send for help to capture us. The farmer met us at the door, and asked us who we were. We told him that we were soldiers, were going to Hiwassa, had exhausted our rations coming over the mountains, and that we called on him in order to buy some supper. He said we could have supper, and walked into the kitchen to give directions to the cook; but, at the same time, he sent after help to capture us. He then came back, and joined us in conversation. Just as we were at supper, two doors leading into the dining-room opened, and four men entered each door, with revolvers cocked, demanding us to surrender. Oh, treachery! treachery! we cried out, but all to no effect. Here we were, after all our hardships and trouble, betrayed once more into the hands of the Philistines. They also captured those we left outside as pickets. Oh, what a night of anxious disappointment this was to us! All our hopes seemed to be blasted. All we had endured and suffered for the past twenty-four days, in hopes of gaining our liberty, and of seeing our friends and homes once more, amounted to nothing. All the consolation we could get from our captors was, that we must go back to prison. You may imagine our feelings; after spending eighteen months in prison, then effected our escape, and had traveled two hundred and fifty-seven miles through woods and over mountains, fording all streams that came in our way in the dead of night, and, after suffering so much from hunger and cold, living in the woods for so long a time, to be then captured after all, was hard. But prisoners we were, and back to prison at Columbia we must go. Our captor's name was John Cornby, a captain of 'Home-guard.' He was proprietor of the house where we were so unfortunate as to go for our supper. He kept us all night, and treated us well. Next morning he turned us over to Lieutenant J. Gibson, of Captain Singleton's company, of Clayton, Georgia. The lieutenant had been to Hiwassa village with dispatches, and was returning, when we were captured; so Captain Cornby delivered us up to him and his party of three men. Those men were deserters from the Rebel army, and formed part of a home company under Captain Singleton. They marched us back over the mountains, and on the second night we reached Captain Singleton's, a small log house in the mountains five miles southwest of Clayton. The captain treated us very well, kept us all night in his house, and next day sent us off to Wallhollow, under guard of Lieutenant Gibson, Marcus Tippins, and James Reamey. After we had traveled some miles, Tippins said if we would give them one thousand dollars we might go where we pleased. He said that they would forge a receipt for our delivery, and sign the name of Captain Moody, to whom we were to be delivered. Of course we could not raise the money. We consulted together, and told them what we could raise, including our jewelry; but this not being enough to satisfy their demands, they marched us on, and that night we staid with one Mr. Gwinn, and were guarded by citizens. Our old-guard went to sleep, and one of our officers made his escape; so, next morning, after they discovered one gone, they became enraged, and tied us all together with a rope, so tight that the blood made its appearance on our wrists—threatening to shoot us down at the first false step we made after we left the place where we staid for the night. They took us off the main road, through the woods, and to the top of 'Stump-house Mountain,' where they made us form a circle. They then cocked their revolvers, and asked us if we were prepared to die, saying that they would not treat us so brutally as we did their men after getting them prisoners—stating that we Yankees killed their men, stripped them of all they had, and then left them unburied; but that they would treat us more humanely by killing us, and then burying us, at the same time calling our attention to some deep pits close by. These pits were dug in the form of a well, and were some two hundred and fifty feet deep. They were used for raising copper, as there was a copper mine underneath. Here, they said, shall be your graves. We begged hard for them not to kill us, asserting our innocence as to ever killing a prisoner; but they would not allow us to say a word in our defense. At the same time, they ordered us to deposit all our effects on the ground, and, after we had done so, they told us to strip off all our clothes. Of course there was no other way but to submit. They then took all our clothes, money, and what little jewelry we had, and gave us old dirty rags to put on—some they had for that purpose. They then told us to pray for ourselves, if we wished to do it. We did pray, and fervently too, and I have reason to believe that God heard our prayers, for just then a man who was hunting came along and saw us. The man's name was Moorehead, and lived in Wallhollow, South Carolina. He asked them what all this meant. They replied that we were Yankees that had escaped from prison, and that they intended to kill us in retaliation for what Sherman had done to their citizens as he passed through Georgia. The man said they should not do it; that we had surrendered, and should be treated as prisoners. He also said that the government was the proper authority to decide who should be killed and who should not, and that he would report them if they did not desist. Then we began to tell him of our past treatment, but were suddenly stopped by a knock on the head with one of their carbines, and threats to shoot us on the spot if we told any more. Finally, after some debate with Mr. Moorehead, they ordered us to get ready and march on to Wallhollow, where we arrived at about 3 o'clock P.M., much to our satisfaction. We were turned over to Captain Moody, who was quite a gentleman, and treated us as such. We stopped there all night, and next morning were visited by the citizens, who gave us invitations to dine with them. I went off with an Irish gentleman, and spent the afternoon with him. I had a splendid breakfast and dinner, and got enough food to last me to headquarters. In the afternoon of that day we took the railcars for Columbia. We were escorted to the dépôt by the citizens, who treated us courteously, saying they wished they were once more in the Union, and several such remarks. At last the cars started, and we bid farewell to our new friends. The train stopped all night at Anderson Court-house, and we were put in the jail, where we remained from Saturday until Monday. Sunday was Christmas, and was the most lonesome day I ever spent in my life. Just think of it; to be locked up in a cold cell two nights and one day, without fire, bed, blanket, or seat; weather cold and freezing. But the good Lord gave us strength to stand all those persecutions. On Monday morning we were taken to the cars and started for Columbia, where we arrived at sundown; stopped that night in Columbia jail, and next morning were put in the Asylum Prison yard with the rest of the officers. I was without clothes, money, or blanket, going on my nineteenth month's imprisonment. In conclusion, I will say that it is the general impression of the people that the Confederacy is ruined.* There is only about one white man to a house. The poor men say that if they could get away from the South they would do so, as they are oppressed in every imaginable way by the Confederate government authorities. They wish themselves back in the old Union. The jails are full of these people, who refuse to join the army "

* Written February, 1865.

CHAPTER XV.

IN THE CELL AT LIBBY.

The following article was contributed by Colonel Litchfield, one of the famous raiders under Kilpatrick in February and March, 1864. He gives the following inside view of cell life at Libby. Read it, and then say what shall be done with those who had authority over them.

" We were captured near Richmond, on the Kilpatrick and Dahlgren raid, about March 1st. Litchfield, Clark, and Kingston were kept in the entrance of Libby for three days under special guard, not allowed to communicate with other officers. While there, were visited frequently by citizens; among these was the wife of the Rebel Secretary of War, Mrs. Seddon, who wished to identify some of the party as of those who paid their compliments to her at Goochland. Her rage exceeded all previous exhibitions—said we were a party of hell-monsters and vagabonds; hoped we would all be hung; hoped her government was strong enough to do it; at any rate, would use her influence to have us put in dungeons, and fed on bread and water *till we rotted.* In pursuance of those suggestions to her noble lord no doubt came the treatment which followed. On the fourth day we were thrust into a dungeon eight by twelve feet, and in the course of the day four negro soldiers, captured from Butler, were unceremoniously put in with us, doubtless to throw *light* upon our condition. In the evening they were taken out and put through the manual of arms, to satisfy the curiosity of the prison officers as to whether the negro was fit for a soldier; then were informed they would be hung at nine o'clock the next morning, and were made to kneel, one after another, on the pavement of the cellar to pray, then brought back to inform us of their doom. That was a solemn night for the poor fellows. One of them sat up all night, spending the time in prayer. Morning came, but no execution. We remained in this crowded condition one week, six officers and four negroes in a dungeon eight by twelve feet, when we were removed to a more commodious cell, and four officers of negro troops put in with us. These were Captain Thomas Thornton, 5th United States Volunteer Cavalry; Lieutenant L. R. Titus, 3d Corps d'Afrique; Lieutenant Brown, and Lieutenant G. B. Coleman, 5th United States Colored Volunteers. In this condition we remained four and a half months; were furnished with no fire, though during the time snow fell to the depth of eight inches; no utensils to eat with; and were at no time allowed to send out for *any* thing, nor allowed to *receive* any thing from friends. As a substitute for a privy, an open tub was set in one corner of the room, the stench from which was almost *insufferable*. At times our room received all the smoke from a pipe protruding from an adjoining window, proving one of our greatest annoyances. The burning of the pitch-pine made the smoke so dense as to completely blind us. When rations were served, officers and negroes were arranged alternately in a row, and the stuff was eaten under guard. While the room overhead was occupied by officers, communication was always kept up, and sufficient favors were received to make our condition bearable. After they left, not only were these comforts taken away, but the rations were reduced to the lowest possible limit on which life could be sustained, consisting of a piece of corn bread made from unbolted meal, one and a half to two and four inches; one gill of filthy black pease, boiled in water; two ounces of rancid bacon. On this filthy and insufficient diet most of the party were taken sick; and, till Surgeon ———, whose name I have forgotten, and is a shame to humanity, left, we were denied hospital privileges. During these four and a half months we were kept as a sort of menagerie for exhibition to the curious negro-breeders and negro-haters, all delighted that the Yankees had found so fit companions. Among our distinguished visitors was 'Belle Boyd,' a lady of somewhat questionable notoriety. All this time, though treated as felons, no charges were preferred against any of the party; but not till after repeated inquiries and remonstrances were we released. On the 16th day of July we started for Macon, Georgia, where we joined the other prisoners.

"The following are the names of the officers confined in the cell : A. C. Litchfield, Lieutenant Colonel 7th Michigan Cavalry; John A. Clark, Captain 7th Michigan Cavalry; Major E. F. Cook, 2d New York Cavalry; —— Kingston, Surgeon 2d New York Cavalry; H. H. D. Merritt, Lieutenant 5th New York Cavalry; R. Bartley, Lieutenant United States Signal Corps; T. Thornton, Captain 5th United States Volunteer Cavalry; L. R. Titus, Lieutenant 3d United States Colored Troops; Lieutenant Brown, 5th United States Colored Troops; Lieutenant Coleman, 5th United States Colored Troops."

CHAPTER XVI.

ESCAPED AND RECAPTURED.

Camp Sorghum, S. C., November 24th.

THANKSGIVING all day. Not much to give thanks for, but thankful it is no worse. In the evening read the 146th Psalm. Thought the seventh verse meant me. Told A—— I thought I could not afford to stay much longer in prison.

Friday, 25th. In camp as usual. Felt unusually discontented; meditated escape. At night baked two loaves of corn bread, the usual number for next day's ration for five. Told P—— it was my last baking.

Saturday, 26th. In the forenoon talked with A—— about building. Had no faith in it, but felt it a duty to try to be comfortable. Told him to "go ahead;" I would help if I staid in camp. Got the loan of an ax. About noon prisoners began to leave. Thought *my* time had come. Put on another piece of a shirt, caught up blanket, said good-by, and started for guard line. Found K—— there, in my state of mind. Tried several points. No success. Watched movements. Saw our game. Picked up a stick of timber, one at each end. Staggered across guard line. Guard objected. "Mistake." Couldn't see it. Walked on round good ways. Threw down stick on "our pile." (?) Went back after "another." (?) Couldn't find it. Walked on. Dodged wood-cutters. Hid in the brush. Lay still all day. Sun went down slowly.

Thought of a great many things. Wondered if it was possible for us to make our escape. Prayed God, if it were His will, He would direct us in every step; if not, that He would defeat us. Felt safe. Sun went down; stars peeped out and down through the tree-tops, and seemed to bid us " go."

Great noise in camp. Rose up quietly. All safe. Thanked God. Took stellar direction. "That's *one* star." It has guided many a fugitive before *us*. Let's "away!" "Away!" Crossed a road. "Away, tiptoe!" "Away still!" "Westward!" "Tiptoe, away!" Venus our guide. "Arcturus behind!" "Away!" "Goodby," Camp Sorghum! "May we never see you again!"

> "Away through bush and bog,
> Over fence and log,
> Over brush and bramble,
> Fast as we could scramble;
> Heath and thickest bushes;
> Now among the rushes;
> Over stream we hurried,
> Not the least bit flurried,"

though stopping every few rods to see if all was right. Spoke only in low whispers. Came to a road. Decided to remain quiet for an hour. Heard others pass. Followed soon. Passed plantation on the left. On! No interruption. Heard negroes singing in the distance. Came in hearing of a house near the road. Women singing. Dog heard us, and barked furiously. Halted. Decided to "fall back in good order." Dog could not see us, but evidently scented us. Made a few steps by way of retreat; dog heard us, and, being scared, broke for the house. K——, like a quarter-horse, struck for the brush. Halted him in less than a quarter of a mile. Flanked the house on left, stumbled over many a bush, and, after an hour's beating about, we struck the road. Followed it part of the time. Flanked another. Plantations. Kept the blind roads as well as we could. Steered west by stars. Heard loud halloaing among negroes; sometimes the hounds. Saturday night, and they were hunting. Came again to main road. Ran on a house. Backed, and flanked it. Got into deep hollow; by-paths. Came near big road; saw lights. Thought it must be Rebel camp. Great noise, and singing and dancing; sounded as though some were preaching, some praying, some shouting, some laughing and halloaing. Think it must have been a negro frolic. Passed large plantation fields thrown open and destroyed; grown up with weeds and bushes. No roads; kept direction by stars. Became tired; laid down and slept for one hour. Went on; began to feel hungry. Heard roosters crowing in the distance, and the sounds thereof provoked hunger. Strongly tempted; thought I would like to have chicken in hand. Meditated the destruction of something to appease appetite. Rooster crowed again. Made straight course by sound; halted in front of house. Rooster wouldn't crow any more. Heard one at the barn; liked his voice better. Approached; went in; desperate work; never stole a chicken in my life, but very hungry; must have something; *very hungry*. Put hand on hen; hen died. Put hand on another; hen *flew away*, and made such a noise that we were obliged to leave on short notice. Traveled three or four miles through the woods and brush; went into quarters at daylight near Lexington, South Carolina. Cooked chicken by holding it over a fire built in a hole dug in the sand; devoured it; delicious! Laid down;

did not sleep much; laid all day. Heard bells ring at church-time in village. Nothing to eat or drink for the balance of the day. Sun went down beautiful and red. Prayed God to direct us.

Sunday, second night, 27th. Starlight. Crept forth carefully from our concealment. Cut clubs with dull case-knives; all the weapons, offensive or defensive, we had. Started cautiously to flank Lexington on the left. Heard waterfall in the distance. Were quite thirsty, hungry, and no provisions. Traveled through the woods. Saw light in the distance. Speculated upon the probabilities of its being a negro hut; decided in the negative; thought there must be some close by. Thought we saw a barn in the distance. Went to it, and found it an old tobacco-house; nothing there. Waited around a long time for negroes; none came. Heard hand-mill. (?) Made us feel more hungry. Thought of the good things that might be near by. Approached house. Dogs became ferocious, and for fear of detection we left. Traveled a good ways. Ran into more dogs, in trying to run into something to eat. Became disgusted, and, withal, very faint. Ate a teaspoonful of salt; felt better, and went on. Good road, but it soon began to lead in wrong direction. Too much north. Tried to twist it round; couldn't do it. Heard more water far off to the right. Some ahead sounded like a river. Feared pickets. Thought we saw several. Came up to an old tan-yard. Took a drink, the first for thirty hours. Took road to the left. Ran into open field. Lost it. Crossed boys on fence. No road. Concluded to steer by stars, and leave the roads to the dogs. Ran into swamp; huge one. Tried to flank it. *Got* flanked, and backed out. Went back to tan-yard. Decided to risk crossing a bridge ahead. Found a mill. No pickets, as we expected. Pushed on. Road twisted round more than ever the wrong way. Got disgusted again. Left the road and steered by the stars. Deep pine forest. Very tired and weak. Sank down to sleep 'neath a large pine-tree. Waked up in an hour refreshed, though very hungry. Started by stars. Ran into a huge swamp. Tried to flank it; no use. Floundered about in the brush for a long time. Went back to the road. A little discouraged. Concluded to follow road. Camp Sorghum began to loom up in imagination, and became almost visible; but "*no!*" will go to the Arctic Ocean before consenting to go back or be taken! On! on! Ran on a house. Dogs more than barked. Some huts in the rear. Blind with hunger. Could have eaten a piece of a dog easily. Passed on, but concluded to try to enter by back way and find negro huts. Took a large circle in field, and came up in rear. Dogs did not see us. Found an old tobacco-house, *empty; disappointed.* K—— suggested a search for potatoes in shed near by. Approached it with breathless silence. Good! found some! Appropriated a peck. Ate a few raw ones, but hastened to the woods. Nearly daylight. Went into camp. Cooked some potatoes; ate. Lay down. Very tired. Heard a wagon passing near by. Concluded we were discovered. Sought for other quarters. Crossed the road. Found pretty good place in half a mile. Crawled into bushes and lay down. Slept a little. Waked. Thought I would find negroes. Heard them in the distance. Crept up to the fence of a plantation. Thought I saw a negro plowing in a field far off. Slipped round cautiously in the thick woods. Approached to within fifteen feet of the fence where he would come. Waited till he would approach. I rose up to call to him; but, what horror! "*white!*" I dropped as quick as though I had been shot; lay low until his back was turned; then broke for quarters, disgusted with the entire white race (South).

Roasted balance of potatoes. Hog came up pretty close. Thought he wanted to be killed. Made a tremendous pass at him with a club. Knocked him down, and thought I had two hams; but before I had time to possess myself fully of them, lo! hams got up and went off with hog, and I was afraid to follow. Failed this time; but all for the best, as sequel will show.

Heard a boy coming toward us whistling and driving goats. Broke up camp in one fourth of a minute; snatched potatoes out of the fire; covered it up; picked up traps, and glided away as noiselessly as possible. It was growing dark; boy seemed to follow us, whistling. We changed direction; boy changed too. Changed again; boy ditto. Changed again; boy went on whistling, all unconscious of us; but he succeeded in driving us into a better road. We lay down close to the road for an hour.

Monday, third night, 28*th*. Got up and went on our way. Began to feel very hungry and tired. Sand about one foot deep. Hard traveling. Halted near a house on the right, and waited for negro. Waited long time. None came near enough to hail. Dog barked, and we were obliged to leave. Trudged on. Traveling very hard. Became weary and desperate for water. Brought up against a house. Dared not pass it on the road. Heard some one spinning. Lay down under a pine a few rods

M

from road. Presently negro came out of house; crossed road near us. We knew him to be a negro by his whistling and singing. He passed near us, but we dared not hail him, for fear of attracting notice from the house. Listened carefully, and heard him enter house about a quarter of a mile on our right. Thought it must be his own. Felt encouraged. Decided to follow him. Approached the house. It proved to be plantation-house. Dog barked. K—— wanted to retreat. Could not agree with him; too thirsty and hungry. We waited in the bushes near by for nearly an hour. Could hear the conversation at the house; not very complimentary to the "Yanks." I became impatient. We advanced cautiously. Dog barked. Heard negroes coming out toward the barn; two of them. Now is the time! Approached one of them. "Spoke him." Negro scared. Whispered him, "Be quiet." "Yes, sah!" "Who lives here?" "Miss R——." "Any white men here?" "No, sah, nary one now, but may be *soon*." "Are you true?" (a term we use in the South, and which the negroes understand perfectly). "Oh yes, sah; never tell on nobody." "Do you know who we are?" "No, sah." "We are Yanks." "Is, sah? I spects you was." "Have you ever seen any before?" "Yes, sah;. two on em done cotched here last night. Dem fust ones I seed." "Where are the white men belonging here?" "Dere's nary white man heah jis now. He's done gone out, an' watching for you uns all. Massa K—— lives jes up dah, and he's out now, too, wid a gun on the road up dah wha'ah you uns wuz, watching for yees."

And so it turned out that our extreme hunger and thirst saved us from capture, and probably from death.

Had we gone but a few steps farther, as would have been the case had we succeeded in taking the "hams" aforesaid, we should have fallen into the trap set for us.

These faithful negroes secreted us in a secure place not far from the house; and, after supplying us with water and uncooked potatoes, for they said there was nothing else about the premises, not even a bit of corn bread, they directed us as well as they could how to avoid the pickets.

Thus far Divine Providence seemed to favor us, resolving all our doubts, and making our disappointments and seeming failures serve our purpose.

To show how faithful and how shrewd these poor slaves are, I will mention one little incident that occurred while in conversation with one of these negroes on the same evening. He was one of those coarse, mortally homely creatures that looked as though he did not know any thing at all. He was giving us some directions how and where to secrete ourselves while they brought us some food, when all at once he exclaimed, in a half whisper, "Kawful dah, kawful! down, down! man comin'!" We could neither see nor hear any one, but we fell flat on the ground. We had no sooner done so, than a man, armed with a gun, approached, hailed the negro, and commenced conversation. It proved to be one of the spies that were watching for us. The man did not observe us, but his dog did. The negro had a dog also; and when dog number one began to make ado about finding us in that curious position, we began to think it was all day with us. But mark the shrewdness of this negro. "Begone dah! begone dah!" he exclaimed. "What yer want to be fightin' *my* dog fo'?" The man, supposing from this observation that it was nothing more than a quarrel between the dogs, passed within ten feet of us, no wiser for having talked with "Cuffee."

But, dear A——, I fear that, if I continue this narration, your book will not be large enough to contain it. I will, therefore, only give you some of the principal incidents that occurred for the next ten or twelve nights. We were obliged to retrace our steps that night a mile or two, when we struck off to our left some eight miles for another road less exposed to pickets, and, after sundry mistakes and swampings similar to those of the previous evening, we went into camp for the day, it having grown light before we reached the other road. A little before daylight this morning it began to rain, promising, from all appearances, to give us a good drenching that day, but, fortunately for us, it did not continue long.

The day was spent as usual, closely secreting ourselves among some old logs and bushes, and cooking the balance of our potatoes. I had my Bible with me, my only stock of property except some MS. I had secreted on my person, and, as I could sleep but little during the day, I busied myself in reading that, and I do assure you it was a solid comfort. I have thought since that I was about as happy as ever I was in my life. I remember that my socks had given out on the previous evening, and no wonder, for they were made up of all manner of patches and pieces—and my shoes were no better—and that I took a part of my shirt (it is needless to say *what particular part*) and repaired said socks, revamping them entirely, or, what is called in the language of shoemakers, "foxed" them round about. Thus passed the day, and night came on, beautiful and clear. The first thing of note was a threatened encounter with a huge bear that was prowling about our pathway. But, owing to a disposition on the part of one of the parties—not the bear—to be a little prudent, there was no fight, but a bully run, in which, I believe, the bear did not participate.

We soon struck a road that seemed to lead in the right direction, which we followed. We soon became intensely thirsty, and in our state of bodily vigor it was almost maddening. I will quote from my diary here again. Became very thirsty; came to a plantation-house; heard some one spinning (and here I would remark it is not an unusual thing in the South to hear the spinning-wheel till near midnight, a species of industry recently sprung up; but I more than half suspect it is carried on chiefly by the slaves). Almost mad for water; concluded to flank the house on the left; thought I smelled water* on that side. Crossed two fields; water became more apparent; prayed God that we might find it. Looked on the left hand, and saw the stars shining on the ground. "Water!" we cried, in a whisper, for we dared not speak. "Thank God!" and we rushed to the side of a beautiful little lake or pond, where we laid down and drank, and drank.

Oh, how good is water! God gave it to us when we most needed it. After drinking we sat down upon the bank. K—— said he thought the stars shone brighter than usual. No wonder. His eyes were brighter, too. We were glad. Ate some sweet potato; drank more water; looked at the stars a while. They seemed to smile on us, and bid us away from the vile dens of oppression. Thought of *dear ones at home* that I had not heard from

---

* This is no fiction. A man suffering from extreme thirst can scent water half a mile, if it be abundant.

for nearly a year. Tears came into my eyes, and we started for the road.

We suffered no more for water that night, for in a few miles we were hemmed in by it, and were obliged to slip off our shoes and stockings, an elaborate ceremony in our cases, and to wade a stream of water deep, and swift, and cold.

This done, we plodded on, passing several large plantations, and, being still hungry, we sought for food every where; but we feared to enter a house, lest we should encounter a white man. Why should we fear our own race and nation? We would rather have met the bear we left behind than a white man here in South Carolina. I quote again from diary. Came to high road; guideboard on high post. Wanted to know where we were, and where we were going; too high to be read. ' K—— proposed to climb it and read. Good! I "boosted" him thus (see cut opposite). When up, K—— lighted a match and read as follows: "Mount Welling, — miles; Charleston, — miles; Columbia, — miles; Hamburg, *via* Ridgehouse Road, 42 miles." That experiment paid, for we had hitherto been ignorant of our whereabouts, and of our place of destiny. Christened it "The Pursuit of Knowledge under Difficulties." Proposed a cut for A——'s "Illustrated Prison Life."

After traveling fifteen or twenty miles this night, we sought shelter by the side of an old log in the densest part of the woods, where we spent the day as on former occasions.

Here a little incident worthy of note occurred. Late in the afternoon we became very hungry, and I determined to creep forth in search of food. I had selected my

The Pursuit of Knowledge under Difficulties.

direction, and was about starting, when I heard the report of a gun but a short distance from us, and in the exact direction I had selected. I concluded not to go. In a similar manner, on another occasion, I was saved by the barking of a dog.

After the stars had made their appearance, and while the new moon hung like a silver horn in the west, we crept quietly forth on this, the fifth night of our travel, and resumed our wearisome march.

It is remarkable how much a person will fall in love with Nature and familiar objects when thus shut out of all human society. We would have considered it a great calamity indeed had we been deprived the privilege of looking at the stars; and when the new moon made its appearance we hailed it with rapturous joy. It seemed that an old friend had come to us to pilot us through our difficult undertaking. Even the clouds seemed friendly, and the wind whispered sweet names of "home and friends" to us.

After traveling some five or six miles, and making several fruitless attempts to replenish our depleted commissary and our collapsed stomachs, we came in sight of a large plantation and buildings near the road. After making careful observations, we came to the conclusion there must be negro quarters somewhere near. This was confirmed by singing, which we heard beyond and in the rear. We therefore determined to flank the large buildings, and bring up at the negro quarters, if we could find them. In this we were guided by the singing, which we could now distinctly hear, and which we knew by the tone to proceed from a negro hut. The booming of the cannon that guides the lost mariner to the ship or the shore could not be a much more welcome sound than this sweet voice was to us. But I will here quote briefly from diary. Nearly starved. Saw a light in negro hut, in large row of them near the road. All looked favorable. Woman kept on singing. Determined to enter. Saw light in two of the huts. Approached hut No. 2, and peeped through the cracks near the chimney; saw two negroes; had been making baskets, and were about going to bed. Between ten and eleven o'clock. Went in; negroes somewhat scared, and I do not much wonder, for we must have looked somewhat frightful. "Who is yeh?"

"We are Yankee officers; will you be true?" "Oh yes, sah! We nose who you is now. We never tells." We begged for something to eat. They said they had nothing, but that they would take us to the next house—hut No. 1—where we could get something. These two men were railroad hands, and were in the employ of the government. Told us that four Yanks had been there that night and got something to eat. Took us to next house. Woman still singing; went in: man asleep; waked him; told him who we were. They understood us perfectly; woman went about getting supper; we were glad. I laid down; could not sleep; too hungry and tired. Man told us all about the country and roads. The news of Sherman's approach was terrifying every body. The road we were on was picketed farther on; told us we had better go through Aiken, twenty-four miles south. Timely advice again. Supper ready—corn bread, sweet potatoes, and fried bacon. Oh, how delicious that latter article! the first we had had for nearly four months. Ate enormously; filled our haversacks with bread and sweet potatoes; got some salt. Started; man went with us some distance, to show us the road. A widow woman lived on plantation. Overseer had gone to C—— on business. Negro said he knew what it was to run away; had tried it several times himself. Good and true people. May God bless them for their kindness to us and others! After giving us careful directions, and bidding us God speed, this good man left us, and we went on our way rejoicing and praising God for negroes.

We were now in a rich and thickly-settled country— that is to say, thickly settled for the South, there being a plantation every few miles; but, fortunately for us, the buildings, for the most part, were at a distance from the road. Made good time. Were much cheered by our good fortune, and the prospect of seeing home and friends. Oh, how our hearts yearned for these! I verily think that, if our desires could have been gratified, we should have been entirely overcome.

Here we found milestones set along the road, and, by carefully feeling them, we could ascertain the distances. On this night we repeated the process of "climbing the guide-post."

In a few hours after eating so hearty a meal I became very sick; was obliged to lie down several times. Suffered till morning, but could not afford to give up. Became very thirsty. Went on till near morning. Feared that we would be obliged to go into quarters without water. I prayed for water, and in less than fifteen minutes I saw the stars reflected in the road from a stream of water. Thank God for water! Traveled about fifteen miles this night, and went into quarters near a beautiful little stream of water, which, in our state of health and dirtiness, was much needed. Here, from our complete seclusion, we were permitted to engage in ablutions both in person and clothing. So calm, and sweet, and still was this day, that it seemed that it must be a Sabbath. Slept but little; read much in Bible, and commenced a diary of our travels.

God had so signally directed us and delivered us hitherto, that we began to feel encouraged, and to believe that he intended to bring us through safe.

Our next night's travel, December 1st, was full of incident and danger, and not less remarkable deliverances. Twice we were met by parties traveling or hunting with dogs; but, by dodging and lying flat on the ground, they passed us without detecting us. Our road was beset by fires, which in some cases we found it difficult to avoid. About three or four o'clock in the morning we were surprised to find ourselves right in the midst of a large town; hotels, stores, large mansions loomed up in the darkness all around us. It was too late to retreat, and we rushed on, and, in our attempt to avoid the main street, we ran into the railroad dépôt. Here it was still more dangerous; but by gliding stealthily from point to point where we could see, keeping our direction as well as we could by the stars, our best friends here in this, where a false step, or the breaking of a stick, the rattle of the gravel, or even a loud breath might have betrayed us to our enemies. But, strange to say, not even a dog barked; and the only signs of civilized life was the crowing of the chickens; and this would not have been a safe business for them if it had been any where else but in town. Perhaps they or their owners were aware of this, for Yanks were numerous all through the country. Soon, however, we came to roads leading out of town, and right glad were we to find them, for we were not long in finding our friendly forest. After many and devious wanderings we found our road. I knew it from its direction, and because I felt safe in it. But by this time we were suffering for water again, not having had any during the night; but, just as I began to pray earnestly for it, I heard a little brook bubbling not more than ten feet from the road. "Thank God for the little bubbler" (I find it in my diary). There is nothing among the common gifts of Providence for which a man, when tired and thirsty, feels more thankful than for water.

The common blessings are those for which we should feel most grateful. What a bountiful supply of good air we have in the world, and what misery we would suffer, even if it were changed in the slightest degree in its composition! And yet how few ever think of it as the gift of God!

After traveling some four or five miles farther, we went into quarters on a high hill covered with low pine bushes. Of these we were accustomed to make booths, so as to escape notice should any one pass near. I find the following written in my diary—written some days after, but relating to this night's journey: "Went into quarters happy and thankful to Almighty God for protection and direction thus far. No water this day, but fortunately we do not feel much thirsty. Slept but little during the day" (and I wish to say here that this is an accomplishment that I never could acquire. It matters but little what time in the night or early in the morning I go to bed, for when the sun rises I wake up; and I must be very tired indeed if I can ever close my eyes to sleep in the daylight). "Read the Bible, and wrote in diary. Beautiful day! Hitherto have had every night clear most of the time, so that we could steer by the stars, though it has been raining frequently during the day. By this and other marks of Divine approbation, I felt pretty sure that God intended, at least, that we should proceed. I am now hid away in the woods by negroes; and, though in the midst of dangers, such is my trust in God that I have not the least fear or uneasiness. I know He will bring us through, if it is best; and if it is not, I don't wish to go. I know He will work the best thing for us. 'The angel of the Lord encampeth round about them that fear Him, to deliver them.'" And it appeared to me that the angel went before us, pointing out the way for us. How could we doubt, then? and why should we fear, since not only the past is a guaranty for the future, but the promises themselves are enough to inspire faith in any one.

Friday, sixth night, December 2d. Stars shone out as usual, and the crescent moon looked us full in the face as we crept forth to resume our journey. This night passed with the usual incidents, varied according to circumstances. Hunger and thirst were our chief tormentors; though, in most instances, we chose rather to endure these light afflictions than to expose ourselves to detection. I remember we had great difficulty in passing a long range of fires extending for half a mile. We found that an army was encamped there, as it was near the railroad leading to Augusta. These passed, we found ourselves in the midst of a very rich and populous country.

About one o'clock in the morning, after making long and careful reconnoissance, we ventured into a negro hut on a very rich plantation, where our wants, and they were pressing, were supplied in the usually liberal manner. Here, I remember, I got a draught of buttermilk, a favorite drink of mine, and the first I had tasted since my capture. This made me think of *home* and *friends* more than ever. Here we also learned of the state of the country, and the probable approach of Sherman; and, as we were now only seven miles from Augusta, the roads being guarded, it stood us in hand to be very careful. We therefore decided to keep the by-roads, and to strike the Savannah River a few miles below Augusta.

So the negroes advised us; but, of all the times we ever had, this one was the most trying; for in the great multiplicity of roads, we could find none that would lead us long enough in one direction to justify us in following it more than a mile or two. Thus perplexed and defeated, and tired and sleepy, we threw ourselves on the ground, and, after committing my way to God, I remember I fell asleep almost instantly. In an hour or two we waked, chilled and numb with cold. I remember, too, that we were suddenly inspired with new resolution, and, selecting a star, we made as straight a course as we could in that direction, heedless of all roads and other obstructions. In our desperation to keep straight on, we passed almost under the eves of some houses, until we struck a road that seemed to lead in the exact direction we desired. This we followed, and soon were made conscious of our near approach to the river by the ringing of steam-boat bells and the noise of wheels in the water. Suddenly a dense fog shut out all stars from us and enveloped us in thick darkness. But it was nearly daylight. In this situation, we thought it best not to attempt the crossing of the river until the next night. We were about to seek quarters for the coming day, which now began to dawn, when our ears were saluted by the welcome sound of negroes singing in the distance. We imagined they were approaching us, and so they were. We stepped to the road-side and waited. Soon they came within hailing distance, and by great efforts—for my voice had become almost paralyzed and useless, either from suffering or disease, perhaps from both—I succeeded in attracting the attention of this party—for there were five or six of them—and made them understand, in our usual way, our situation.

They expressed the liveliest sympathy for us, and cautioned us not to go a rod farther on that road, as there were guards stationed all along it, and for miles on the river; that every ferry-boat and flat had been removed or sunk, for fear of the "Yanks." They advised our immediate return to their quarters, assuring us that there were no "white men" within several miles of the plantation. So we did, and here I must relate what followed.

These quarters we had passed but an hour before with great caution, for fear of waking the inmates; but had we known who and what they were, we would have approached them with impunity. It was a collection of some half a dozen houses, rather better than the average, tenanted by perhaps twice that number of families. We were conducted to the main building, and, what was unusual, it had two apartments. Here we were introduced to "Granny," the presiding personage of the little colony. She was an old lady of ninety-six, and yet she retained all the vivacity and sprightliness of a woman of forty or forty-five years of age. She was tall and commanding in appearance, and, save that she was a little bent with age, was a model of what slave-dealers would have pronounced "a valuable piece of property." She told me she had nearly all her life belonged to the same man, having raised her master and buried him. She could not tell now to whom she belonged, but supposed she was a part of "the estate." She set about preparing breakfast for us, and, while sitting there waiting and watching—for we could not banish the thought that we were in danger every moment of being discovered by some white man; but, on being assured that there were none on the plantation, and that it was now seldom visited, since the white inhabitants and many of the blacks had been taken to the "front" to oppose Sherman, and being assured that the children were already dispatched to different points as sentinels to announce the approach of any one in time for us to secrete ourselves, we began to feel very much at home. I well remember what a relief I experienced from the intense strain of protracted anxiety when I was assured by this old lady, in her warm and impressive manner, of our entire security. From her we learned many particulars in reference to the treatment of slaves in that region of country. To many a story of heart-rending cruelty did we listen. Oh, how my heart swelled with indignation, and my cheek burned with shame at her simple and yet graphic description of the sufferings of the slaves and the brutality of their masters. All her own children but one had been sold and driven off before her eyes, and she had witnessed a whole generation rise and pass away. But a recital of these incidents would only be a repetition of what is heard and known to exist all through the more Southern slave-holding states.

This old lady was devoutly pious, and her word and counsel were the law and gospel of all that little community. And oh, with what a prophetic rapture she looked upon the coming deliverance of her race from bondage! As she spoke, her otherwise grave countenance beamed with almost angelic raptures; and I confess that more than once my eyes filled with tears as my own spiritual vision caught the rapture of her dream, and looked far down the stream of time, and saw her race and people blessed, honored, and elevated to nationality and freedom.

In her conversation, she addressed me in the terms of the bondman, "massa," which I forbade, for I felt more like bowing down to *her* than *she to me.* I felt like a child listening to the instructions of a parent, and more than once I was reminded of my own dear sainted mother.

After breakfast, which was by no means a poor or unwelcome one, we were secreted in a small stable but a few rods from the group of houses. Here, buried up in the soft hay, I tried to sleep, but my mind was too much affected by what I had seen and heard, and too much occupied with a hope of finally escaping, to allow of much slumber.

While we were in the house, we were visited by the numerous members of the group of families there, all anxious to show some kindness. We seemed to be objects of great curiosity and interest. Each one would approach us cautiously, extending a hand to welcome us to their hospitalities, and, after we were secreted in the stable, we were visited that day by others from adjoining plantations, though they were very careful not to expose us.

This plantation, to which we had been so providentially directed by our mistakes and perplexities on the preceding night, proved to be the only one in the whole neighborhood, for five or six miles, where we would have been at all safe. It is one of the largest and richest in the South, extending several miles along the river. It is the estate of the notorious Thomas Lamar, the kidnapper of the slave-ship "Rover" notoriety. It will be remembered by many that this vessel, some six or eight years ago, after vainly trying to land its cargo of

350 negroes from the coast of Africa at the ports of Charleston and Savannah, ran up the river, landed its cargo on this plantation, and then pushed out into the stream, and was burned to avoid detection. Lamar was tried for his life in the civil courts at Augusta, escaped the just penalty of hanging because he was rich, and a slave-owner and breeder, went to Charleston in a few years, and died of yellow fever. The property is now in the hands of his brother-in-law, Barney S. Dunbar, who is living in great style with a black concubine, has four or five children, which he owns as slaves; but he himself is now hid in the swamp, some four miles distant, to avoid the conscription officer. He is a rank secessionist, but swears he won't fight. This information I got from the negroes. And while said Barney is compelled to lie out in the swamp, I, his mortal enemy, whom he would gladly shoot, am nicely stowed away in his stable, preaching heresy to his slaves, which slaves carry food to him twice a day, but save the best of it for me. Oh, how these slaves love their masters! They have things about their own way now, and a jolly time they have.

It will be remembered that nearly or quite one half of the cargo of slaves above referred to, numbering some 600 in all, died on the passage; of the balance, every woman is dead, and many of the men; some of the younger boys are still living. They are rare specimens indeed. Their language is scarcely intelligible, though one or two with whom I conversed are very bright and intelligent.

I will here copy again from my diary, as the shortest way of getting at what followed.

Saturday, eighth night, December 3d. This night was the first we spent in sleep since we started. It was acceptable, indeed, though somewhat interrupted by a genuine African dance, held by the negroes of the plantation in the open air, around several blazing fires made from pine knots. This exercise, from its wild and fantastic nature, attracted our attention somewhat. Whether or not it was given in honor of our arrival we never learned.

About 9 o'clock, A.M., December 4th, our breakfast was sent to us, and consisted of biscuit, beefsteak, baked potatoes, fried eggs, and coffee (rye or wheat). This was the best meal we had had in the Confederacy. We praised God in our hearts and took courage. Heard heavy cannonading in the forenoon toward the front. We knew that Sherman was coming; and, as we could learn through the negroes, the country all around was in perfect terror, all except the negroes. In most cases they, too, in the presence of their masters, were terribly scared, but when by themselves, or with us, their joy knew no bounds; it became perfectly wild and extravagant. But let a white man not a Yank approach them, and they were ready to die of terror for fear "Massa Sherman" would come, and they would all be carried off or killed by the "Yanks."

Was Sherman indeed coming? Oh, how we prayed that that cannonading might come nearer, and that our lines might come rolling on, crashing over the broken and fleeing columns of the enemy, until we should be included in the captures; but we were doomed to disappointment. Sherman did not know *we* were there, and we had no means of informing him. Perhaps he would not have changed the programme of the campaign, or his line of "march to the sea" much, if he had even been informed of the strong position we held. But this consideration was not the more comforting to us. Lay still all day. Read and wrote some.

Sunday night, December 4th. Went to bed, expecting another good sleep, but about 11 o'clock P. M. were roused up by Cuffee, the driver on the plantation, half frightened out of his senses, exclaiming, in a husky whisper, "Say! say, massa! massa! Come out dah! come, come, *quick!* Gor A'mighty, *hurry!* White man in de house huntin' for yees! Hurry, hurry! God's sake, *hurry!* Break for de hollah down dah!"

The next moment he was gone, and out of hearing and out of sight, and we were "piling out" in double-quick time, and we *did* "break for hollah" sure enough, blundering over bush, and brake, and brier pell-mell, regardless of head, or heels, or any thing else, except escape from "de white man" aforesaid. Tumbled down a small precipice; brought up in an old brier-patch; tore our clothes badly, besides receiving sundry *other* wounds that we cared less about, till presently we found ourselves, panting and almost breathless, in a deep ravine, listening to what was going on at the houses. We could hear distinctly a man cursing roundly, and apparently in great displeasure, at what he denominated as some "*dog on* rascality about heyah sumwhar;" said he expected they were hid now some place about the house. Cuffee declared they were not, and affirmed his honesty and integrity with such vehemence that the master (for it proved to be Barney Dunbar) was obliged to give up the search.

We supposed, from the occurrence, that we had been betrayed by some one, and that we were the individuals alluded to in this mild conversation; but it was otherwise. "Barney" was after two other "Yanks" that had been seen the night before going toward the river. Our danger, however, was none the less, for, armed as he was with two loaded revolvers, one of which he carried in each hand, and a coward at that, he would not hesitate at any deed of meanness.

The result was, however, we nearly perished with the cold in the woods that night, not daring either to return to the stable or to lie down where we were; and, fearing lest we should be pursued, we had gone so far into the woods that the negroes could not find us that night. About daylight our ears were saluted by the shrill blast of a horn, and the loud call of the negroes. We mistook this for the signal of our pursuit, and we waited patiently the issue. But it soon occurred to me that it was the usual morning call, and so it proved.

I then crawled on my hands and knees up to within speaking distance of the house, in hopes to learn something of the true state of affairs. Did not succeed. We then fell back to the woods again, to wait farther developments. In a few moments I heard some one chopping far back in the timber, where I knew Charlie, the blacksmith on the plantation, had been the day before.

This Charlie was a knowing one, and had accompanied his master through the Mexican War. He had assumed the special charge of us. Proceeding carefully in the direction of the chopping, to our utter relief we found him; whereupon he gave us the history of the whole mystery, adding that "Granny" had been hunting for us from the time it was light enough to see, and that she was in great distress lest she should not see us again. We soon relieved her anxiety, however, and she, in turn, relieved our hunger by a good breakfast.

After spending two more days and a night with these clever people, and after they had washed and mended our soiled and tattered garments, supplying us with whatever they could *possibly* spare, tearing up some of their best new cotton cloth to make us haversacks and towels, taking their stockings off their own feet and giving them to us, "Granny" giving me the best pair she had (God bless the old saint!); after cooking meat, and bread, and potatoes, and filling these haversacks for us, and after we were satisfied that Sherman had passed Augusta, and was making for Savannah, and after repeated prayers for our safety and success, these good people grasped our hands with all the fervid warmth and affection of parents and children, and bade us "good-by," and we turned our faces toward the North Star, setting out on a journey of nearly three hundred miles to reach the mountains of Eastern Tennessee.

It was with real sadness and many misgivings that we left these people, for they assured us that they would be able to keep us all winter, and they would gladly do it, rather than have us risk our lives again. But the ties of kindred and home, friends and country, were stronger than their solicitations, and, about 10 o'clock P.M., December 6th, we addressed ourselves to the perilous undertaking, not, however, without repeatedly invoking God's blessing and protection.

But our expectations were soon cut short, for, after two nights' hard traveling, and the usual number of incidents and dangers passed, on the morning of the 8th of December, at about four o'clock, it being very dark and cloudy, though it had been clear nearly all night, we were startled by the loud baying of hounds, and the voice of a man calling to us within a few feet of us. He was mounted on a splendid horse, and I could see, by the dim reflection from the clouds, that he was dressed in Rebel clothes. He hailed us with "Who are you?" "Travelers," we replied. After repeating the question, and receiving the same answer, he replied, "All right," and passed on. But we suspected mischief, and prepared for the worst. After traveling about half a mile or more, we suddenly dodged from the road into an open field on our left, crossed fences and fields, retraced and crossed our track time and again, making large circles and detours through thickets and across ravines; and, after wandering in this manner for two or three hours, it being now broad daylight, we threw a few pine boughs together to screen us from open sight, and then threw ourselves upon the ground to rest.

But I had no sooner straightened out my weary limbs, than I heard, far in the distance, the deep baying of the "*bloodhounds.*" I said to my companion, "Do you hear that?" "Yes," hissed through his clinched teeth. We listened. The baying grew louder. We were silent for a moment. Neither looked at the other; but we well knew what was passing before us. In those few moments, oh, how our visions of home faded—how our hopes crumbled—how our hearts *sickened!* All our past toils and our future expectations crowded into one bitter moment —one terrible resolve, and it was past. "Father, Thy will be done!" relieved me, and I said, "Up, let us be going!" and, gathering up our few "traps," we were moving forward at a rapid pace, we knew not where, neither did we care much. Soon we ascended a steep hill, from which we saw a plantation in the distance. Thinking that a house might serve us in close pursuit, we went toward it, but, discovering a stream of water passing through the fields, and no house being in sight, we concluded to cross the stream and conceal ourselves beneath a high bank on the opposite side. This we did, and for a few moments we could hear nothing from our pursuers. A faint hope flashed upon us that possibly we had eluded them.

But soon the loud yelp and yell, accompanied by the hunter's horn, assured us that they still were on our track; and on, on they came, and, having struck our fresh trail, we soon saw them descending the hill-side, led by a monster black hound, trained to the exalted position of "leading a pack."

At first sight of them, we resolved to stand our ground and defend ourselves as best we could, and, in case of necessity, to leap into the water, which was half-breast deep near us. But, on a nearer approach, K—— suggested that we "climb;" and thinking perhaps our resistance might form a pretext for insult and injury by our captors, I accepted the suggestion, and, mounting the bank, we sprang up into the boughs of an oak; but, no sooner had we cleared our distance, than the hounds came bounding full six feet high up the tree after us. Fortunately, we were beyond their reach, which fact seemed to aggravate their ferocity.

I had, then and there, a few moments' profitable reflection. Looking down into those deep mouths gaping upon me, and those hideous teeth that had torn the flesh of many a *man*, I thought of the many helpless women

Recaptured.

and children that had been mangled by them—of the poor slaves that had been hunted down like wild beasts, and then, when at bay, had been shot and wounded, so that the dogs could "*go in and wool the nigs,*" as they termed this interesting performance.

But soon our attention was called to our captor, who was at this time just descending the hill-side in hot pursuit, armed with a double-barreled shot-gun. Approaching nearer, he began to curse us in true Southern style, not excepting the Southern slang, and closing with the epithet "*Abolitionist,*" with a qualifying word.

Coming closer, he asked us if we "surrendered," at the same time making sundry demonstrations with his gun. I replied "that I did not see what else we could do, as we could not go much farther in our last direction (pointing up the tree), and we were not prepared to contend with his dogs."

With many chivalrous remarks and demonstrations, he approached us, ordering us to throw down our clubs, blankets, and haversacks. By this time he was joined by three other men, also mounted and armed, and, after a brief consultation, we were ordered down from the tree. We replied that we were now their prisoners, and we hoped they would call off their dogs before we descended. To this they replied that the dogs would not hurt us *much*.

My friend, being below me, was obliged to descend first; and no sooner had he come within reach of these monsters than they all sprang upon him, tearing his clothes, and otherwise injuring him. On our earnest expostulation against such treatment, the dogs were partially removed! but, on my coming down, they fell upon me in a similar manner, but did me no injury.

After searching us for arms and evidence (for we had no money), about the first question they asked was, "What do you uns all want to come down heah fo' to free all our niggers?" I replied, "We were not in that business *now*." Whereupon there sprang up quite a spirited argument in reference to the two sections of our country, and their respective institutions and policies, in which I took pains to tell them in plain terms what I thought of slavery, and what I thought of the policy of hunting down United States officers with bloodhounds as though they were beasts of prey; and, finding that we *would* talk, and only laughed at their pretended severity, they soon began to exhibit a much better spirit, and finally invited us to the house, where the lady prepared a good breakfast for us, to which we did ample justice.

Several ladies from the neighborhood had come in to see the "live Yanks" that had been caught that morning, and I improved the opportunity of delivering as strong an Abolition lecture as ever I did in my life. I felt that the occasion demanded it, and God gave me words of utterance that brought tears to their eyes. Out of pity, perhaps, for our unfortunate condition, they did not attempt to deny much of what I said, but replied in a despairing way, "Oh, I wish this cruel war was ended!" I was satisfied that they were sincere, at least, in *that* wish. I told them I hoped it would not end so long as there was any opposition to the government left; and especially as long as any of the curse that caused the war existed.

After dinner, we were marched to Edgefield jail, eight miles distant, through a most pitiless, pelting rain that froze as it fell; so that, when we arrived there, we were just as wet as though we had been plunged into the river, and so benumbed with cold that it was with difficulty we could stand. In this plight, the enrolling-officer who had command of the place ordered us thrown into a cell, through the iron bars of which the wind howled in hideous mockery of our fate.

I bethought me of one more appeal, and it was not in vain, for the jailor was a mason; and on my certifying to the same fact, we were taken to the basement, where an old negro had kindled a fire, and there we were permitted to dry our rags before being locked up. Had not this act of kindness been done, we certainly must have perished before morning.

We had been allowed to retain what rations were in our haversacks, except what the hounds ate (and that was about one half), and, in examining me, they had failed to find my manuscript and diary that I had concealed in my nether garments. Had they found these, I should have swung, I suppose, from the first good limb, or perhaps been made food for their hounds. With what rations we had, and the *little* afforded us at the jail, we managed to keep alive till I had an opportunity to send a note to Mrs. G——, a good Union lady living in the place, who sent the following in reply, accompanied by a most excellent dinner:

"Edgefield, South Carolina, December 11th, 1864.

"LIEUTENANT ——: DEAR SIR,—Your very gentlemanly note is before me. I did not know until its reception that there were any United States officers in the place. I will come over this evening at three o'clock. Any thing I can do for either of you will give me much satisfaction. 1 have been able to do but very little, owing to my circumstances being limited; but I am willing to divide the last iota I have, rather than that any one in your situation should suffer. I would certainly have sent you something to eat had I known of your being there.   Yours very truly,
"MRS. W. W. G——."

Oh, how thankful I was to her and to God for thus

remembering us in our distress. Having but one old blanket, and an old rag or two in the cell, we suffered *much* from cold, as by this time it was *very inclement.* Waking in the morning (for we slept from sheer exhaustion), we were shivering with cold, and were obliged to resort to a system of violent exercise to keep from freezing. Thus we managed for two or three days and nights; but, after Mrs. G——'s note, we suffered no more from hunger. She communicated the facts to a Mr. B——, a wealthy and influential citizen of the place, whose heart was for the Union, and he and his good lady vied with Mrs. G—— in sending us good things, which fact coming to the knowledge of the enrolling-officer, we were ordered to leave for Columbia, South Carolina, *via* Post Ninety-six, that afternoon.

Our conveyance to Ninety-six, thirty miles distant, was a two-horse hack. This was a relief to us, and we became more and more reconciled to return. While halting a few moments before leaving town, I saw Mr. B—— with a bundle under his arm, which he endeavored to conceal from the crowd. Approaching the hack, he dropped his bundle at my feet, at the same time giving me a sly wink. Gathering it up, I found it to contain about two dozen excellent biscuits. This made us all right for the balance of the way. We were guarded by two young men of wealthy parentage; had been in the service some time, and understood military etiquette. One of them was a nephew of John C. Calhoun, the other a son of Dr. Jennings, a leading member of the South Carolina Legislature. On our way we talked freely on politics, and of the policy of the respective governments. Soon the negro question was broached, and I was asked to give my opinion on it, which I did with my usual frankness. This enraged the driver, who, by the way, I had learned was a man of high standing, but had resorted to stage-driving to avoid conscription; and, being a little intoxicated, he was very abusive in his language. I therefore refused to talk with him; but, after being repeatedly insulted and threatened by him, I told him plainly that no gentleman would make use of the language he had done in an argument, and especially to a prisoner; upon which he struck me in the face with his fist, and, becoming exasperated, he caught up an iron wrench, and assaulted me with a determination to kill me. Failing in this, the guards interfering, he began to beg for a pistol to shoot me. This was refused him by the guards, on the ground that they considered him more in fault than I was; but for some time he was bent on taking my life. I then had an opportunity of seeing an infuriated ruffian, and I thought of the tender mercies of the slave-driver.

Becoming a little pacified, we drove on a mile or two, and, halting at a country tavern or grog-shop, and finding some of his boon companions there, he related the affair to them, declaring that "he ought to have killed me," and farther, "that he meant to do it yet." Thereupon they all began to clamor for my blood. I had the felicity at that place of hearing what they in South Carolina thought of Abolitionists, for this was my chief offense. Arrangements were progressing favorably for hanging me, when the guards again interfered and saved my life.

Nothing farther of interest occurred on our way to Ninety-six, where we were placed on board the cars, and were soon on our way back to prison at Columbia, where we arrived on the morning of the 13th of December, having been absent seventeen days and nights; thankful to God for His many mercies and deliverances, but *not very* thankful to the Rebels for again returning us to prison.

CHAPTER XVII.

FIVE WEEKS AMONG THE LOYAL LEAGUE AT CHARLESTON.

"I LEFT Roper Hospital in company with the other officers confined there, and marched up King Street, to take the cars for Columbia, South Carolina. I escaped from the guard by stepping out of the ranks and running up a pair of stairs into a daguerrian room. The artist, at that moment, was at the front, looking at the prisoners passing. I at once passed into the back yard unperceived by any one, and secreted myself under the stairs, remaining there until after dark that night. I then scaled a high wall into another yard, which seemed as difficult to escape from as the first. While there, I was joined by another officer who had escaped, and, by aiding each other, we succeeded in getting out of that yard into another. This yard had formerly been occupied as a livery-stable-yard, but the building had been burned, the bare walls remaining. While standing there, devising some plan to get into the street, one of our shells struck the old wall, scattering the bricks, mortar, and dust all over us, but, fortunately, without damage to either of us. We at length succeeded in opening one of the burned doors, and emerged into the street. We at once made our way to the house of a citizen, whom we had been assured before was friendly to us. We were both dressed in Rebel uniform, and, as we came up to the stoop, what was our surprise to see another of our officers sitting there, who had also just escaped. He appeared very much alarmed, supposing us to be Confederate soldiers. The lady of the house at once pointed us to an out-house, where we would be safe for the present, while her husband had time to see to the other officer. As soon as he was disposed of, we were brought into the house, and furnished with supper and lodging. In the morning our host went and made arrangements with another party to take charge of us, and keep us in a less exposed place, till they could perfect a plan to get us out of the city. Just before leaving for our new boarding-place, a Mrs. —— called on us, and we had a very pleasant interview. Before she left, she gave us two nice large sponge-cakes, a bottle of wine, and farther told us if we were so unfortunate as to be recaptured, which she hoped we would not, to inform her, and any thing she could do for us should be done. Our second friend lived by himself, in a neat little house, surrounded by a high fence. Here we had the liberty of the yard and house, and were safe from exposure day and night. Our friend invited in his Union friends to see us, so we had plenty of company, and they all were lavish in bringing us presents to supply our wants. After a sojourn of one week with him, we were invited back to our first friend's for the purpose of arranging matters to leave the city. That evening I went out with friend No. 1, after disguising myself in a white coat, to find a party and see about a boat to take us to ——. While in the street we came in sight of a house surrounded by guards, and a Rebel officer trying to gain admittance. We at once turned into another street, but soon encountered a like scene just before us. We were on the opposite side of the street, and, as the officer saw us, he crossed over, stopped us, and made inquiry as to who lived in *that house*, stating that he was looking for escaped Yankee officers that they knew were being secreted in the houses by the citizens. He eyed me very closely, but not suspecting me or my friend, let us pass on unmolested, which I considered a fortunate escape for me. Fearing for the safety of the one who remained at his house, my friend soon left me, after giving me the proper direction, and returned to his own house to take care of the one left there. I soon found the place without difficulty, but the moon had now risen, and it was too light for farther operations *that* night. My companion soon joined me. The next day friend No. 3 came and took me in the daytime, still disguised, to see the city, and in our walk we visited every wharf, dock-yard, arsenal, and battery in the city. At one point we staid over two hours, where I could see our 'dear old flag' floating in the breeze, and so near was I that I could count the stripes plainly; also watched the firing of our guns, and took a sketch of the harbor, which I expected to use soon. At night we were all assembled again at the house of friend No. 3, where we had a bountiful supper, my friend having been piloted there, as soon as dark, by the wife of friend No. 3; after which we were taken to the house of friend No. 4—a safe place for us till some plan could be devised for us to escape from the city. We remained there about two weeks, waiting for the nights to become dark, during which time we received the kindest treatment and best of care. During this time we formed the acquaintance of a large number of Union friends, both male and female, all of whom seemed willing and anxious to do what they could for our comfort, and to assist us in making our escape. The night we left, the colored man belonging to No. 4 came to see us. His master had been arrested on suspicion of aiding Union officers in escaping. It was at once decided that we had better change our quarters, and the servant of the lady of the house went with us, and secreted us in the house of friend No. 5, in another part of the city less suspicious, but we kept up correspondence with the party all the time we remained in the city, and subsequently learned that nothing could be proven against him, and he was released. While here, a plan was fixed upon for our escape as follows: a negro woman, who had escaped from up the country, came to the city disguised as a man. She stole her son from his master on her way there, and, learning that Federal officers were in the city trying to get within our lines, volunteered to take a party out with her and make an escape down the bay. This colored woman and her son got a boat, and the night was fixed for a start. At dark they repaired to the boat to bail out the water, while the officers were to follow later in the evening. While engaged in that work, a second party of Federal officers came to the same wharf to escape in another boat. Shortly after, an officer in charge of a guard came down (for it seems the negroes had been betrayed), and, seeing the negroes running, gave the order to fire, but, instead of firing at the negroes, one of the shots took effect in the officer's *knee*. All but two of the negroes escaped by jumping into the water, and remaining until the excitement was over. The Federal officers, meanwhile, were secreted by a fence, and made their escape by running and hiding in the burnt district. While on our way to the wharf, an Irishwoman informed us of the state of affairs, and advised us not to go in that direction. We returned to the house of No. 5, where we remained till the following day, when suddenly an officer with a guard confronted the house; due notice of which was given us, and we escaped through the back yard to the house of friend No. 6.

"We remained here several days, closely concealed by our trusty friend, for there was some excitement in the city over the report that Yankee prisoners were being harbored by some of the inhabitants, and it was deemed unsafe for us to go out much. One evening, however, one of our party ventured to call upon one of the loyal ladies who had been so kind to us, but whose husband was a bitter Rebel, and was engaged in blockade-running, and was at that time away.

"While enjoying the pleasant hours of the evening with his loyal friend, steps were heard in the front yard, and soon the voice of the husband was heard in the hall. There was no opportunity to escape, and the only thing that could be done was to hide, and trust to luck. But *where?* was another difficult question.

"A closet in the ladies' bedroom was the only refuge. Mrs. —— hurried him into it, and was just fastening the door, when her husband stood at the bedroom door, and, trying it, *found it locked.* She sprung to open it, and encountered her 'liege lord' in a towering passion, who demanded to know of this strange proceeding.

"He at once accused her of infidelity, of receiving visits from gentlemen in his absence, and farther, he had heard one in the house as he came in the hall, and demanded to know the truth of the whole matter.

"She could only reply, in tears, that she *was true* to him; that all the visits she had ever received were only friendly ones, and she begged him not to condemn her, but believe all she told him.

"Being dissatisfied with this explanation, he farther demanded to know what had become of the man who was there when he came in. His wife made no reply, and he began to search the room, when, *oh horrible!* in the closet he found a MAN full dressed in Rebel uniform.

"'You villain! what are you here for? Guilty, both of you; bring me my pistol, till I punish the guilty pair. Police! help!' shouted the husband.

"'Don't, my dear husband, kill him, for he is not guilty; let him go.'

"'Confess all, or I will kill you both,' said the enraged husband.

"'As God lives, we are innocent of any crime,' pleaded the suffering wife.

"'Away with such talk, you guilty wretches; I will not hear it,' said the now infuriated husband, as he rushed out of the room to get his pistol, while the unfortunate man jumped out of the first window and made good his escape. How the affair ended I never learned, as I left the city shortly after, and none of us cared to meet the blockade-runner again, or subject his wife to so severe a trial.

"*Her loyalty cost a price.*

"Matters quieted down after a few days, and another plan was proposed by our friends of the Loyal League to get us inside our lines at Morris Island. The plan was, to disguise us as Englishmen, get passes for us to cross the bridge over Cooper River, and proceed to ——, where a gentleman was ready for a consideration (which our friends supplied) to take us to Morris Island.

"The time arrived, and, to allay suspicion, it was proposed that I should start first, and go in the daytime, and if I succeeded the others were to follow. I was nicely fitted out in citizen's dress, with an English riding-hat. My passes, procured by one of the League, represented me as an English tourist, and I started out.

"I passed through the city without molestation, meeting several other of the officers disguised as foreigners, and walking with members of the 'League.' I passed the pickets at one end of the bridge, had had my passes examined by the lieutenant in charge of the guard at the other, and was just passing along, when one of the guards, a member of the 32d Georgia, who had guarded us elsewhere, said to the lieutenant, 'I know that man; he is a YANK.' 'Halt there, you Yank!' *and I halted.* 'Here, corporal, take two men, and take this man back to the provost marshal's office in the city, and turn him over as a suspicious character,' was the next news that greeted my ears. 'Farewell, my visions of home and friends,' said I to myself, as I plodded back between my guards. The examination at the provost marshal's was too close for me to wool them, and I was written down as a Yankee prisoner of war. I was sent to the jail a few days, and then forwarded to Columbia, where I joined the other officers at Camp Sorghum, from whom I had been separated five weeks."*

---

* Captain Tilford escaped again from Camp Sorghum, after being there two or three days, and made our lines.—A. O. A.

CHAPTER XVIII.

REBEL BARBARITIES.

WE propose, in the following brief record, to indicate by a few facts, which we know to be truly and fairly stated, the manner in which Union prisoners have been dealt with by the Rebel authorities. To some the record will be distasteful; for there are many who desire to believe no evil of Davis and his fellows, however indisputable the proofs. To many a tender-hearted reader it may seem too horrible for decent recital. Yet it is a true record, and in the history of the rebellion will form an important chapter, to be read with tears, indeed, but written in adamant.

The illustrations on the following pages will bring to the eye features of cruelty which could not well be described by the pen. They have been selected, not because they were more effective than a hundred others which we might give, but because we had not space to give all. We have limited our illustrations to a special class of our prisoners, namely, those who from exposure and lack of food have lost their feet. These illustrations are the exact fac-similes of photographs. They do not come to us from a distance. A large number of the victims have been for a long time within an hour's ride of this city. Of the class represented in our illustrations, there were, in the prisoners paroled and sent to Wilmington on the 26th of March, two hundred and eighty-seven cases. These had, from starvation and frost in Southern prisons, lost their feet wholly or in part. These cases were placed in the hands of Chaplain J. J. Geer, of the 183d Ohio Volunteers. Chaplain Geer, from whom we received the photographs, and whose statements are perfectly reliable, has done much for the comfort of these unfortunate men. But his statements do not stand alone. Others have visited the hospital in which the prisoners were confined. One of them writes:

"I wish every eye in the land could rest on the poor fellows in the Geer Hospital, and especially every one who believes in treating leniently this rebellion, could go as I did, from bed to bed, and see the blankets lifted to expose a pair of stumps *from which the feet had rotted off*

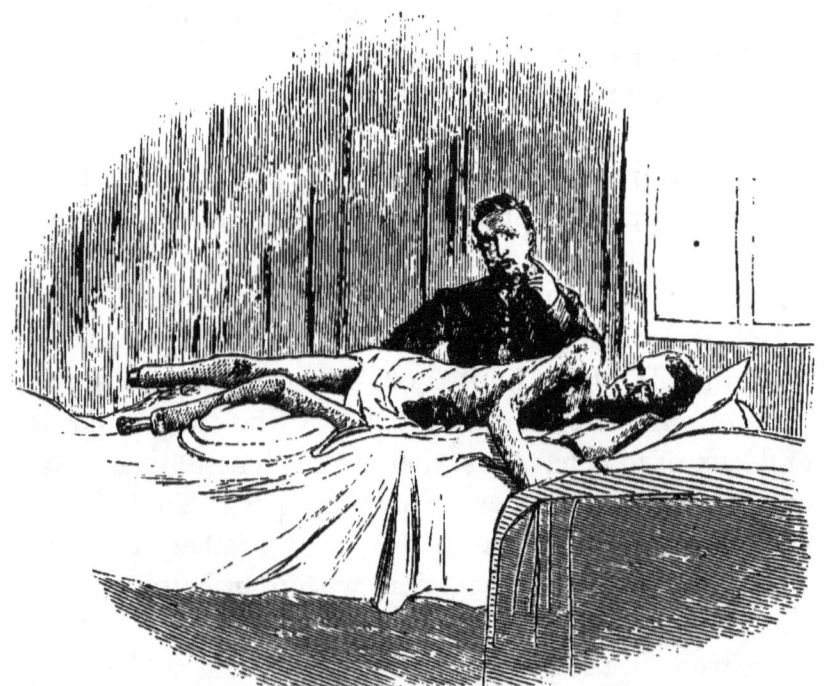

John W. January, Corporal Co. B, 4th Illinois.

by cold and exposure. And this not in one case, nor two, nor ten, nor twenty, but scores! Men who had committed no crime, but were honorable soldiers, brave, loyal, true to their government, but made prisoners by the fortunes of war, and, as such, entitled to food and comfortable shelter. As I went from bed to bed, and from ward to ward, and found, now a son of Massachusetts, next a boy from Maine, then a soldier from Michigan, or from Indiana, or New York, differing from one another only in some new and more horrid form of gangrene of the feet and legs, which left the bone protruding sometimes six inches beyond the flesh, decaying, putrid, offensive, while they could be strengthened with food a few days and made able to bear an amputation, I felt almost unable to endure the strain upon my sensibilities."

These unhappy prisoners have under oath given the record of their terrible experience, which, in many cases, is too loathsome for detail. You do not want to know, gentle reader, to what means these men swear they were obliged to resort to keep from absolutely starving. Only the very strong survived at all, and these come back to us pitiable wrecks of what they once were—how pitiable let our illustrations show. Nearly all whose affidavits have been taken, attest that they were robbed of their clothing, receiving in its place a dirty blanket or a bundle of tattered rags. In regard to all the prisons the uniform testimony is that no shelter of any kind was provided for the prisoners; that they were thrown into stockades and exposed to all sorts of weather; and that they had not received rations adequate to sustain vitality.

Byron Churchill swears that when he was captured he was, by the sanction of Rebel authority, robbed of all his clothing except his shirt and drawers; that the prisoners, for want of other shelter, burrowed in the ground; and that, "by reason of exposure, starvation, cruelties, and countless outrages inflicted on him by the Rebels while a prisoner in their hands, a part of the time he was bereft of his reason, lost all the toes on his left foot," and has otherwise been reduced to the condition shown in the illustration.

Smith and Churchill.

John H. Matthews, a corporal in Company F, of the 4th Pennsylvania, testifies that he enlisted in this company August 29th, 1861; was taken prisoner October 12th, 1863, in Meade's retreat from Culpepper, and that, after various marchings and countermarchings, he was taken to Richmond. For three days he was without any food. He testifies that, in long marches which the prisoners were compelled to make from one place of confinement to another, the Rebel authorities issued, for three days' rations, one pint of shelled corn. This prisoner lost the use of both his feet.

John H. Matthews, Corporal Co. F, 4th Pennsylvania.

Calvin Bates testifies that, "by reason of exposure and other inhumanities practiced upon him at Andersonville, his feet decayed, so that both of them have since been cut off at the ankle with scissors, and that previous to his imprisonment he was in good health.

Calvin Bates (Fig. 1), Corporal Co. E, 20th Maine.

Many of these sworn statements were the words of dying men. Others still live, monuments of the wanton cruelty of the Rebel authorities.

We have stated that there were two hundred and eighty-seven cases of the character represented by our illustrations. On the ninth of April there were still left at Andersonville, Georgia, 2500 poor fellows, who remained there because they were unable to march.

As soon as these prisoners return to us they are treated with all possible kindness. None of those heroes who have died on the battle-field are more worthy of remem-

Calvin Bates (Fig. 2).

brance than such men as Doctors Palmer and Buzzell, who literally worked themselves to death in their efforts to alleviate the sufferings of our prisoners. Many of these famished prisoners come to us so exhausted that they are unable to receive proper food, and many of them die from the change in diet.

Dr. J. C. Dalton, Professor of Physiology and Microscopic Anatomy in the College of Physicians and Surgeons in this city, thus reports respecting the general condition of the prisoners delivered up at Wilmington:

"The better cases were walking about the streets, perhaps barefooted, or with no other clothing than a pair of white cotton drawers and an old blanket or over-coat, both equally ragged. In these, the slow, dragging gait, listless manner, and cavernous, inexpressive look of the face, together with the general emaciation, formed a peculiar aspect, by which they alone attracted the attention of the passer-by, and by which they were at once distinguished from the other convalescent soldiers. There was no occasion to inquire in Wilmington which were our returned prisoners; after half a day's experience any one could distinguish them at a glance. Many of them, who had strength to crawl about in this manner, were prevented from doing so by the want of clothing. Major Randlete, the provost marshal of Wilmington, told me that on one day forty of these men came into our lines *absolutely as naked as they were born.* I inquired of a considerable number of them, whom I saw in the hospitals confined to their beds, naked or with only a shirt, and covered with a hospital blanket, what had become of their clothing, and was told that they had thrown away what remained as soon as they could obtain shelter, because it was so ragged, filthy, and full of vermin. One of them, on being told that the Sanitary Commission had sent them flannel shirts and drawers, caught at the word with a childish eagerness, and repeated the good news to his companions with a faint, half-imbecile smile, as long as I was within hearing. With the great majority of the feebler ones personal cleanliness was a thing which they appeared to have entirely forgotten. They no longer retained sufficient strength, either of mind or body, to appreciate or correct the degradation to which months of unavoidable uncleanliness had reduced them. In the most extreme cases the condition of the mind, as well as the expression of the face, was absolutely *fatuous*, and the aspect of the patient was not that of a strong man reduced by illness, but that of an idiotic pauper, who had been such from his birth. Nevertheless, several of the surgeons informed me that the condition of the patients had visibly improved since their reception, and that I could not then form an adequate idea of what it was when they entered our lines. In that case it must have been lamentable beyond description.

"The testimony of both men and officers was uniform as to the causes of their unnatural condition. These causes were, first, starvation, and, second, exposure. Only such officers and men as could procure money were able to obtain any thing like sufficient nourishment. Some of them told me that during the entire winter they had received absolutely no meat; a pint of corn-meal, often with the cob ground in, sometimes with and sometimes without salt, a handful of "cow-peas," and sometimes sorghum molasses, constituted their usual ration. When in hospital, they had only very thin corn-meal gruel and a little corn-bread. To the debility occasioned by this insufficient food was added that resulting from exposure. It was a common thing for a prisoner, immediately on being taken, to be stripped of his clothing—shoes, socks, pantaloons, shirts, and drawers—and to be left with only an old and worn-out pair of drawers, and perhaps an equally worn-out shirt and blanket given him in exchange. This robbery of clothing was also practiced more or less upon officers. Even an assistant surgeon, who was captured within four miles of Richmond, told me that he was robbed of his flannel shirt while standing in front of the Libby Prison, and in presence of the Rebel officer in charge of the squad. This was immediately after his arrival in the city, and when he had been, for the three days succeeding his capture, entirely without food. With the scanty clothing thus left them the men were kept during the winter, often without any shelter, excepting such as they could contrive to provide by excavating a sort of rifle-pit in the ground, and covering it with old blankets or canvas, as their supply of fuel was insufficient, and sometimes entirely wanting. Even in the hospitals their suffering from cold was very great.

"One of the most melancholy sights in Wilmington

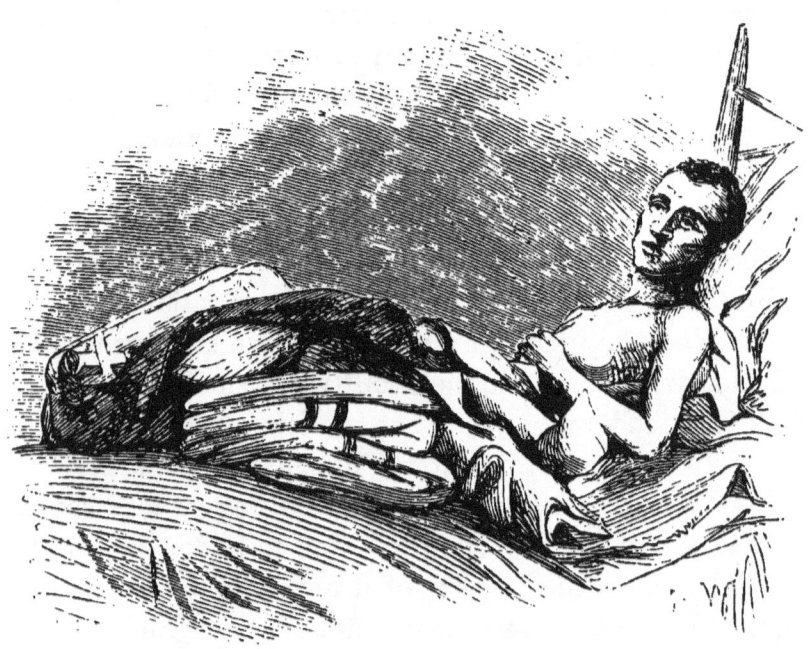

Benjamin T. Daugherty, Co. K, 31st Illinois (Fig. 1).

was that to be seen at the 'Geer' hospitals. In these hospitals were collected all those patients who had lost their feet, either wholly or in part, by freezing, from their exposure during the past winter, and this in a well-wooded country. In some of them two or three toes only, on one or both feet, were gangrened, and in process of sep-

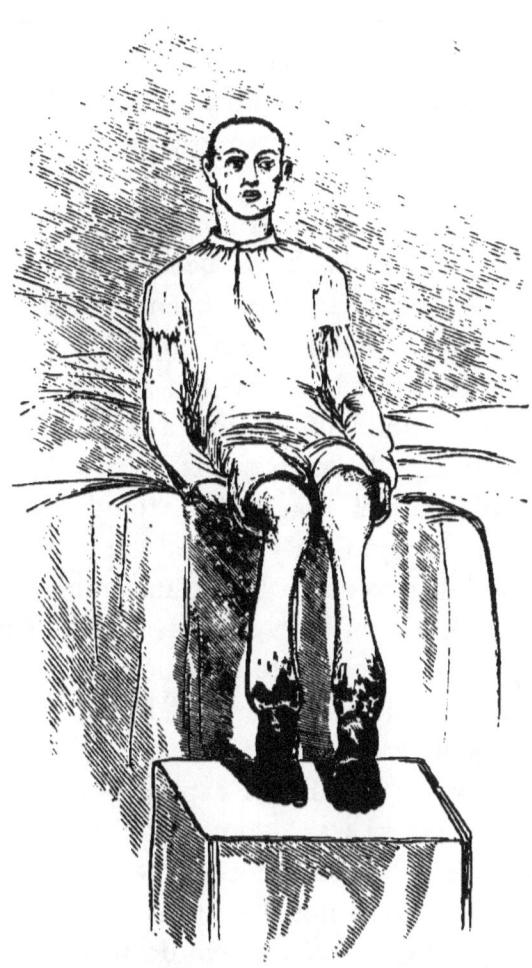

Benjamin T. Daugherty, Co. K, 31st Illinois (Fig. 2).

O

arating by ulceration; in others, both feet had entirely separated, and the patients were awaiting the time when their general strength and the condition of the stump would warrant a final amputation. In many cases the patients ascribed this gangrene directly to frost-bites received on particular occasions; in others, to their illness from which they were suffering — generally fever combined with exposure. My own impression, derived from the result of many inquiries, was that it was generally due to a continuous depression of the vital energies from starvation and neglect, resulting gradually in a destruction of the life of those parts most exposed to the cold and the weather."

But the record of cruelty is not confined to the special class of cases which we have been considering. It is known that our prisoners have been treated with every sort of indignity. Letters from home have been withheld. Rewards have been offered to the Rebel guard for shooting any who should cross a certain limit known as the dead line. These rewards were offered with a knowledge of the fact that many would thus be killed who trespassed thoughtlessly beyond the limits, and many more from a desire to end a life so miserable. These rewards were a premium both on murder and suicide. It has been proven by reliable testimony that the Libby Prison at Richmond was undermined for the purpose of blowing it up in case any of our cavalry raids should succeed in entering the Rebel capital — thus retaliating for a legitimate act of war by an act of useless and wanton cruelty inflicted upon innocent men.

These cruelties were not the result of accident, but of a deliberate purpose. By this we do not mean that the

Southern people were committed to these acts. In many cases their humanity compelled them, though in opposition to the authorities, to attempt the alleviation of the sufferings which they witnessed. When our wasted prisoners entered Wilmington, before the capture of that city, many of the citizens tried to supply them with food, but were kept from doing so by an armed force of Rebel soldiers. In a letter written to General Winder by Colonel Ould, March 17th, 1863, the latter says:

"The arrangements I have made (for exchanging prisoners) works largely in our favor. We get rid of a set of miserable wretches, and receive some of the best material I ever saw."

Henry S. Foote, the Rebel Senator, offered to go before a court of justice and testify to the fact that a portion of the Rebel Congress once visited Mr. Davis to remonstrate against the treatment of Union prisoners, and the petition was refused by Mr. Davis and his cabinet on the ground of policy merely. We have read in history of terrible cruelties inflicted upon the defenseless in revolutionary times. We understand how it was in the streets of Paris, when poor men had cried for bread in vain, and at length resorted to violence. There is some poor plea, too, for those who, in the excitement of battle, cry "No quarter!" and slay their prisoners on the spot. But who ever heard before of men who called themselves Christians coolly and on principle starving men to death for no other crime than that of fighting for their country? And yet Mr. Mitchel, the new editor of the *Daily News*, tells us that Davis has waged an honorable war, according to all the high usages of a Christian and civilized age.

The rebellions of which history takes note have had various aspects. Rebel leaders have not always been instigators of arson and murder. There have been Rebels who have even elicited the respect of honorable minds. But Davis and his fellows have chosen for themselves a blacker record. Not content to have been the cause of the most needless war ever waged, they have affiliated themselves with crimes which are revolting to every Christian civilization except that of the chivalrous, slaveholding South.

APPENDIX.

The following Appendix is not as perfect as I could wish, yet as much so as it was possible to make it from the limited means at my command. The names were taken from the (Rebel) adjutant's book at Columbia. I have furnished the post-office address of the officers as far as I could obtain them.

Those marked thus * died at Columbia, S. C.

APPENDIX.

Names.	Rank.	Regiment.	When captured.	Where captured.	Residence.
Aldrich, C. S.	Capt.	85th N. Y. Vol.	Apr. 20th, 1864.	Plymouth, N. C.	Canandaigua, N. Y.
Austin, J. W.	1st Lieut.	5th Iowa Cav.	Nov. 25th, 1863.	Mission Ridge, Ga.	Lansing, Iowa.
Alters, J. B.	Capt.	75th O. Vol.	Aug. 1st, 1864.	Gainesville, Fla.	Spring Dale, O.
Algbaugh, Wm.		51st Pa. Vol.	May 12th, "	Spottsylvania C.H.,Va.	Morristown, Pa.
Alger, A. B.	Lieut.	22d O. Batt'y.	Jan. 3d, "	Jonesville, Va.	Mansfield, O.
Avery, W. B.	Capt.	132d N. Y. Vol	July 25th, 1863.	North Carolina.	
Allender, W. F.	Lieut.	7th Tenn. Cav.	Mar. 24th, 1864.	Union City, Tenn.	Memphis, Tenn.
Adair, W. A.	"	51st Ind. Vol.	May 3d, 1863.	Rome, Ga.	North Salem, Ind.
Albro, S. A.	"	80th Ill. Vol.	"	"	Upper Alton, Ill.
Adams, J.	"	"	"	"	Nashville, Ill.
Allstaedt, C. L.	Adjt.	54th N. Y. Vol.	July 1st, 1863.	Gettysburg, Pa.	Newark, N. J.
Ahern, M.	Lieut.	10th W. Va. Vol.	Jan. 3d, 1864.	Greenland Gap, Va.	
Ahert, T. H.	"	45th N. Y. Vol.	July 1st, 1863.	Gettysburg, Pa.	New York City.
Adams, C. A.	Capt.	1st Vt. Cav.	Oct. 11th, "	Brandy Station, Va.	Wallingford, Vt.
Alban, H. H.	"	21st O. Vol.	Sept. 25th, "	Chickamauga, Ga.	
Andrews, H. B.	"	17th Mich. Vol.	May 12th, 1864.	Spottsylvania C.H.,Va.	
Apple, H.	Lieut.	1st Md. Cav.	June 9th, 1863.	Brandy Station, Va.	
Anderson, C. S.	"	3d Iowa Vol	July 12th, "	Jackson, Miss.	Lincoln, Ill.
Allee, A.	"	16th Ill. Cav.	Jan. 3d, 1864.	Jonesville, Va.	Paris, Mo.
Abernathy, H. C.	A. Adjt.	"	"	"	Fostoria, O.
Acker, G. D.	Lieut.	123d O. Vol.	June 25th, 1863.	Winchester, Va.	
Adkins, P.	"	2d Tenn. Vol.	Nov. 25th, "	Rodgersville, Tenn.	
Aigan, John	Capt.	5th R. I. Art'y.	May 12th, 1864.	Croton, N. C.	Pawtucket, R. I.
Adams, J. G. B.	Lieut.	19th Mass. Vol.	June 25th, "	Petersburg, Va.	Groveland, Mass.
Alexander, E. P.	"	26th Mich. Vol.	" 16th, "	"	Detroit, Mich.
Anderson, H. M.	"	3d Mc. Vol.	" 20th, "		
Anderson, J. F.	"	2d Pa. Art'y.	" 2d, "	Gum Spa, Va.	Philadelphia, Pa.
Anderson, R. W.	"	122d O. Vol.	" 15th, 1863.	Gaines's Mill, Va.	Columbus, O.
Andrus, W. R.	"	16th Conn. Vol.	Apr. 20th, 1864.	Winchester, Va.	East Berlin, Conn.
Abbey, A. L.		8th Mich. Cav.	Aug. 5th, "	Plymouth, N. C.	Armada, Mich.
Arthur, J. A.	Capt.	8th Ky. Cav.	" 3d, 1863.	Rosswell, Ga.	
				Elkton, Ky.	

APPENDIX. 319

Name	Rank	Regiment	Date	Place	Residence
Arthurs, S. C.	Capt.	67th Pa. Vol.	June 15th, 1863.	Winchester, Va.	Brookville, Pa.
Allen, S.	"	85th N.Y. Vet. Vol.	Apr. 20th, 1864.	Plymouth, N. C.	Black Creek, N. Y.
Adams, S. B.	"	"	"	"	Lenox, O.
Andrews, S. T.	Lieut.	"	"	"	Black Creek, N. Y.
Albright, J.	Capt.	87th Pa. Vol.	June 15th, 1863.	Winchester, Va.	York, Pa.
Abbott, A. O.	Lieut.	1st N. Y. Drag.	May 7th, 1864.	Todd's Tavern, Va.	Portageville, N. Y.
Armstrong, T. S.	"	122d O. Vol.	June 15th, 1863.	Winchester, Va.	Gratiot, O.
Airey, W.	Capt.	15th Pa. Cav.	Dec. 28th, "	Dandridge, Tenn.	Philadelphia, Pa.
Appleget, A. S.	Lieut.	2d N. J. Cav.	June 12th, 1864.	Moscow, Tenn.	Hightstown, N. J.
Allen, Robert	"	2d N. J. Drag.	" 22d, "	Petersburg, Va.	
Auer, M.	Capt.	15th N. Y. Cav.	May 20th, "	Front Royal, Va.	Syracuse, N. Y.
Anshutz, H. T.	Lieut.	12th W. Va. Vol.	June 15th, 1863.	Winchester, Va.	Moundville, W. Va.
Adams, H. W.	"	89th O. Vol.	Sept. 20th, "	Chickamauga, Ga.	Frankfort, Ill.
Austin, G. A.	R. Q. M.	14th & 15th Ill. V. Batt.	Oct. 4th, 1864.	Acworth, Ga.	Woodstock, Ill.
Albin, H. S.	Lieut.	79th Ill. Vol.	Sept. 19th, 1863.	Chickamauga, Ga.	Tuscola, Ill.
Andrews, E. E.	"	22d Mich. Vol.	" 20th, "	"	Milford, Mich.
Alden, G. C.	R. Q. M.	112th Ill. Vol.	May 24th, 1864.	Cass Station, Ga.	Annawan, Ill.
Ashworth, J. H.	Colonel.	1st Ga. U. Vol.	Nov. 5th, "	Gimber Co., Ga.	
Adams, W. C.	Lieut.	2d Ky. Cav.	" 28th, "	Waynesboro', Ga.	Star Furnace, Ky.
Amory, C. B.	Capt.	A. A. Gen.	July 30th, "	Petersburg, Va.	Jamaica Plains, Mass.
Allleck, E. T.	Adjt.	170th O. Nat. G'd.	" 24th, "	Winchester, Va.	Bridgeport, O.
Alexander, A. H.	Capt.	103d Pa. Vol.	Apr. 20th, "	Plymouth, N. C.	Callensburg, Pa.
Abbott, E. A.	Lieut.	23d O. Vet. Vgl.	" "		Olmsted Falls, O.
Belger, James	Capt.	1st R. I. Art'y.	May 16th, 1864.	Drury's Bluff, Va.	
Baker, S. S.	Lieut.	6th Mo. Vol.	Oct. 29th, 1863.	Bear Creek, Mo.	
Butler, C. P.	"	29th Ind. Vol.	Sept. 19th, "	Chickamauga, Ga.	Peru, Ill.
Baird, J. F.	"	1st W. Va. Vol.	" 11th, "	Moorefield, Va.	Wheeling, W. Va.
Bricker, W. H.	"	3d Pa. Vol.	Aug. 23d, "	Baker's Cross Roads.	Newville, Pa.
Bick, W. C.	Capt.	62d Pa. Vol.	May 5th, 1864.	Wilderness, Va.	
Braiday, Count S.	Lieut.	2d N. J. Cav.	June 11th, "	La Grange, Miss.	Vienna, Austria.

APPENDIX.

Names.	Rank.	Regiment.	When captured.	Where captured.	Residence.
Bulow, A.	Lieut.	3d N. J. Cav.	July 6th, 1864.	Petersburg, Va.	Redding, Conn.
Burdick, C. H.	Capt.	1st Tenn. Cav.	June 10th, "	Stilesboro', Ga.	Wellsville, N. Y.
Bartram, D. S.	Lieut.	17th Conn. Vol.	July 1st, 1863.	Gettysburg, Pa.	Friendship, N. Y.
Brown, J. A.	Capt.	85th N.Y.Vet.Vol.	Apr. 20th, 1864.	Plymouth, N. C.	Cuba, N. Y.
Bradley, A. B.	R. Q. M.	"	18th, "	"	Pittsburg, Pa.
Butts, L. A.	Lieut.	"	20th, "	"	Gettysburg, Pa.
Bowers, G. W.	Capt.	101st Pa. Vol.	" "	"	Hartford, Conn.
Benner, H. S.	"	"	" "	"	New Britain, Conn.
Bowers, G. A.	Lieut.	16th Conn. Vol.	" "	"	Bridgeport, Conn.
Blakeslee, B. F.	"	"	" "	"	Butler, Pa.
Bruns, H.	"	"	" "	"	Circlesville, Pa.
Bryson, R. R.	"	103d Pa. Vol.	" "	"	York, Pa.
Burns, S. D.	"	"	" "	"	Rainsburg, Pa.
Bierbower, W.	"	87th Pa. Vol.	June 15th, 1863.	Winchester, Va.	Harrisburg, Pa.
Beegle, D. F.	"	101st Pa. Vol.	Apr. 20th, 1864.	Plymouth, N. C.	Baltimore, Md.
Bryan, J. H.	"	184th Pa. Vol.	June 22d, "	Petersburg, Va.	"
Berry, A.	Capt.	3d Md. Cav.	Feb. 11th, "	"	"
Bruiting, G.	Lieut.	5th Md. Cav.	June 15th, 1863.	Winchester, Va.	Rome, N. Y.
Bascomb, R.	"	50th N. Y. Vol.	Apr. 20th, 1864.	Plymouth, N. C.	
Baldwin, M. R.	Capt.	2d Wis. Vol.	July 1st, 1863.	Gettysburg, Pa.	
Blake, ——	Lieut.	3d Me. Vol.	June 20th, "	Aldie, Va.	
Brown, W. H.	"	93d O. Vol.	Jan. 17th, 1864.	Dandridge, Tenn.	Dayton, O.
Beard, J. V.	"	89th O. Vol.	Sept. 20th, 1863.	Chickamauga, Ga.	
Byron, C.	Capt.	3d O. Vol.	May 3d, "	Rome, Ga.	
Banks, R. V.	"	13th Ken. Cav.	Dec. 14th, "	Clynch Mt., Va.	New England, O.
Burch, J.	"	42d Ind. Vol.	Sept. 20th, "	Chickamauga, Ga.	Winslow, Ind.
Bailey, G. W.	Lieut.	3d O. Vol.	May 3d, "	Rome, Ga.	Columbus, O.
Brownell, F. G.	"	51st Ind. Vol.	" "	"	Dayton, O.
Booher, A. H.	"	73d Ind. Vol.	" "	"	Westville, Ind.
Brown, J. L.	"	"	" "	"	
Barlow, J. W.	"	51st Ind. Vol.	" "	"	London, Ind.

APPENDIX. 321

Name	Rank	Regiment	Date	Battle	Residence
Bath, W.	Lieut.	132d N. Y. Vol.	Feb. 2d, 1864.	Newbern, N. C.	
Bending, H. R.	Capt.	61st O. Vol.	July 2d, 1863.	Gettysburg, Pa.	Circleville, O.
Bush, J. G.	"	16th Ill. Cav.	Jan. 3d, 1864.	Jonesville, Va.	
Blimm, L. B.	"	100th O. Vol.	Sept. 8th, 1863.	Limestone, Tenn.	
Baldwin, C. W.	Lieut.	2d N. J. Vol.	May 5th, 1864.	Wilderness, Va.	New York City.
Bartley, R.	"	U. S. A. Sig. Corps.			
Bradley, G.	Capt.	2d N. J. Vol.	May 14th, 1864.	Spottsylvania, Va.	
Brandt, C. W.	Lieut.	1st N. Y. Vet. Cav.	Mar. 10th, "	Key's Ford, Va.	Belmont, N. Y.
Boutin, C. W.	Capt.	4th Vt. Vol.	June 23d, "	Petersburg, Va.	Chester, Vt.
Barrett, D. W.	"	89th O. Vol.	Sept. 20th, 1863.	Chickamauga, Ga.	Ramesboro', O.
Brandt, O. R.	Lieut.	17th O. Vol.	"	"	Lancaster, O.
Byers, S. H. M.	Adjt.	5th Iowa Vol.	Nov. 25th, "	Mission Ridge, Tenn.	Newton, Iowa.
Barker, H. P.	Lieut.	1st R. I. Cav.	June 18th, "	Middleburg, Va.	
Boone, S. G.	"	88th Pa. Vol.	July 1st, "	Gettysburg, Pa.	Reading, Pa.
Bisbee, L. C.	"	16th Me. Vol.	"	"	Canton Mills, Me.
Bisbee, G. D.	"				
Button, G. W.	"	22d Mich. Vol.	Sept. 20th, "	Chickamauga, Ga.	Farmington, Mich.
Barker, H. E.	"	22d N. Y. Cav.	May 8th, 1864.	Wilderness, Va.	
Butler, T. H.	Colonel	5th Ind. Cav.	July 31st, 1864.	Limestone Ch., Ga.	Clifty, Ind.
Bowen, C. D.	Capt.	18th Conn. Vol.	June 16th, "	Winchester, Va.	
Bennett, B.	"	22d N. Y. Cav.	" 29th, 1864.	Ream's Station, Va.	Hammondsport, N. Y.
Brush, Z. T.	Lieut.	100th O. Vol.	Sept. 8th, 1863.	Limestone, Tenn.	Clyde, O.
Bigley, C. H.	"	82d N. Y. Vol.	June 22d, 1864.	Petersburg, Va.	
Burns, M.	"	13th N. Y. Cav.	July 6th, "	Aldie, Va.	New York City.
Bassett, M. M.	"	53d Ill. Vol.	" 13th, 1863.	Jackson, Miss.	
Bostwick, N.	Capt.	20th O. Vol.	June 11th, 1864.	Trevillian Station, Va.	
Brown, C. A.	Lieut.	1st N. Y. Art'y.	May 18th, "	White Church, Va.	Vienna, Ill.
Benson, J. F.	Capt.	120th Ill. Vol.	June 12th, "	North Miss., Miss.	
Bosford, W. R.	Lieut.	1st N. Y. Vol.	May 17th, "	Spottsylvania, Va.	
Burns, J.	"	57th Pa. Vol.	July 2d, 1863.	Gettysburg, Pa.	Clark's Post, Pa.
Barton, J. L.	"	49th Pa. Vol.	May 10th, 1864.	Spottsylvania, Va.	
Beebee, B. C.	Capt.	13th Ind. Vol.	"	Drury's Bluff, Va.	Seneca Falls, N. Y.

322 APPENDIX.

Names.	Rank.	Regiment.	When captured.	Where captured.	Residence.
Buchanan, W.	Lieut.	76th N. Y. Vol.	May 5th, 1864.	Wilderness, Va.	Cohoes, N. Y.
Benson, A. N.	Capt.	1st D. C. Cav.	June 27th, "	Ream's Station, Va.	
Barkley, C.	Lieut.	149th Pa. Vol.	July 1st, 1863.	Gettysburg, Pa.	Albany, N. Y.
Blane, W.	"	43d N. Y. Vol.	May 6th, 1864.	Wilderness, Va.	Derby, Conn.
Bristol, J. H.	"	1st Conn. Cav.	" 5th, "	"	Rockland, Me.
Burpee, E. A.	Capt.	19th Me. Vol.	June 19th, "	Petersburg, Va.	
Bryant, J. W.	"	5th N. Y. Cav.	May 17th, "	Guinea's Station, Va.	Bridgeport, Conn.
Bicbel, H.	"	6th Conn. Vol.	" 14th, "	Drury's Bluff, Va.	Norridgewock, Me.
Bixby, H. L.	Lieut.	9th Me. Vol.	June 1st, "	Cold Harbor, Va.	Philadelphia, Pa.
Byrns, J. M.	Capt.	2d Pa. R. C. Vol.	July 1st, 1863.	Gettysburg, Pa.	
Barrett, J. A.	"	7th Pa. R. C. Vol.	May 5th, 1864.	Wilderness, Va.	Shippensburg, Pa.
Burkholder, D. W.	Lieut.				
Beal, E.	Capt.	8th Tenn. Vol.	Apr. 21st, "	Bull's Gap, Tenn.	
Bayard, G. A.	"	148th Pa. Vol.	June 22d, "	Petersburg, Va.	
Brunn, S.	Lieut.	81st Ill. Vol.	" 11th, "	Ripley, Miss.	
Brady, W. H.	"	2d Del. Vol.	" 22d, "	Petersburg, Va.	Wilmington, Del.
Breon, J.	"	148th Pa. Vol.	" 17th, "	"	Potter's Mills, Pa.
Bischoff, P.	"	6th U. S. Art'y.	Apr. 12th, "	Fort Pillow, Miss.	St. Louis, Mo.
Burnett, G. M.	"	4th Ind. Cav.			Terre Haute, Ind.
Blair, B. F.	Adjt.	123d O. Vol.	June 15th, 1863.	Winchester, Va.	Norwalk, O.
Boyce, T. W.	Lieut.	"	"	"	
Breckenridge, F. A.	"				Monroeville, O.
Boyd, W. J.	"	5th Mich. Cav.	" 29th, 1864.	Ream's Station, Va.	
Brown, W. L.	"	17th Tenn. Vol.	Oct. 20th, 1863.	Philadelphia, Tenn.	
Burrows, S. W.	"	1st N. Y. Vet. Cav.	June 13th, 1864.	Monterey, Va.	
Brown, S.	A. M. Mate	U. S. Navy	Oct. 23d, 1863.	Rapp River, Va.	
Beman, W. M.	Capt.	1st Vt. Cav.	" 11th, "	Brandy Station, Va.	Lockport, Ill.
Bonz, E. P.	"	20th Ill. Vol.	May 24th, "	Raymond, Miss.	Vincenttown, N. Y.
Bryan, G.	Adjt.	18th Pa. Cav.	Nov. 18th, "	Germania Ford, Va.	New York City.
Bath, H.	Lieut.	45th N. Y. Vol.	July 1st, "	Gettysburg, Pa.	South Easton, N. Y.
Beadle, M.	"	123d N. Y. Vol.	" 2d, "	"	

APPENDIX. 323

Name	Rank	Regiment	Date	Battle	Residence
Bigelow, A. J.	Capt.	79th Ill. Vol.	Sept. 19th, 1863.	Chickamauga, Ga.	Kansas, Ill.
Borches, L. T.	"	67th Pa. Vol.	June 16th, "	Winchester, Va.	Dyberry, Pa.
Borches, T. F.	Lieut.	"	" 15th, "	"	Honesdale, Pa.
Brown, G. L.	"	101st Pa. Vol.	Apr. 20th, 1864.	Plymouth, N. C.	Milton, Pa.
Blanchard, Geo. A.	Capt.	85th Ill. Vol.	July 19th, "	Atlanta, Ga.	Havanna, Ill.
Bradford, John	Lieut.	4th N. J. Vol.	Oct. 15th, 1863.	Chantilly, Va.	Hoboken, N. J.
Barnes, O. P.	"	3d O. Vol.	May 3d, "	Rome, Ga.	Barnesville, O.
Bremen, S.	Capt.	3d Mich. Vol.	" 5th, 1864.	Wilderness, Va.	Georgetown, Mich.
Brickenhoff, M.	Lieut.	42d N. Y. Vol.	June 22d, "	Petersburg, Va.	New York City.
Barse, J. R.	"	5th Mich. Cav.	Oct. 19th, 1863.	Buckland Mills, Va.	
Bliss, A. T.	Capt.	10th N. Y. Cav.	June 29th, 1864.	Petersburg, Va.	Peterboro', N. Y.
Buckley, H.	Lieut.	4th N. Ill. Vol.	May 16th, "	Bermuda Hund'ds,Va.	New York City.
Bader, H.	"	29th Mo. Vol.	Nov. 27th, 1863.	Ringgold, Ga.	Cape Girardeau, Mo.
Blae, J. G.	"	3d O. Vol.	May 3d, "	Rome, Ga.	Cardington, O.
Boughton, S. H.	"	71st Pa. Vol.	July 2d, "	Gettysburg, Pa.	
Barnes, A. T.	"	14th and 15th Ill. Vet. Batt.	Oct. 4th, 1864.	Acworth, Ga.	
Beasley, J. L.	"	81st Ill. Vol.	Sept. 2d, 1864.	East Point, Ga.	Fredonia, Ill.
Baker, H. D.	"	120th Ill. Vol.	June 3d, "	Lagrange, Miss.	Golconda, Ill.
Burke, T. F.	Capt.	16th Conn. Vol.	Apr. 20th, "	Plymouth, N. C.	Hartford, Conn.
Barnes, W. J.	"				
Bennett, W. F.	"	39th Iowa Vol.	Oct. 5th, 1864.	Altoona, Ga.	Osceola, Iowa.
Bussett, W. H.	Lieut.	79th Ill. Vol.	Sept. 19th, 1863.	Chickamauga, Ga.	Arcola, Ill.
Botts, W. O.	"	10th Wis. Vol.	" 20th, "	"	
Biggs, J.	"	123d Ill. Vol.	"	"	
Bennett, F. J.	"	18th U. S. Inf.	"	"	
Brown, J. C.	"	15th "	"	"	
Bryant, M. C.	"	42d Ill. Vol.	"	"	Dayton, O.
Butler, W. O.	"	10th Wis. Vol.	"	"	Kankakeo City, Ill.
Brooks, E. P.					
Barringer, A.	Adjt.	44th N. Y. Vol.	June 3d, 1864.	Cold Harbor, Va.	Nassau, N. Y.
Ballard, S. H.	Lieut.	6th Mich. Cav.	July 2d, 1863.	Gettysburg, Pa.	Grand Rapids, Mich.

APPENDIX.

Names.	Rank.	Regiment.	When captured.	Where captured.	Residence.
Brown, J. H.	Capt.	17th Iowa Vol.	Oct. 13th, 1864.	Dalton, Ga.	Des Moines, Iowa.
Byron, S.	Lieut.	2d U. S. Inf.	Apr. 11th, "	Catlett's Station, Va.	
Blaire, Geo. E.	"	17th O. Vol.	Sept. 20th, 1863.	Chickamauga, Ga.	Lancaster, O.
Bishop, F. P.	"	4th Tenn. Cav.	Aug. 15th, 1864.	Westport, Ga.	
Bowen, C. T.	"	4th R. I. Vol.	July 30th, "	Petersburg, Va.	Wickford, R. I.
Bateman, Wm.	"	9th Mich. Cav.	Dec. 8th, "	Brier Creek, Ga.	Ypsilanti, Mich.
Baird, Wm.	"	23d U. S. C. T.	July 30th, "	Petersburg, Va.	China, Mich.
Barnum, S. D.	Capt.	"	"	"	North Rome, Pa.
Biller, J. N.	Lieut.	2d Pa. Art'y.			Martinsburg, W. Va.
Baker, W. F.	Capt.	87th Pa. Vol.	" 9th, 1864.	Monocacy, Md.	Gettysburg, Pa.
Bowley, F. S.	Lieut.	30th U. S. C. T.	" 30th, "	Petersburg, Va.	Worcester, Mass.
Boetger, C.	"	2d Md. Vol.			Baltimore, Md.
Bogle, A.	Major	35th U. S. C. T.	Feb. 20th, "	Olustee, Fla.	Boston, Mass.
Barnard, W. A.	Lieut.	20th Mich. Vol.	July 30th, "	Petersburg, Va.	Lansing, Mich.
Blasse, Wm.	"	43d N. Y. Vol.	May 6th, "	Wilderness, Va.	Albany, N. Y.
Buffum, M. P.	Lt. Col.	4th R. I. Vol.			Providence, R. I.
Brown, C. O.	Lieut.	31st Me. Vol.	July 30th, 1864.	Petersburg, Va.	Moro, Me.
Beecham, R. K.	"	23d U. S. C. T.	" "	"	Sun Prairie, Mo.
Briscoe, A. M.	"	Cole's Md. Cav.	" 29th, "	Hagerstown, Md.	Baltimore, Md.
Burbank, H. H.	Capt.	32d Me. Vol.	" 30th, "	Petersburg, Va.	Limerick, Me.
Bearce, H. M.	Lieut.	"	"	"	West Minot, Me.
Bittenger, C. L.	"	76th Pa. Vol.	" 11th, 1863.	Fort Wagner, S. C.	
Bartlett, O. E.	Capt.	31st Me. Vol.	" 30th, 1864.	Petersburg, Va.	Skowhegan, Me.
Braidley, A. J.	Lieut.	54th Pa. Vol.	" 25th, "	Genettstown, Va.	
Bell, C. A.	Lt.&A.D.C.	"	" 24th, "	Kernstown, Va.	
Burton, R.	"	9th N. Y. Art'y.	" 9th, "	Monocacy, Md.	
Beebe, H. E.	"	22d N. Y. Cav.	May 8th, "	Wilderness, Va.	
Coleman, S. S.	Lieut.	12th Ky. Cav.	Oct. 11th, 1863.	Sweetwater, Tenn.	Pittsburg, Pa.
Chalfant, J. T.	Capt.	11th Pa. Vol.	May 5th, 1864.	Wilderness, Va.	Inkster, Mich.
Call, C. H.	"	29th Ill. Vol.	June 23d, "	Ledere, Miss.	

APPENDIX.

Name	Rank	Regiment	Date	Place	Residence
Caswell, H.	Lieut.	95th Ill. Vol.	Apr. 19th, 1864.	Big Black, Miss.	Putnam, Conn.
Carpenter, E. D.	"	18th Conn. Vol.	June 15th, 1863.	Winchester, Va.	Lind, Wis.
Caldwell, C.	"	1st Wis. Cav.	Apr. 13th, 1864.	Cleaveland, Tenn.	Springfield, O.
Cook, A. A.	"	9th O. Cav.	"	Florence, Ala.	Kanawha, W. Va.
Castorph, C. H.	Capt.	7th W. Va. Cav.	Dec. 19th, 1863.	Jackson River, W.Va.	East Randolph, N. Y.
Cusler, B. G.	Lieut.	154th N. Y. Vol.	July 1st, "	Gettysburg, Pa.	
Cook, A. L.	Capt.	2d Pa. Vol.	May 14th, "	Holly Springs, Miss.	McComb, O.
Cusac, I	"	21st O. Vol	Sept. 20th, "	Chickamauga, Ga.	
Canfield, S. S.		"	"	"	
Catin, M.					
Coffin, V. L.	Lieut.	31st Me. Vol.	June 7th, 1864.	Cold Harbor, Va.	Harrington, Me.
Chandler, G. A.	"	5th "	July 24th, 1863.	White Plains, Va.	
Coren, J. H.	"	1st W. Va. Cav.	Apr. 30th, "	Bridgeport, Pa.	
Culver, F. B.	"	123d O. Vol.	June 16th, "	Winchester, Va.	
Carothers, J. J.	"	"	May 3d, "	Raymond, Miss.	
Claghorn, A. C.	"	21st O. Vol.	Sept. 20th, "	Chickamauga, Ga.	Boston, Mass.
Carey, S. E.	"	13th Mass. Vol.	July 3d, "	Gettysburg, Pa.	
Campbell, L. A.	"	152d N. Y. Vol.	June 22d, 1864.	Petersburg, Va.	Cherry Valley, N. Y.
Carnes, W. C.	Capt.	2d Tenn. Vol.	Nov. 6th, 1863.	Rodgersville, Tenn.	
Center, A. P.	"	"	"	"	
Carroll, E.	Lieut.	11th Tenn. Vol.	Feb. 22d, 1864.	Lulu, Va.	
Carr, C. W.	"	4th Vt. Vol.	June 23d, "	Petersburg, Va.	Leesport, Pa.
Cunningham, J.	"	7th Pa. R. C. Vol.	May 5th, "	Wilderness, Va.	Philadelphia, Pa.
Coslett, C.	"	115th Pa. Vol.	June 22d, "	Petersburg, Va.	Jersey City, N. J.
Cooper, R.	"	7th N. J. Vol.	"	"	Philadelphia, Pa.
Crawford, C. H.	"	183d Pa. Vol.	May 12th, "	Spotsylvania, Va.	Bennington, Vt.
Cromack, S. O.	"	77th N. Y. Vol.	" 6th, "	Wilderness, Va.	New Haven, Vt.
Correll, H.	"	2d Vt. Vol.	"	"	New York City.
Cornell, C. H.	"	95th N. Y. Vol.	" 5th "	"	Boston, Mass.
Cutter, C. H.	"	"	"	"	
Creasey, G. W.	"	35th Mass. Vol.	" 24th, "	North Anna River, Va.	Newburyport, Mass.
Clute, R. H.	"	59th "	"	"	Chelsea, Mass.

326 APPENDIX.

Names.	Rank.	Regiment.	When captured.	Where captured.	Residence.
Cross, H. M.	Lieut.	59th Mass. Vol.	May 24th, 1864.	North Anna R., Va.	Newburyport, Mass.
Chapin, H. A.	"	95th N. Y. Vol.	" 5th, "	Wilderness, Va.	"
Clyde, J. D.	Capt.	76th N. Y. Vol.	" "	"	Cherry Valley, N. Y.
Cahill, W.	Lieut.	"	" "	"	Solon, N. Y.
Casler, J. L.	"	"	" "	"	Otsego, N. Y.
Chisman, H.	"	7th Ind. Vol.	" 6th, "	Plymouth, N. C.	Cincinnati, O.
Cooper, A.	"	12th N. Y. Cav.	Apr. 20th, "	Cold Harbor, Va.	Oswego, N. Y.
Cribben, H.	"	140th N. Y. Vol.	June 2d, "	Mechanicsville, Va.	Rochester, N. Y.
Curtis, G. M.	"	"	" "	"	"
Caldwell, J. S.	"	16th Ill. Cav.	" 3d, "	Jonesville, Va.	Chicago, Ill.
Caslin, C. S.	"	151st N. Y. Vol.	Nov. 29th, 1863.	Mine Run, Va.	"
Crossley, S.	"	118th Pa. Vol.	June 2d, 1864.	Mechanicsville, Va.	Philadelphia, Pa.
Chauncey, C. R.	Capt.	34th Mass. Vol.	May 15th, "	New Market, Va.	Westfield, Mass.
Carlisle, L. B.	Lieut.	145th Pa. Vol.	June 16th, "	Petersburg, Va.	Latbersburg, Pa.
Conover, S. D.	Capt.	125th Ill. Vol.	Sept. 21st, 1863.	Chickamauga, Ga.	Squaw Village, N. J.
Cole, O. L.	Lieut.	50th Ill. Vol.	" 20th, "	"	Elgin, Ill.
Cain, J. H.	"	104th N. Y. Vol.	July 1st, "	Gettysburg, Pa.	Albany, N. Y.
Cassell, E. F.	"	11th Iowa Vol.	" 22d, "	Atlanta, Ga.	Illinois City, Ill.
Chambers, J. H.	"	103d Pa. Vol.	Apr. 20th, "	Plymouth, N. C.	Apollo, Pa.
Cottingham, E.	"	35th O. Vol.	Sept. 20th, 1863.	Chickamauga, Ga.	
Coddington, J. P.	Vet. Surg.	8th Iowa Cav.	July 30th, 1864.	Newnan, Ga.	Dubuque, Iowa.
Cole, A. F.	Capt.	59th N. Y. Vol.	June 22d, "	Petersburg, Va.	Lowville, N. Y.
Curtiss, W. H.	Adjt.	19th Mass. Vol.	" "	"	Randolph, Mass.
Clark, J. W.	Lieut.	59th N. Y. Vol.	" "	"	Butler, O.
Clark, J. H.	"	1st Mass. Art.	May 12th, "	Spottsylvania, Va.	Boston, Mass.
Case, D. L., Jr.	Adjt.	102d N. Y. Vol.	" 18th, "	"	Lansing, Mich.
Cope, J. D.	Lieut.	116th Pa. Vol.	July 20th, "	Atlanta, Ga.	Uniontown, Pa.
Core, J. W.	"	6th W. Va. Cav.	June 22d, "	Petersburg, Va.	
Coulter, W. J.	"	15th Mass. Vol.	" 26th, "	Springfield, Va.	Clinton, Mass.
Cubbetson, W. M.	"	30th Ind. Vol.	Sept. 19th, 1863.	Chickamauga, Ga.	
Casey, J.	"	45th N. Y. Vol.	June 22d, 1864.	Petersburg, Va.	Tuckahoe, N. Y.

APPENDIX. 327

Name	Rank	Regiment	Date	Place	Residence
Carter, W. H.	Lieut.	5th Pa. R. C. Vol.	May 10th, 1864.	Spottsylvania, Va.	Elimsport, Pa.
Chittenden, J. L.	"	5th Ind. Cav.	July 31st, "	Sunshine Ch., Ga.	Knoxville, Ill.
Canney, W. H.	"	69th N. Y. Vol.	June 22d, "	Petersburg, Va.	New York City.
Cameron, P.	"	16th N. Y. Cav.	Feb. 22d, "	Leesburg, Va.	
Campbell, W. F.	"	51st Pa. Vol.	May 12th, "	Spottsylvania, Va.	Slifer, Pa.
Cameron, J. F.	"	5th Pa. Cav.	June 27th, "	Petersburg, Va.	Philadelphia, Pa.
Carr, J. P.	Capt.	93d Ind. Vol.	" 12th, "	Salem, Miss.	Austin, Ind.
Clegg, M.	"	5th Ind. Cav.	July 31st, "	Clinton, Ga.	
Curtice, H. A.	Lieut.	157th N. Y. Vol.	July 1st, 1863.	Gettysburg, Pa.	Courtland, N. Y.
Coffin, J. A.	"	"	"	"	
Collins, W. A.	Capt.	10th Wis. Vol.	Sept. 20th, "	Chickamauga, Ga.	Milwaukee, Wis.
Carlisle, J. B.	Lieut.	2d W. Va. Cav.	" 11th, "	Smith Co., Va.	Ironton, O.
Christopher, W.	"	"	July 4th, "	Raleigh, Va.	Willow Grove, Pa.
Chandler, G. W.	"	1st	" 2d, "	Gettysburg, Pa.	Birmingham, O.
Chatburn, J.	"	150th Pa. Vol.	" 1st, "	"	Farmington, Me.
Childs, J. W.	"	16th Mc. Vols.	"	"	Germantown, Pa.
Chase, H. R.	"	1st Vt. H. Art.	June 23d, 1864.	Petersburg, Va.	Guilford Centre, Vt.
Conover, W. H.	"	22d N. Y. Cav.	" 9th, "	Turner's Bridge, Va.	Norwich, N.Y.
Clark, J. A.	Capt.	7th Mich. Cav.	Mar. 2d, "	Mechanicsville, Va.	
Cook, W. B.	Lieut.	140th Pa. Vol.	July 2d, 1863.	Gettysburg, Pa.	Candor, Pa.
Califf, B. F.	"	2d W. S. S. S.	May 5th, 1864.	Wilderness, Va.	Salem, Mass.
Cook, E. F.	Major.	4th	Mar. 3d, "	Stevensburg, Va.	
Cooke, H. P.	Capt. & A. A. Gen.	2d N. Y. Cav.	May 2d, 1863.	Wilderness, Va.	Deckerstown, N.J.
Crocker, H.	Lieut.	1st N. J. Cav.	June 9th, "	Brandy Station, Va.	Port Jervis, N. Y.
Camp, T. B.	Capt.	52d Pa. Vol.	July 3d, 1864.	Fort Johnson, S. C.	Camptown, Pa.
Clark, L. S.	"	62d N. Y. Vol.	May 30th, "	Hanover C. H., Va.	Saratoga Springs, N Y
Chapin, H. C.	"	4th Vt Vol.	June 23d, "	Petersburg, Va.	Elmira, N. Y.
Conyngham, J. B.	Lieut. Col.	52d Pa. Vol.	July 3d, "	Fort Johnson, S. C.	
Christopher, J.	Capt.	16th U. S. Inf.	Sept. 19th, 1863.	Chickamauga, Ga.	Oswego, N. Y.
Cochran, M. A.	"	"	"	"	Washington, D. C.
Causten, M. C.	Lieut.	19th	" 20th, "	"	

328 APPENDIX.

Names.	Rank.	Regiment.	When captured.	Where captured.	Residence.
Chubbuck, D. B.	Lieut.	19th Mass. Vol.	Sept. 22d, 1864.	Petersburg, Va.	Springfield, O.
Carpenter, S. D.	"	3d O. Vol.	May 3d, 1863.	Rome, Ga.	"
Carley, A. A.	Capt.	73d Ind. Vol.	Apr. 30th, "	Alabama.	
Connelly, R. J.	Lieut.	73d Ill. Vol.	May 3d, "	Rome, Ga.	
Carwright, A. G.	Capt.	85th N. Y. V. Vol.	Apr. 20th, 1864.	Plymouth, N. C.	Philip's Creek, N. Y.
Clark, M. L.	"	101st Pa. Vol.	"	"	Mansfield, Pa.
Compher, A.	"	"	"	"	Rainsburg, Pa.
Clapp, J. B.	Adjt.	16th Conn. Vol.	"	"	Wethersfield, Conn.
Case, A. G.	Lieut.	"	"	"	Simsbury, Conn.
Cratty, E. G.	Capt.	103d Pa. Vol.	"	"	Butler, Pa.
Coats, H. A.	"	85th N. Y. V. Vol.	"	"	Wellsville, N. Y.
Crooks, S. J.	Colonel.	22d N. Y. Cav.	June 30th, 1864.	Ream's Sta., Va.	Rochester, N. Y.
Case, F. S.	, Capt.	2d O. Cav.	" 29th, "	"	Wellington, O.
Cutler, J.	"	34th O. Vol.	July 18th, 1863.	Witheville, Va.	
Coglin, T.	"	14th N. Y. H. Art.	June 17th, 1864.	Petersburg, Va.	
Cord, T. A.	Lieut.	19th U. S. Inf.	Sept. 20th, 1863.	Chickamauga, Ga.	Danville, Ind.
Cloadt, J.	Capt.	119th N. Y. Vol.	July 1st,	Gettysburg, Pa.	
Calkins, W. W.	Lieut.	104th Ill. Vol.	Sept. 20th, "	Chickamauga, Ga.	Ottawa, Ill.
Craig, J.	Capt.	1st W. Va. Vol.	" 11th, "	Moorefield, Va.	Wheeling, W. Va.
Colville, J. W.	"	5th Mich. Vol.	June 22d, 1864.	Petersburg, Va.	E. Saginaw, Mich.
Crossby, T. J.	"	157th Pa. Vol.	July 2d, 1863.	Gettysburg, Pa.	Titusville, Pa.
Cohen, M.	"	4th Ky. Vol.	Sept. 2d, "	Stevensburg, Ky.	Louisville, Ky.
Copeland, J. R.	"	7th O. Vol.	Nov. 6th, "	Rodgersville, Tenn.	Locust Grove, O.
Crops, F. A. M.	Lieut.	77th Pa. Vol.	Sept. 19th, "	Chickamauga, Ga.	
Curtis, R.	"	4th Ky. Vol.	" 21st, "	Stevenson's Gap, Ky.	Louisville, Ky.
Clements, J.	"	15th Ky. Vol.	June 27th, "	Jackson, Miss.	Hewalton, Ind.
Caldwell, D. B.	"	75th O. Vol.	July 2d, "	Gettysburg, Pa.	
Cubbison, J. C.	"	101st Pa. Vol.	Apr. 20th, 1864.	Plymouth, N. C.	
Crawford, H. P.	Capt.	2d Ill. Cav.	June 11th, 1863.	Ormande, Miss.	
Chase, E. E.	"	1st R. I. Cav.	"	Middleburg, Va.	
Coffin, G. A.	Adjt.	29th Ind. Vol.	Sept. 19th, "	Chickamauga, Ga.	Irish Ripple, Pa.

APPENDIX.

Name	Rank	Regiment	Date	Place	Residence
Cockran, T. G.	Lieut.	77th Pa. Vol.	Sept. 19th, 1863.	Chickamauga, Ga.	Chambersburg, Pa.
Conrad, W. F.	Capt.	25th Iowa Vol.	May 24th, "	Raymond, Miss.	
Carperts, L. M.	"	18th Wis. Vol.	Oct. 5th, 1864.	Altoona, Ga.	
Cox, J. L.	Lieut.	21st Ill. Vol.	Sept. 20th, 1863.	Chickamauga, Ga	Hutsonville, Ill.
Cunningham, M.	"	42d N. Y. Vol.	"	"	Norwich, Conn.
Charters, A. M.	"	17th Iowa Vol.	Oct. 13th, 1864.	Tilton, Ga.	Leavenworth, Kansas.
Carpenter, J. Q.	"	150th Pa. Vol.	July 1st, 1863.	Gettysburg, Pa.	Germantown, Pa.
Campbell, B. F.	Capt.	2d Mass. Art.	Apr. 20th, 1864.	Plymouth, N. C.	
Clark, H. L.	Lieut.	10th Mich. Vol.	Oct. 19th, "	Rough & Ready Sta., Ga.	Springfield, Mass.
Copeland, W. A.	"				
Cuniffe, II.	"	13th Ill. Vol.	Nov. 24th, 1863.	Lookout M'tain, Ga.	
Carpenter, E. N.	Capt.	6th Pa. Cav.	May 7th, 1864.	Todd's Tavern, Va.	Germantown, Pa.
Clemmons, T.	Lieut.	13th Ill. Vol.	Nov. 24th, "	Lookout M'tain, Ga.	
Crocker, Geo. A.	Capt. & A. A. Gen.		Oct. 11th, 1863.	Brandy Sta., Va.	New York City.
Cook, W. C.	Adjt.	9th Mich. Cav.	Dec. 4th, 1864.	Waynesboro', Ga.	Tecumseh, Mich.
Cowles, H. F.	Lieut.	18th Conn. Vol.	June 15th, 1863.	Winchester, Va.	Norwich, Conn.
Cramer, C. P.	"	21st N. Y. Cav.	July 17th, 1864.	Petersburg, Va.	West Troy, N. Y.
Clancey, C. W.	Lieut. Col.	52d O. Vol.	" 19th, "	Peach Tree Cr., Ga.	Smithfield, O.
Corum, Geo.	Lieut. & R. Q. M.	2d Ky. Cav.	Nov. 28th, "	Waynesboro', Ga.	Greenupsburg, Ky.
Case, M. B.	Lieut.	23d U. S. C. T.	July 30th, "	Petersburg, Va.	Owattona, Minn.
Cline, D. J.	"	75th O. V. M. I.	Aug. 17th, "	Gainesville, Fla.	Logan Hocking, O.
Conn, C. G.	"	1st M. S. S.	July 30th, "	Petersburg, Va.	Elkhart, Mich.
Cook, J. L.	"	6th Iowa Vol.	May 14th, 1863.	Holly Springs, Miss.	St. Louis, Mo.
Cunningham, M.	"	1st Vt. H. Art.	June 23d, 1864.	Petersburg, Va.	
Copeland, C. D.	"	58th Mass. Vol.	July 30th, "	"	Fall River, Mass.
Chamberlain, V. B.	Capt.	7th Conn. Vol.	" 11th, 1863.	Fort Wagner, S. C.	
Catlin, J. E.	Lieut.	45th Pa. Vol.	" 30th, 1864.	Petersburg, Va.	Wellsboro', Pa.
Cashell, C. P.	"	12th Pa. Cav.	" 29th, "	Cherry Run, Md.	
Clark, M. W.	Capt.	11th Iowa Cav.	Feb. 17th, 1865.	Columbia, S. C.	Columbus City, Iowa.

APPENDIX.

Names.	Rank.	Regiment.	When captured.	Where captured.	Residence.
Channel, J. R.	Lieut.	1st Ill. Art.	Feb. 15th, 1865.	Lexington, S. C.	Ottawa, Ill.
Day, J. W.	"	17th Mass. Vol.	" 1st, 1864.	Newbern, N. C.	Averill, Mass.
Damrell, W. S.	"	13th Mass. Vol.	May 21st, "	Spottsylvania, Va.	Boston, Mass.
Dearing, G. A.	"	16th Mc. Vol.	July 1st, 1863.	Gettysburg, Pa.	
Dufer, T. J.	"	5th Mich. Cav.	Oct. 10th, "	Robinson's River, Va.	
Dickerson, A. A.	"	16th Conn. Vol.	Apr. 20th, 1864.	Plymouth, N. C.	Hartford, Conn.
Donaghy, J.	Capt.	103d Pa. Vol.	" "	"	Allegany City, Pa.
Davis, W. G.	Lieut.	27th Mass. Vol.	May 16th, "	Drury's Bluff, Va.	
Day, A. P.	"	15th Conn. Vol.	Apr. 20th, "	Plymouth, N. C.	New Haven, Conn.
Dewees, J. H.	Major.	13th Pa. Cav.	June 24th, "	Malvern Hill, Va.	Philadelphia, Pa.
Daniels, E. S.	Capt.	35th U. S. C. T.	May 23d, "	Florida, Fla.	Old Cambridge, Mass.
Dietz, Henry	"	45th N. Y. Vol.	July 1st, 1863.	Gettysburg, Pa.	New York City.
Dodge, C. C.	"	20th Mich. Vol.	June 2d, 1864.	Mechanicsville, Va.	Marshall, Mich.
Dieffenbach, A. C.	Lieut.	73d Pa. Vol.	Nov. 25th, 1863.	Mission Ridge, Tenn.	Philadelphia, Pa.
Dewees, T. B.	"	2d U. S. Cav.	June 9th, "	Brandy Sta., Va.	
Dooley, A. T.	"	51st Ind. Vol.	May 3d, "	Rome, Ga.	New Winchester, Ind.
Downing, O. J.	Capt.	2d N. Y. Cav.	" 12th, 1864.	Richmond, Va.	Rochester, N. Y.
Denny, W. N.	"	57th Ind. Vol.	" 3d, 1863.	Rome, Ga.	Vincennes, Ind.
Delano, J. A.	Lieut.	51st Ind. Vol.	" "	"	Marietta, Ind
Davis, Q. R.	"	123d O. Vol.	June 15th, "	Winchester, Va.	Marcellus, O.
Derrickson, J. G.	Capt.	66th N. Y. Vol.	" 22d, 1864.	Petersburg, Va.	New York City.
Dean, S. V.	Lieut.	145th Pa. Vol.	" 16th, "	"	West Springfield, Pa.
Daily, W. A.	Capt.	8th Pa. Cav.	Oct. 12th, 1863.	Sulphur Spa, Va.	Philadelphia, Pa.
Davis, C. G.	Lieut.	1st Mass. Cav.	" "	"	
Doruschke, B.	Capt.	26th Wis. Vol.	July 1st, "	Gettysburg, Pa	Pontiac, Mich.
Dennis, J. B.	"	7th Conn. Vol.	May 14th, 1864.	Petersburg, Va.	Philadelphia, Pa.
Davis, L. R.	"	7th O. Vol.	Nov. 25th, 1863.	Lookout M'tain, Ga.	
Drake, L.	Lieut.	22d Mich. Vol.	Sept. 20th, "	Chickamauga, Ga.	Marengo, Iowa.
Dutton, W. G.	"	67th Pa. Vol.	June 15th, "	Winchester, Va.	
Dillon, C. D.	"	7th Iowa Cav.	July 30th, "	Corinth, Miss.	
Drennan, J. S.	"	1st Vt. II. Art.	June 20th, 1864.	Petersburg, Va.	Morrisville, Vt.

APPENDIX. 331

Name	Rank	Regiment	Date	Place	Residence
Deane, T. J.	Lieut.	5th Mich. Cav.	Oct. 10th, 1863.	James City, Va.	Wayne, Mich.
Dunn, J.	"	64th N. Y. Vol.	June 3d, 1864.	Cold Harbor, Va.	New York City.
Dunning, A. J.	"	7th N. Y. Art.	" 22d, "	Petersburg, Va.	
Davenport, T. F.	Capt.	75th O. Vol.	Aug. 17th, "	Gainesville, Fla.	Canterbury, Conn.
Davis, H. C.	Lieut.	18th Conn. Vol.	June 15th, 1863.	Winchester, Va.	
Davis, T. C.	Capt.	38th Ill. Vol.	Sept. 20th, "	Chickamauga, Ga.	
Dirlan, C. L.	Lieut.	72d Ill. Vol.	June 12th, 1864.	Ripley, Miss.	Clyde, O.
Doughton, O. G.	Capt.	111th O. Vol.	Sept. 8th, 1863.	Jonesboro', Tenn.	Stryker, O.
Day, J. R.	Lieut.	3d Me. Vol.	June 20th, "	Gum Spa, Va.	Waterville, Me.
Donovan, J.	Capt.	2d N. J. Vol.	May 6th, 1864.	Wilderness, Va.	Elizabeth, N. J.
Dusbrow, W.	Capt.	40th N. Y. Vol.	" 12th, "	Spottsylvania, Va.	New York City.
Dyre, E. B.	Lieut.	1st Conn. Cav.	June 29th, "	Ream's Sta., Va.	Derby, Conn.
Dinsmore, A.	Capt.	5th Pa. Cav.	Oct. 13th, 1863.	Auburn, Va.	
Duzenburgh, A.	"	35th N. Y. Vol.	July 22d, 1864.	Decatur, Ga.	
Dorris, W. C.	Lieut.	111th Ill. Vol.		Atlanta, Ga.	
Dodge, H. G.	"	2d Pa. Cav.	" 24th, "	Charles City C. H., Va.	Philadelphia, Pa.
Dixon, A.	Capt.	104th N. Y. Vol.	" 1st, 1863.	Gettysburg, Pa.	
Dunn, M.	Major.	19th Mass. Vol.	June 22d, 1864.	Petersburg, Va.	
Doane, E. B.	Capt.	8th Iowa Cav.	July 30th, "	Newnan, Ga.	Salem, Iowa.
Davidson, J.	Lieut.	6th N. Y. Art.	Oct. 11th, 1863.	Brandy Sta., Va.	Haverstraw, N. Y.
Drake, J. W.	"	136th N. Y. Vol.	July 3d, "	Gettysburg, Pa.	Dansville, N. Y.
Downs, C.	"	33d N. J. Vol.	" 20th, 1864.	Atlanta, Ga.	Patterson, N. J.
Duven, J. W.	"	115th N. Y. Vol.	Feb. 20th, "	Ossen Pond, Ga.	
Dushane, J. M.	Capt.	5th N. H. Vol.	June 3d, "	Cold Harbor, Va.	Keene, N. H.
Davis, W. H.	"	142d Pa. Vol.	July 1st, 1863.	Gettysburg, Pa.	Connellsville, Pa.
Dircks, C. S. F.	"	4th Md. Vol.	May 5th, 1864.	Wilderness, Va.	Baltimore, Md.
Devine, J. S.	Lieut.	1st Md. Tenn. Vol.	June 26th, 1863.	Davidson Co., Tenn.	
Diemer, M.	"	71st Pa. Vol.	July 3d, "	Gettysburg, Pa.	Philadelphia, Pa.
Dingley, F.	"	10th Mo. Vol.	May 16th, 1864.	Jackson, Miss.	Palmyra, Mo.
Durfee, W. H.	"	7th R. I. Vol.	July 13th, "	"	
Durboyne, G.	"	5th R. I. Vol.	May 5th, 1864.	Crotan, N. C.	Newport, R. I.
		66th N. Y. Vol.	June 17th, "	Petersburg, Va.	

332   APPENDIX.

Names.	Rank.	Regiment.	When captured.	Where captured.	Residence.
Donohoy, G. B.	Capt.	7th Pa. Res.	May 5th, 1864.	Wilderness, Va.	Huntingdon, Pa.
Dieffenbach, W. H.	Lieut.	3d Iowa Cav.	June 12th, "	Ripley, Miss.	Centreville, Iowa.
De Lay, R.	"	11th N. H. Vol.	" 17th, "	Petersburg, Va.	Strafford, Vt.
Demmick, O. W.	"	142d Pa. Vol.	July 1st, 1863.	Gettysburg, Pa.	Stroudsburg, Pa.
Drake, C. H.	Capt.	16th Mich. Vol.	" 3d, "	"	
Dygest, K. S.	Lieut.	72d O. Vol.	June 12th, 1864.	Salem, Miss.	Fremont, O.
Dick, I.	Capt.	93d Ind. Vol.	"	"	Patriot, Ind.
Davis, L. B.	"	1st Ky. Cav.	May 25th, 1863.	Fishing Cr., Ky.	
Dillon, F. W.	Lieut.	15th Wis. Vol.	Sept. 20th, "	Chickamauga, Ga.	Chippewa Falls, Wis.
Dahl, O. R.	"	94th O. Vol.	"	"	Franklin, O.
Dickey, M. V.	"	71st Pa. Vol.	July 2d, "	Gettysburg, Pa.	
Davis, Byron	Capt.	89th O. Vol.	Sept. 20th, "	Chickamauga, Ga.	Bainbridge, O.
Day, F.	Lieut.	22d Mich. Vol.	"	"	
Dalton, G. A.	"	44th Wis. Vol.	Oct. 5th, 1864.	Altoona, Ga.	
Dickerson, E.	"	16th U. S. Inf.	Sept. 19th, 1863.	Chickamauga, Ga.	
Durnam, T. J.	"	10th Ky. Vol.	"	"	Cannonsburg, Mich.
Dunn, H. C.	"	24th Mo. Vol.	Oct. 12th, 1864.	Tilton, Ga.	Rocktown, Ill.
Driscoll, D.	"	44th Ill. Vol.	Sept. 20th, 1863.	Chickamauga, Ga.	Richmond, Ind.
Davis, F. J.	"	35th Ind. Vol.	"	"	Boston, Mass.
Dugan, J.	Lieut. & A. Q. M.	4th Mass. Cav.	Oct. 24th, 1864.	Magnolin, Fla.	
Dorr, H. G.	Lieut.	9th N. J. Vol.	July 30th, "	Petersburg, Va.	Trenton, N. J.
Drake, J. M.	Capt.	1st Mich. S. S.	"	"	Detroit, Mich.
Dicey, F. C.	Lieut.	31st U. S. C. T.	"	"	Poughkeepsie, N. Y.
Downing, H. A.	Capt.	45th Pa. Vol.	"	"	Bainbridge, Pa.
Dibeler, J. B.	Lieut.	95th O. Vol.	"	"	Big Plains, O.
Davidson, J. W.	Major.	51st Ind. Vol.	July 30th, 1864.	Petersburg, Va.	Vincennes, Ind.
Denny, W. N.	Lieut.	9th N. H. Vol.	"	"	Milford, N. H.
Drew, G. H.					
Everett, Chas.	Lieut.	70th O. Vol.	Aug. 26th, "	Atlanta, Ga.	Cleveland, O.

APPENDIX. 333

Name	Rank	Unit	Date	Place	Residence
Eastman, F. R.	Lieut.	2d Pa. Cav.	June 22d, 1864.	St. M.'s Church, Va.	Mt. Clemens, Mich.
Elkin, J. L. F.	Adjt.	1st N. J. Vol.	May 6th, "	Wilderness, Va.	New Brunswick, N. J.
Eastmond, O.	Capt.	1st N. C. U. Vol.	Apr. 20th, "	Plymouth, N. C.	New York City.
Evans, T. E.	Lieut.	52d Pa. Vol.	July 3d, "	James Island, S. C.	Hyde Park, Pa.
Evestone, J. W.	"	13th Ind. Vol.	" 22d "	Atlanta, Ga.	Washington, Iowa.
Ellinwood, W. B.	"	10th Wis. Vol.	Sept. 20th, 1863.	Chickamauga, Ga.	Oshkosh, Wis.
Edwards, D. C.	"	2d Md. Vol.	Jan. 4th, 1864.	Burlington, Va.	
English, D.	Major.	11th Ky. Cav.	July 31st, "	Sunshine Ch., Va	Owenton, Ky.
Elder, S. S.	Capt.	1st U. S. Art'y.	June 24th, "	Petersburg, Va.	
*Eckings, T. K.	Lieut.	3d N. J. Vol.	May 8th, "	Spottsylvania, Va.	
Evans, B. W.	Capt.	4th O. Cav.	" 6th, "	Wilderness, Va.	Kirkersville, O.
Errickson, J. H.	Lieut.	57th N. Y. Vol.	Oct. 14th, 1863.	Bristow Station, Va.	Brooklyn, N. Y.
Eberheart, H. H.	Capt.	120th O. Vol.	May 24th, "	Raymond, Miss.	Wooster, O.
Eagan, M.	"	15th W. Va. Vol.	" 19th, 1864.	Meadow's Bluff, Va.	
Evans, N. C.	"	184th Pa. Vol.	June 22d, "	Petersburg, Va.	Rainsburg, Pa.
Eglin, A. R.	"	45th O. Vol.	Nov. 15th, 1863.	Knoxville, Tenn.	Kenton, O.
Ewen, M.	"	21st Wis. Vol.	Sept. 20th "	Chickamauga, Ga.	Fond Du Lac, Wis.
Eagan, John	Lieut.	1st U. S. Art'y.	July 1st, 1864.	Ream's Station, Va.	
Elder, John	"	8th Ind. Vol.	" 22d, "	Atlanta, Ga.	
Edwards, T. D.	Ass't. Eng.	U. S. Navy.	Apr. 20th, "	Plymouth, N. C.	
Edminston, S.	Lieut.	89th O. Vol.	Sept. 20th, 1863.	Chickamauga, Ga.	
Evans, H. F.					
Eaur, M.	Capt.	15th N. Y. Cav.			
Elheny, J. L. F.	Adjt.	1st N. J. Vol.			New Brunswick, N. J.
Flick, M.	Lieut.	67th Pa. Vol.	June 15th, 1863.	Winchester, Va.	Rainsburg, Pa.
Fritz, J.	"	11th Tenn. Vol.	Feb. 22d, 1864.	Lee County, Tenn.	
Fay, S. A.	"	85th N. Y. Vet.Vol.	Apr. 20th, "	Plymouth, N. C.	Olean, N. Y.
Frost, C. W.	"	"	"	"	Rochester, N. Y.
Freeman, D. W. D.	Capt.	10'st Pa. Vol.	"	"	Irish Ripple, Pa.
Fiske, J. E.	"	2d Mass. Art'y.	"	"	Grantville, Mass.
Fish, O. M.	Lieut.				Boston, Mass.

Names.	Rank.	Regiment.	When captured.	Where captured.	Residence.
Fluke, A. L.	Lieut.	103d Pa. Vol.	Apr. 20th, 1864.	Plymouth, N. C.	Kittaning, Pa.
Fahs, J.	Capt.	87th Pa. Vol.	June 15th, 1863.	Winchester, Va.	York, Pa.
Foot, M. C.	Lieut.	92d N. Y. Vol.	Apr. 20th, 1864.	Plymouth, N. C.	Cooperstown, N. Y.
Fontaine, J.	"	73d Pa. Vol.	Nov. 25th, 1863.	Mission Ridge, Tenn.	Washington, D. C.
Fairbanks, J.	"	72d O. Vol.	June 12th, 1864.	Salem, Miss.	Rollersville, O.
Follett, W. H.	"	2d Mass. Art'y.	Nov. 22d, 1863.	Chancellorsville, Va.	Quincey, Mass.
Fry, Alfred	"	73d Ind. Vol.	May 3d, "	Rome, Ga.	Crown Point, Ind.
Fish, G. W.	"	3d O. Cav.	"	"	Hamilton, O.
Frasier, J.	Colonel.	140th Pa. Vol.	June 22d, 1864.	Petersburg, Va.	
Fleming, C. K.	Major.	11th Vt. Vol.	" 23d, "	"	Bellows Falls, Vt.
Foster, J. W.	Capt.	42d Ill. Vol.	Sept. 20th, 1863.	Chickamauga, Ga.	Belvidere, Ill.
Fales, J. M.	Lieut.	1st R. I. Cav.	June 18th, "	Middleburg, Va.	
Finney, G. E.	Adjt.	19th Ind. Vol.	May 5th, 1864.	Wilderness, Va.	Elizabethtown, Ind.
Fowler, J. H.	Lieut.	100th O. Vol.	Sept. 8th, 1863.	Limestone, Tenn.	
Fox, G. B.	Major.	75th O. Vol.	Aug. 17th, 1864.	Gainesville, Ga.	Cincinnati, O.
Farr, W. V.	Capt.	106th Pa. Vol.	June 22d, "	Petersburg, Va.	
Forbes, W. H.	Major.	2d Mass. Cav.	July 6th, "	Addie Station.	
Ford, E. W.	Capt.	9th Min. Vol.	June 11th, "	Salem, Miss.	Austin, Min.
Ferris, J. M.	Lieut.	3d Mich. Vol.	" 1st "	Gaines's Mills, Va.	
Fairchild, H.	"	10th Wis. Vol.	Sept. 20th, 1863.	Chickamauga, Ga.	Platteville, Wis.
Funk, J. W.	Capt.	39th N. Y. Vol.	May 10th, 1864.	Spotsylvania, Va.	New York City.
Faye, E. M.	Lieut.	42d N. Y. Vol.	" 12th, "	"	"
Furgerson, J.	"	1st N. J. Vol.	" "	"	Philadelphia, Pa.
Flannery, D.	"	4th N. J. Vol.	" "	"	Trenton, N. J.
Fowler, H. M.	"	15th N. J. Vol.	" "	"	Newark, N. J.
Fisk, W. M.	Capt.	73d N. Y. Vol.	May 6th, 1864.	Wilderness, Va.	New York City.
Floeger, G. W.	Lieut.	11th Pa. R. C. Vol.	" 5th, "	"	Butler, Pa.
Fagan, C. A.	"	"	" "	"	Ebensburg, Pa.
French, H.	"	3d Vt. Vol.			Hartford, Vt.
Francis, J. L.	Capt.	135th O. Vol.	July 3d, 1864.		
Field, A.	"	94th N. Y. Vol.	" 1st, 1863.	Gettysburg, Pa.	Weedsport, N. Y.

APPENDIX.

Name	Rank	Regiment	Date	Battle	Residence
Fritchy, A. W.	Lieut.	26th Mo. Vol.	Nov. 26th, 1863.	Mission Ridge, Tenn.	St. Louis, Mo.
Fortescue, L. R.	"	Signal C., U. S. A.	July 4th "	Emmettsburg, Md.	Middleborne, W. Va.
Fellows, M.	"	149th Pa. Vol.	" 1st, "	Gettysburg, Pa.	
Fisher, R.	"	17th Mo. Vol.	Nov. 27th, "	Ringgold, Ga.	St. Louis, Mo.
Fenner, W.	"	2d R. I. Vol.	July 2d, "	Port Hudson, Miss.	Providence, R. I.
Fox, J. D.	"	16th Ill. Cav.	Jan. 3d, 1864.	Jonesville, Ga.	Aurora, Ill.
Fritze, C.	"	24th Ill. Vol.	Sept. 20th, 1863.	Chickamauga, Ga.	Chicago, Ill.
Fisher, L. W.	"	4th Vt. Vol.	June 23d, 1864.	Petersburg, Va.	Danville, Vt.
Fatzer, S.	"	108th N. Y. Vol.	" 17th, "	"	Rochester, N. Y.
Fontaine, E.		7th Pa. R. C. Vol.	May 5th, "	Wilderness, Va.	
Flamsburgh, D.	Capt.	4th Ind. Batt'y.	"	"	
Forney, D.	Lieut.	30th O. Vol.	July 22d, 1864.	Atlanta, Ga.	Coshocton, O.
Fisher, S.	"	93d Ind. Vol.	Aug. 11th, "	Salem, Miss.	
Fiedler, J.	Capt.	Eng'r C., U. S. A.	" 7th, "	Jonesboro', Ga.	
Finney, D. S.	Lieut.	14th and 15th Ill. Vet. Batt.	Oct. 4th, "	Acworth, Ga.	Beardstown, Ill.
Fairfield, O. B.	"	89th O. Vol.	Sept. 20th, 1863.	Chickamauga, Ga.	
Fitzpatrick, L.	"	146th N. Y. Vol.	May 5th, 1864.	Wilderness, Va.	Brooklyn, N. Y.
Fales, L. D. C.	"				
Freeman, H. B.	"	18th U. S. Inf.	Sept. 19th, 1863.	Chickamauga, Ga.	Jeffersonville, Ind.
Foster, H. C.	"	23d Ind. Vol.	June 21st, 1864.	Kennesaw Mt., Ga.	Boston, Mass.
Foley, John	"	59th Mass. Vol.	July 30th, "	Petersburg, Va.	Utica, N. Y.
Faass, Louis	"	14th N. Y. Art'y.	"	"	Albion, Mich.
Frost, R. J.		9th Mich. Cav.			
Fall, J. P.	Capt.	32d Me. Vol.	Oct. 27th, 1864.	Stone Mountain, Ga.	South Berwick, Me.
Filler, J. H.	Major.	55th Pa. Vol.	July 30th, 1864.	Petersburg, Va.	Bedford, Pa.
Fay, W. W.	Capt.	56th Mass. Vol.	"	"	
George, G. J.	Lieut.	40th Ill. Vol.	June 27th, 1864.	Kennesaw Mt., Ga.	Vienna, Ill.
Gillespie, J. B.	Capt.	120th Ill. Vol.	" 12th, "	Ripley, Miss.	
Gunn, T. M.	Lieut.	21st Ky. Vol.	" 15th, "	Kennesaw Mt., Ga.	Shelbyville, Ky.
Gilbert, E. C.	Capt.	152d N. Y. Vol.	" 22d, "	Petersburg, Va.	Butternuts, N. Y.

APPENDIX.

Names.	Rank.	Regiment.	When captured.	Where captured.	Residence.
Gill, A. W. H.	Capt.	14th N. Y. Vol.	May 5th, 1864.	Wilderness, Va.	Brooklyn, N. Y.
Greble, C. E.	"	8th Mich. Cav.	Nov. 18th, 1863.	Knoxville, Tenn.	Battle Creek, Mich.
Green, J. H.	Lieut.	100th O. Vol.	Sept. 8th, "	Limestone, Tenn.	Fremont, O.
Gotshall, J.	Adjt.	55th Pa. Vol.	May 16th, 1864.	Drury's Bluff, Va.	
Godown, J. M.	Lieut.	12th Ind. Vol.	July 22d, "	Atlanta, Ga.	Ft. Wayne, Ind.
Grover, J. E.	"	6th Ind. Cav.	Sept. 16th, 1863.	Bean's Station, Tenn.	
Gayer, H.	"	133d W. Va. Mil.	" 12th, "	Centreville, Va.	Rockcase, W. Va.
Gatch, O. C.	Capt.	89th O. Vol.	" 20th, "	Chickamauga, Ga.	Milford, O.
Gross, J. M.	"	18th Ky. Vol.	" "	"	
Galbraith, H. E.	"	22d Mich. Vol.	" "	"	Lexington, Mich.
Goetz, J.	"	"	" "	"	Mt. Clemens, Mich.
Gray, W. L.	"	151st Pa. Vol.	July 1st, 1863.	Gettysburg, Pa.	
Gross, C. M.	Lieut.	110th O. Vol.	June 15th, "	Winchester, Va.	Covington, O.
Grant, G. W.	"	88th Pa. Vol.	July 1st, "	Gettysburg, Pa.	Reading, Pa.
Grant, H. D.	"	117th N. Y. Vol.	May 16th, 1864.	Drury's Bluff, Va.	
Gray, R. H.	"	15th U. S. Inf.	Sept. 20th, 1863.	Chickamauga, Ga.	Cleveland, O.
Gariss, A. J.	Adjt.	1st Md. Cav.	June 9th, "	Brandy Station, Va.	Baltimore, Md.
Gates, A. L.	Lieut.	10th Wis. Vol.	Sept. 20th, "	Chickamauga, Ga.	Hustisford, Wis.
Goodwin, J. A.	"	1st Mass. Cav.	May 11th, 1864.	Beaver Dam, Va.	Medford, Mass.
Gamble, G. H.	Adjt.	8th Ill. Cav.	" 3d, 1863.	Rome, Ga.	
Gates, R. C.	Lieut.	18th U. S. Inf.	Sept. 20th, "	Chickamauga, Ga.	
Gilmore, J. A.	"	79th N. Y. Vol.	July 10th, "	Jackson, Miss.	
Gamble, H.	"	73d Ind. Vol.	May 3d, "	Rome, Ga.	Monroeville, O.
Grant, E.	Capt.	1st Vt. Cav.	June 29th, 1864.	Stony Creek, Va.	
Granger, C. M.	Lieut.	88th N. Y. Vol.	" 22d, "	Petersburg, Va.	
Goodrich, J. O.	Adjt.	85th N.Y.Vet.Vol.	Apr. 20th, "	Plymouth, N. C.	Scottsville, N. Y.
Glazeer, W. W.	Lieut.	2d N. Y. Cav.	Oct. 19th, 1863.	Buckland Mills, Va.	Fowler, N. Y.
Goodin, A.	"	82d O. Vol.	July 3d, "	Gettysburg, Pa.	
Gordon, C. O.	"	1st Me. Cav.	June 24th, 1864.	St. M.'s Church, Va.	Phillips, Me.
Green, E. H.	Capt.	107th Pa. Vol.	May 21st, "	Spottsylvania, Va.	Maytown, Pa.
Gimber, H. W.	"	150th Pa. Vol.	July 1st, 1863.	Gettysburg, Pa.	Philadelphia, Pa.

APPENDIX. 337

Gilman, ——	Lieut.	3d Me. Vol.	Aldie, Va.	June 20th, 1863.	Mayfield, N. Y.
Gotland, C.	"	134th N. Y. Vol.	Gettysburg, Pa.	July 1st, "	
Gotman, D.	Capt.	10th N. Y. Cav.	Brandy Sta., Va.	June 9th, "	Cambridge, Ill.
Griffin, H. G.	Lieut.	112th Ill. Vol.	Knoxville, Tenn.	Nov. 18th, "	
Gordon, E.	"	81st Ind. Vol.	Chickamauga, Ga.	Sept. 20th, "	Kingston, Tenn.
Geasland, S. A.	"	11th Tenn. Cav.	Cumberl'd Gap, Tenn.	Feb. 22d, 1864.	
Guy, F. C.	"	11th Pa. Vol.	Gettysburg, Pa.	July 1st, 1863.	Donegal, Pa.
Green, C. W.	"	44th Ind. Vol.	Chickamauga, Ga.	Sept. 22d, "	
Goss, J. W.	"	1st Mass. Art'y.	Petersburg, Va.	June 22d, 1864.	Ipswich, Mass.
Grafton, B.	Capt.	64th O. Vol.	Chickamauga, Ga.	Sept. 20th, 1863.	Marion, O.
Gatos, J.	"	33d O. Vol.	"	"	
Grant, A.	"	19th Wis. Vol.	Petersburg, Va.	July 28th, 1864.	Muncie, Ind.
Green, G. W.	"	19th Ind. Vol	Gettysburg, Pa.	" 1st, 1863.	Churchville, N. Y.
Goodrich, A. L.	"	8th N. Y. Cav.	Stony Creek, Va.	June 29th, 1864.	Pittsburg, Pa.
Gamble, N. P.	Lieut.	63d Pa. Vol.	Harper's Ferry, Va.	July 19th, 1863.	Hyde Park, Pa.
Garbet, D.	"	77th Pa. Vol.	Chickamauga, Ga.	Sept. 19th, "	
Good, T. G.	"	1st Md. Cav.	Brandy Sta., Va.	June 9th, "	Shickshinny, Pa.
Gordon, H. M.	"	143d Pa. Vol.	Wilderness, Va.	May 5th, 1864.	Philadelphia, Pa.
Gray, P.	"	77th Pa. Vol.	Chickamauga, Ga	Sept. 19th, 1863.	Brookfield, Vt.
Gallagher, J.	"	4th O. V. Vols.	Petersburg, Va.	June 23d, 1864.	Pensacola, Fla.
Galloway, J. L.	Capt. & A. A. G.		Osceola, Fla.		
Green, E. A.	Lieut.	81st Ill. Vol.	Ripley, Miss.	June 11th, 1864.	Monroe, Mich.
Green, J. L.	Capt.&A.A. G.U.S.A		Trevillian's Sta., Va.		
Gove, W. A.	Lieut.	3d Mass. Cav.	Louisiana.	Nov. 28th, 1863.	East Boston, Mass.
Grant, S.	"	6th Mich. Ar'ty.	Louisville, Ky.	" 8th, "	Schoolcraft, Mich.
Griffin, T.	Adjt.	55th U. S. C. T.	Ripley, Miss.	June 11th, 1864.	Pulaski, Ill.
Gore, J. B.	Lieut.	115th Ill. Vol.	Lookout M'tain, Tenn.	Sept. 24, 1863.	Taylorsville, Ill.
Gross, T.	"	21st Ill. Vol.	Chickamauga, Ga.	" 20th, "	Bement, Ill.
Gordon, G. C.	Capt.	24th Mich. Vol.	Gettysburg, Pa.	July 1st, "	Detroit, Mich.
Gerhardt, H.	Lieut.	24th Ill. Vol.	Chickamauga, Ga.	Sept. 20th, "	

APPENDIX.

Names.	Rank.	Regiment.	When captured.	Where captured.	Residence.
Gageby, J. H.	Lieut.	19th U. S. Inf.	Sept. 20th, 1863.	Chickamauga, Ga.	Johnstown, Pa.
Gutjahr, C.	Capt.	16th Ill. Vol.	May 12th, 1864.	Dalton, Ga.	
Galloway, ——	Lieut.	15th U S. Inf.	Sept. 20th, 1863.	Chickamauga, Ga.	Johnstown, Pa.
Grayham, P.	Capt.	54th Pa. Vol.	May 16th, 1864.	New Market, Va.	Ashland, Iowa.
Godley, M. L.	Lieut.	17th Iowa Vol.	Oct. 13th, "	Tilton, Ga.	
Gould, D.	Capt.	33d W. Va. Vol.	Sept. 12th, 1863.	Centreville, Va.	
Grey, W. H.	Lieut.	14th Ill. Cav.			Vandalia, Ill.
Gude, A.	Capt.	51st Ind. Vol.			Bruseville, Ind.
Glenn, S. A.	"	89th O. Vol.	" 20th, "	Chickamauga, Ga.	Hillsboro', O.
Grey, Philip	Lieut.	72d Pa. Vol.	May 9th, 1864.	Mattaponi River, Va.	
Huey, Pennock	Colonel.	8th Pa. Cav.	June 24th, 1864.	Samaria Ch., Va.	Westchester, Pa.
Hetsler, J. W.	Capt.	9th O. Cav.	Apr. 18th, "	Florence, Ala.	Calina, O.
Hicks, D. W.	Lieut.		" 20th	Plymouth, N. C	
Halsey, T. J.	Major.	11th N. J. Vol.	June 22d, "	Petersburg, Va.	Dover, N. J.
Hutchinson, J.	Lieut.	2d W. Va. Mt. Inf.	Sept. 24th, 1863.	Chattahoochie R., Ga.	Pittsburg, Pa.
Huffman, J. W.	"	5th Iowa Vol	Nov. 25th, "	Mission Ridge, Ga.	
Hinds, H. H.	"	57th Pa. Vol.	July 2d, "	Gettysburg, Pa.	Montrose, Pa.
Hagler, J. S.	Capt.	5th Tenn. Vol.	May 21st, "	East Tennessee.	
Helms, M. B.	Lieut.	1st W. Va. Vol.	Sept. 11th, "	Moorefield.	Rosbby's Rock, W. Va.
Hall, C. B.	"	"	" "	"	
Hallenburg, G.	Capt.	1st O. Vol.	" 20th, "	Chickamauga, Ga.	Louisville, Ky.
Hall, A. M.	"	9th Min. Vol.	June 12th, 1864.	Jackson, Miss.	
Haneley, T.	Capt.	79th Ill. Vol.	Sept. 19th, 1863.	Chickamauga, Ga.	Marshall, Ill.
Hubbard, H. R.	Lieut.	119th Ill. Vol.	Feb. 22d, 1864.	Mississippi.	
Huffman, J. W.	"	5th Iowa Vol.	Nov. 25th, 1863.	Mission Ridge, Pa.	Birmingham, Iowa.
Heffley, A.	Capt.	142d Pa. Vol.	July 1st, "	Gettysburg, Pa.	Berlin, Pa.
Hays, A. H.	"	7th Tenn. Cav.	Mar. 24th, 1864.	Union City, Tenn.	Lovington, Tenn.
Hare, T. H.	Lieut.	5th O. Cav.	Nov. 4th, 1863.	Waterloo, Tenn.	
Helm, J. B.	"	101st Pa. Vol	April 20th, 1864.	Plymouth, N. C.	Shellsburg, Pa.
Heffley, C. P.	"	142d Pa. Vol	July 1st, 1863.	Gettysburg, Pa.	Berlin, Pa.

APPENDIX. 339

Name	Rank	Regiment	Date	Place	Residence
Hubbell, F. A.	Lieut.	67th Pa. Cav.	June 15th, 1863.	Winchester, Va.	Honesdale, Pa.
Heffner, W.	"	"	"	"	Pottsville, Pa.
Harrington, B. F.	"	18th Pa. Cav.	" 18th, "	Germania Ford, Va.	Waynesburg, Pa.
Hart, E. R.	"	1st Vt. Art'y.	" 23d, 1864.	Petersburg, Va.	Hartford, Vt.
Hanson, J. B.	"	1st Mass. Art'y.	" "	"	Danvers, Mass.
Hodge, W. E.	"	5th Md. Vol.	" 15th, 1863.	Winchester, Va.	Baltimore, Md.
Hawkins, S. W.	"	7th Tenn. Cav.	Mar. 24th, 1864.	Union City, Tenn.	Huntingdon, Tenn.
Henry, C. D.	"	4th O. Cav.	Sept. 20th, 1863.	Chickamauga, Ga.	Tiffin City, O.
Hays, W. W.	"	34th O. Vol.	July 18th, "	Wytheville, W. Va.	
Hodge, J. F.	"	55th Pa. Vol.	May 16th, 1864.	Drury's Bluff, Va.	
Hall, R. F.	"	75th O. Vol.	Aug. 17th, "	Gainesville, Va.	Cincinnati, O.
Haight, J. T.	"	8th Iowa Cav.	July 31st, "	Newnan, Ga.	Tipton, Iowa.
Hastings, T. J.	"	15th Mass. Vol.	Jan. 22d, "	Petersburg, Va.	Wooster, Mass.
Hock, A.	Capt.	63d N. Y. Vol.	July 1st, 1863.	Gettysburg, Pa.	
Hill, G. W.	Lieut.	7th Mich. Cav.	May 16th, 1864.	Yellow Tavern, Va.	Detroit, Mich.
Heslit, J.	"	3d Pa. Cav.	Nov. 27th, 1863.	Parker's Store, Va.	Philadelphia, Pa.
Hazel, E. J.	"	6th Pa. Cav.	May 7th, 1864.	Todd's Tavern, Va.	Baltimore, Md.
Hanon, J.	"	115th Ill. Vol.	Sept. 20th, 1863.	Chickamauga, Ga.	Taylorsville, Ill.
Herrick, L. C.	"	1st N. Y. Cav.	Mar. 10th, 1864.	Charleston, Va.	Syracuse, N. Y.
Hine, J. J.	"	100th O. Vol.	Sept. 8th, 1863.	Tilton, Tenn.	
Herbert, R.	"	50th Pa. Vol.	May 12th, 1864.	Spottsylvania, Va.	Lebanon, Pa.
Harris, S.	"	5th Mich. Cav.	Mar. 2d, "	Richmond, Va.	
Heppard, T. H.	"	101st Pa. Vol.	Apr. 20th, "	Plymouth, N. C.	Philadelphia, Pa.
Hamilton, W.	"	2d Mass. Art'y.	" "	"	West Amesbury, Mass.
Hastings, G. L.	"	24th N. Y. Batl.	" "	"	Oswego, N. Y.
Horton, S. H.	"	101st Pa. Vol.	June 20th, "	Petersburg, Va.	
Huff, H. B.	Capt.	184th Pa. Vol.	" 22d, "	"	Altoona, Pa.
Hampton, C. G.	Lieut.	15th N. Y. Cav.	Feb. 20th, "	Upperville, Va.	Brockport, N. Y
Hurd, W. B.	"	170th Mich. Cav.	May 12th, "	Spottsylvania, Va.	Jackson, Mich.
Heil, J.	Capt.	45th N. Y. Cav.	July 1st, 1863.	Gettysburg, Pa.	New York City.
Hauf, N.	Lieut.				"
Hitt, W. R.	Capt.	113th Ill. Cav.	June 10th, 1864.	Brins Cr'ss Rds., Miss.	Urbana, O.

340 APPENDIX.

Names.	Rank.	Regiment.	When captured.	Where captured.	Residence.
Harris, W.	Capt.	24th Mo. Cav.	Mar. 24, 1864.	Union City, Tenn.	Mount Vernon, Mo.
Hobbie, C. A.	"	17th Conn. Cav.	May 19th, "	Wetatka, Fla.	Stamford, Conn.
Holden, E.	Lieut.	1st Vt. Cav.	Sept. 26th, "	Richard's Ford, Va.	Barre, Vt.
Hedges, S. P.	Adjt.	112th N. Y. Vol.	June 16th, "	Drury's Bluff, Va.	Jamestown, N. Y.
Hinds, H. C.	Lieut.	102d N. Y. Vol.	July 20th, "	Atlanta, Ga.	Richfield Springs, N. Y.
Hall, W. P.	Major.	6th N. Y. Cav.	June 8th, "	King Will'm's Co., Va.	Brooklyn, L. I.
Hart, R. K.	Capt.	19th U. S. Inf.	Sept. 20th, 1863.	Chickamauga, Ga.	
Hodge, A.	"	80th Ill. Vol.	May 3d, "	Rome, Ga.	Fosterbury, Ill.
Harvey, Wm. H.	Lieut.	51st Ind. Vol.	" "	"	
Hay, D.	Capt.	80th Ill. Vol.	" "	"	
Harmer, R. J.	Lieut.		" "	"	
Hart, C. M.	"	45th Pa. Vol.	Dec. 24th, "	Clinch Mt., Tenn.	Wellsboro', Pa.
Hopper, J.	"	2d N. Y. Cav.	June 22d, 1864.	Petersburg, Va.	
Hand, G. T.	"	51st Pa. Vol.	May 3d, 1863.	Rome, Ga.	Shelbyville, Ind.
Hartzog, R. H. O.	Capt.	1st N. Y. Cav.	Apr. 23d, 1864.	Shenandoah Val., Va.	New York City.
Hagler, J. S.	"	5th Tenn. Vol.	May 21st, 1863.	Morgan Co., Tenn.	
Hintz, H.	"	16th Conn. Vol.	Apr. 20th, 1864.	Plymouth, N. C.	Hartford, Conn.
Hunt, C. O.	Lieut.	5th Me. Bat'y.	June 18th, "	Petersburg, Va.	
Halpin, G.	"	116th Pa. Vol.	July 2d, 1863.	Gettysburg, Pa.	Philadelphia, Pa.
Hagenback, J. C.	"	67th Pa. Vol.	June 15th, "	Winchester, Va.	"
Hagan, P. A.	"	7th Md. Vol.	Oct. 19th, "	Haymarket, Va.	
Hulland, W. R.	"	5th Md. Cav.	July 31st, 1864.	Sunshine Ch., Va.	Coastbury, Ill.
Hawkins, H. E.	Capt.	78th Ill. Vol.	Sept. 22d, 1863.	Mission Ridge, Ga.	Tell City, Ind.
Heer, T. A.	"	28th O. Vol.	June 5th, 1864.	Newhope, Va.	
Hart, G. D.	"	5th Pa. Cav.	" 10th, "	Petersburg, Va.	
Hull, G. W.	Lieut.	135th O. Vol.	July 3d, "	North Mount, Ga.	
Hoyt, H. B.	Capt.	40th N. Y. Vol.	May 5th, "	Wilderness, Va.	Rochester, N. Y.
Hamilton, H. E.	Lieut.		" "	"	"
Hezelton, D. W.	"	22d N. Y. Cav.	June 29th, "	Stony Creek, Va.	Peterboro', N. Y.
Hovey, H.	"	78th Ill. Vol.	Sept. 22d, 1863.	Mission Ridge, Ga.	
Hume, D. J.	Capt.	19th Mass. Vol.	June 22d, 1864.	Petersburg, Va.	Boston, Mass.

Name	Rank	Regiment	Date	Place	Residence
Holaham, C. P.	Lieut.	19th Pa. Cav.	June 12th, 1864.	Ripley, Miss.	Philadelphia, Pa.
Hamilton, H. N.	"	59th N. Y. Vol.	" 22d, "	Petersburg, Va.	Belleville, O.
Hoppin, H. P.	"	2d Mass. Art'y.	Apr. 20th, "	Plymouth, N. C.	Cambridge, Mass.
Hutchison, E. S.	"	11th U. S. Inf.	June 2d, "	Mechanicsville, Va.	
Hutchison, R. C.	Capt.	8th Mich. Vol.	May 6th, "	Wilderness, Va.	
Hoyt, W. H.	Lieut.	16th Iowa Vol.	July 22d, "	Atlanta, Ga.	Camanche, Iowa.
Hart, P. H.	"	19th Ind. Vol.	Sept. 20th, 1863.	Chickamauga, Ga.	Edensburg, Ind.
Hughes, R. M.	"	14th Ill. Cav.	July 31st, 1864.	Sunshine Ch., Va.	Vandalia, Ill.
Hencldy, L. D.	"	10th Wis. Vol.	Sept. 20th, 1863.	Chickamauga, Ga.	Wanpan, Wis.
Harkness, R.	"	"	"	"	Elkhorn, Wis.
Hewitt, J.	Major.	105th Pa. Vol.	May 12th, 1864.	Spotsylvania, Va.	
Hastings, C. W.	Lieut.	12th Mass. Vol.	" 24th, "	North Anna Riv., Va.	Taylorsville, Pa.
Heston, J.	Capt.	4th N. J. Vol.	" 12th, "	Spotsylvania, Va.	Sing Sing, N. Y.
Hayes, E.	Capt.	95th N. Y. Vol.	" 6th, "	Wilderness, Va.	Mechanicsburg, Cumb'd. Co., Pa.
Heffelfinger, J.	Lieut.	7th P. R. V. Corps.	" 5th, "	"	
Harvey, J. L.	"	2d Pa. Art'y.	June 2d, "	Mechanicsville, Va.	Philadelphia, Pa.
Hobart, M. C.	Capt.	7th Wis. Vol.	May 5th, "	Wilderness, Va.	Fall River, Wis.
Hock, R. B.	"	12th N. Y. Cav.	Apr. 20th, "	Plymouth, N. C.	New York City.
Holman, W. C.	Lieut.	9th Vt. Vol.	Feb. 2d, "	Newport, N. C.	West Braintree, Vt.
Hadley, H. V.	"	7th Ind. Vol.	May 6th, "	Wilderness, Va.	Indianapolis, Ind.
Hall, C.	"	13th Wis. Cav.	Sept. 20th, 1863.	Chickamauga, Ga.	
Hayden, J. A.	Capt.	11th P. R. V. C'ps.	May 5th, 1864.	Wilderness, Va.	Union Town, Pa.
Hill, J. B.	Lieut.	17th Mass. Vol.	Feb. 17th, "	Newbern, N. C.	Averill, Mass.
Hallett, M. V. B.	"	2d Pa. Cav.	July 12th, "	Ream's Station, Va.	Osceola, Pa.
Hodge, W. L.	Capt.	120th Ill. Vol.	June 10th, "	North Mississippi.	Golconda, Ill.
Henry, A. J.	Lieut.	"	" 12th, "	Ripley, Miss.	
Hamlin, S. G.	Capt.	134th N. Y. Vol.	July 1st, 1863.	Gettysburg, Pa.	Glennville, N. Y.
Hoalladay, V. G.	Lieut.	2d Ind. Cav.	July 30th, 1864.	Carrolton, Ga.	Wintersett, Ind.
Havens, D.	"	85th Ill Vol.	" 19th, "	Peach-tree Creek, Ga.	Manito, Ill.
Hays, C. A.	"	111th Pa. Vol.	" 20th, "	Atlanta, Ga.	Eagle, Pa.
Hastings, J. L.	Adjt.	7th Pa. R. V. C'ps.	May 5th, "	Wilderness, Va.	Salona, Pa.

342   APPENDIX.

Names.	Rank.	Regiment.	When captured.	Where captured.	Residence.
Haines, H. A.	Capt.	184th Pa. Vol.	June 16th, 1864.	Petersburg, Va.	
Hunter, A. W.	Lieut.	2d U. S. Art'y, C'd.	Apr. 12th, "	Fort Pillow, Tenn.	New Hudson, Mich.
Harris, J. W.	"	2d Ind. Cav.	May 9th, "	Varnell, Ga.	Terre Haute, Ind.
Heltemus, J. B.	Capt.	18th Ky. Vol.	June 23d, "	Dalton, Ga.	
Herzbery, F.	Lieut.	66th N. Y. Vol.	" 17th, "	Petersburg, Va.	New York City.
Henry, J. M.	"	154th N. Y. Vol.	July 1st, 1863.	Gettysburg, Pa.	Olean, N. Y.
Harris, G.	"	79th Ind. Vol.	Sept. 20th, "	Chickamauga, Ga.	
Holt, W. C.	Capt.	6th Tenn. Vol.	Mar. 24th, 1864.	Beliar, Tenn.	Trenton, Tenn.
Harrison, C. E.	Lieut.	89th O. Vol.	Sept. 20th, 1863.	Chickamauga, Ga.	Higginsport, O.
Huey, R.	"	2d E. Tenn. Vol.	Nov. 6th, "	Rogerville, Tenn.	
*Henderson, J. H.	"	14th & 15th Ill. Vet. Batt.	Oct. 4th, 1864.	Acworth, Ga.	Greenfield, Ill.
Haight, J. T.	"	8th Iowa Cav.	July 30th, "	Newnan, Ga.	Tipton, Iowa.
Higley, E. H.	"	1st Vt. Cav.	June 29th, "	Stony Creek, Va.	Castleton, Vt.
Hendryks, W. H.	"	11th Mich. Batt'n.			
Hull, G. W.	"	135th O. Vol.	Sept. 12th, 1863.	Chickamauga, Ga.	Brownsville, O.
Hamilton, W. B.	"	22d Mich. Vol.	" 20th, "	"	Romeo, Mich.
Hendrick, F.	Capt.	1st N. Y. Cav.	June 15th, "	Winchester, Va.	New York City.
Huston, J.	Lieut.	95th O. Vol.	" 10th, 1864.	Tishamingo Cr., Miss.	Clayhick, O.
Henderson, R.	"	1st Mass. Art'y.	" 22d, "	Petersburg, Va.	Lawrence, Mass.
Howe, C. H.	"	21st Ill. Vol.	Sept. 20th, 1863.	Chickamauga, Ga.	
Haldeman, J.	"	129th Ill. Vol.			
Hefflefinger, J.	"	88th Ind. Vol.	Sept. 20th, "	Chickamauga, Ga.	Mechanicsburg, Pa.
Hymer, S.	Capt.	115th Ill. Vol.	Oct. 13th, 1864.	Mill Creek, Ga.	Rushville, Ill.
Hienrod, P.	"	105th Ill. Vol.	" 27th, "	Adairsville, Ga.	Waterford, Pa.
Hackett, A. N.	Lieut.	110th O. Vol.	July 9th, "	Monocacy, Md.	Massillon, O.
Huntley, C. C.	"	16th Ill. Cav.	Jan. 3d, "	Janesville, Va.	Huntley, Ill.
Hand, S. P.	"	43d U. S. C. T.	June 30th, "	Petersburg, Va.	Binghamton, N. Y.
Hurst, T. B.	"	7th Pa. Res. V. C.	May 5th, "	Wilderness, Va.	Dillsburg, Pa.
Hale, G. W.	"	101st O. Vol.	Sept. 19th, 1863.	Chickamauga, Tenn.	Upper Sandusky, O.
Hopf, Geo.	"	2d Md. Vol	July 3d, 1864.	Petersburg, Va.	Baltimore, Md.

APPENDIX. 343

Name	Rank	Regiment	Date	Place	Residence
Hescock, H.	Capt.	1st Mo. Arty.	Sept. 3d, 1863.	Chickamauga, Tenn.	St. Louis, Mo.
Hill, O. M.	Lieut.	23d U. S. C. T.	July 30th, 1864.	Petersburg, Va.	Orleans Co., N. Y.
Hall, C. T.	"	13th Mich. Vol.	Sept. 19th, 1863.	Chickamauga, Ga.	Battle Creek, Mich.
Heck, F. W.	Capt.&A.Q.	2d Md. Vol.	July 30th, 1864.	Petersburg, Va.	Baltimore, Md.
Hill, V. H.	Capt.&A.Q.M.U.S.V.		Oct. 14th, "	Atlanta, Ga.	Manchester, N. H.
Hogeland, D. B	Capt.	76th Pa. Vol.	July 11th, 1863.	Fort Wagner, S. C.	Mercer, Pa.
Hood, John	Lieut.	80th Ill. Vol.	May 3d, "	Rome, Ga.	
Hogue, J. B.	"	4th Pa. Cav.	July 30th, 1864.	Lewis Mills, Va.	
Holmes, A. J.	Capt.	37th Wis. Vol.	" 31st, "	Petersburg, Va.	
Haywood, L. E.	Lieut.	58th Mass. Vol.	" 30th, "	"	
Irwin, C. L.	Lieut.	78th Ill. Vol.	Sept. 22d, 1863.	Mission Ridge, Ga.	Columbus, Ill.
Irwin, S. E.	"	3d Iowa Vol.	July 2d, "	Jackson, Miss.	
Irwin, W. H.	Adjt.	103d Pa. Vol.	Apr. 20th, 1864.	Plymouth, N. C.	Alleghany City, Pa.
Imbric, J. M.	Capt.	3d O. Vol.	May 3d, 1863.	Rome, Ga.	Wellsville, O.
Isett, J. H.	Major.	8th Ind. Cav.	July 30th, 1864.	Newnan, Ga.	Wappello, Iowa.
Irsch, F.	Capt.	45th N. Y. Vol.	" 1st, 1863.	Gettysburg, Pa.	New York City.
Isham, A. B.	Lieut.	7th Mich. Cav.	May 11th, 1864.	Yellow Tavern, Va.	Detroit, Mich.
Ingledew, L.	Capt.&C.S.U. S.V.		" 24th, "	Kingston, Ga.	Janesville, Wis.
*Jackson, R. W.	Lieut.	21st Wis. Vol.	Sept. 20th, 1863.	Chickamauga, Ga.	Oshkosh, Wis.
Jenkins, J. H.	Adjt.	"	"	"	"
Johnson, H. A.	"	3d Me. Vol.	May 5th, 1864.	Wilderness, Va.	
James, H. H.	Lieut.	6th Ind. Cav.	Jan. 19th, "	Big Spa, Tenn.	
Jones, S. F.	Capt.	80th Ill. Vol.	May 3d, 1863.	Rome, Ga.	Montezuma, Ind.
Johnson, G.	Lieut.	16th Conn. Vol.	Apr. 20th, 1864.	Plymouth, N. C.	Jones's Creek, Ill.
Judd, J. H.	"	27th Mass. Vol.	May 16th, "	Drury's Bluff, Va.	Hartford, Conn.
Jacobs, J. W.	Capt.	4th Ky. Vol.	July 31st, "	Fayetteville, Ga.	East Hampton, Mass.
John, E. P.	Lieut.	135th O. Vol.	" 3d "	Northwest Virginia.	
Johnson, J. C.	Capt.	149th Pa. Vol.	" 2d, 1863.	Gettysburg, Pa.	Couder's Port, Pa.
Jobe, B. A.	"	11th Pa. R. V. C.	May 30th, 1864.	Cold Harbor, Va.	Salem Cross Roads, Pa.

Names.	Rank.	Regiment.	When captured.	Where captured.	Residence.
Johnson, V. W.	Lieut.	10th N. Y. Cav.	Oct. 14th, 1863.	Auburn, Va.	Wolcott, N. Y.
Jones, J. A.	"	21st Ill. Vol.	Sept. 20th, "	Chickamauga, Ga.	Olney, Ill.
Johnson, C. K.	"	1st Me. Cav.	June 24th, 1864.	Samaria Ch., Va.	Carmel, Me.
Jemmings, J. T.	Capt.	75th O. Vol.	Nov. 15th, 1863.	Knoxville, Tenn.	Kenton, O.
Jones, D.	"	14th N. Y. Art'y.	June 14th, 1864.	Petersburg, Va.	Utica, N. Y.
Judson, S. C.	"	106th N. Y. Vol.	May 6th, "	Wilderness, Va.	Ogdensburg, N. Y.
Jenkins, H.	"	40th Mass. Vol.	" 16th, "	Drury's Bluff, Va.	
Jackson, C. G.	"	84th Pa. Vol.	" 6th, "	Wilderness, Va.	Berwick, Pa.
Jones, J. P.	Lieut.	55th O. Vol.	July 2d, 1863.	Gettysburg, Pa.	Norwalk, O.
Jenkins, G. W.	"	9th W. Va. Vol.	May 9th, 1864.	Cloyd's Mt., W. Va.	Portland, O.
Jones, C. W.	"	16th Pa. Cav.			Duncannon, Pa.
Justus, J. C.	"	2d Pa. R. V. C.	May 24th, "	North Anna Riv., Va.	Philadelphia, Pa.
Jackson, J. C.	"	4th Ind. Cav.			Oshkosh, Wis.
Jackson, J. S.	"	22d Ill. Vol.	Apr. 19th, 1863.	Chickamauga, Ga.	Salem, Ill.
Jones, S. E.	"	7th N. Y. Art'y.	June 16th, 1864.	Petersburg, Va.	
Jones, H.	"	5th U. S. Cav.	Oct. 29th, 1863.	Elk Run, Va.	
Jones, W.	"	38th O. Vol.	" 19th, 1864.	Rough & R'd'y Sta., Ga.	Charles, O.
Jones, M. J.	Capt.	115th Ill. Vol.	" 13th, "	Dalton, Ga.	Rushville, Ill.
Johnson, R.	Lieut.	6th N. Y. Cav.	June 25th, 1863.	Gainesville, Va.	Ogdensburg, N. Y.
Johnson, J. W.	1st Mass. Art'y.		" 22d, 1864.	Petersburg, Va.	Methuen, Mass.
Johnson, W. N.	Army Correspondent.		" 13th, "	Staunton, Va.	
Jones, Alfred	Lt.&R.Q.M.	50 Pa. Vet. Vol.	July 30th, "	Petersburg, Va.	Reading, Pa.
Johnson, J. D.	Capt.	10th N. J. Vol.	May 7th, "	Wilderness, Va.	Hainesport, N. J.
Jordan, E. C.	Lieut.	7th Conn. Vol.	July 11th, 1863.	Fort Wagner, S. C.	Bridgeport, Conn.
Jacks, J.	"	15th W. Va. Vol.	" 18th, 1864.	Scrickus Ferry, Va.	
Kelly, D. O.	"	100th O. Vol.	Sept. 8th, 1863.	Limestone, Tenn.	Kelly's Island, O.
Krohn, P.	"	5th N. Y. Cav.	June 1st, 1864.	Ashland, Va.	Oswego, N. Y.
Keeler, A. M.	Capt.	22d Mich. Vol.	Sept. 20th, 1863.	Chickamauga, Ga.	Disco, Mich.
Kendall, T.	Lieut.	15th U. S. Inf.	" "	"	Brooklyn, N. Y.

Keniston, J.	Lieut.	100th Ill. Vol.	Sept. 20th, 1863.	Chickamauga, Ga.	Joliet, Ill.
Keith, C. E.	"	19th Ill. Vol.	"	"	Chicago, Ill.
Knowles, E. M.	"	42d Ind. Vol.	"	"	
Kreuger, W.	"	2d Mo. Vol.	"	"	
Kreps, F. A. M.	"	77th Pa. Vol.	"	"	
Kane, S.	Capt.	38th Ind. Vol.	"	"	
Kelly, D. A.	Adjt.	1st Ky. Vol.	Nov. 14th, 1863.	East Tennessee.	New York City.
Kendrick, E.	Lieut.	10th N. J. Vol.	May 14th, 1864.	Falling Waters, Va.	Salineville, O.
Kerr, S. C.	Adjt.	126th O. Vol.	" 6th, "	Wilderness, Va.	Reading, Pa.
Kendall, H. T.	Lieut.	50th Pa. Vol.	" 7th, "	"	Barnesville, O.
Kelly, A.	"	126th O. Vol.	" 6th, "	"	Bart, Pa.
Keen, J.	"	7th Pa. V. R. C.	" 5th, "	"	
Kuchin, A.	"	5th Md. Vol.	June 15th, 1863.	Winchester, Va.	
Kees, G. W.	"	18th Conn. Vol.	"	"	Broadheadsville, Pa.
Kreiger, A.	"	67th Pa. Vol.	"	"	
Knowles, R. A.	"	116th O. Vol.	"	"	
Knapp, F. H.	"	9th O. Cav.	Apr. 12th, 1864.	Florence, Ala.	Piqua, O.
Kennuly, J. D.	"	8th O. Cav.	June 19th, "	Liberty, Ga.	Trimble, Athens, O.
Kempton, J. F.	"	75th O. Vol.	Aug. 17th, "	Gainesville, Fla.	
Kline, D. J.	"	"	"	"	
Kennedy, J. W.	"	134th N. Y. Vol.	July 1st, 1863.	Gettysburg, Pa.	New York City.
Kankel, E.	"	45th N. Y. Vol.	"	"	Baltimore, Md.
Kandler, H.	Capt.	1st Md. Art'y.	June 21st, 1864.	Salem, Va.	Port Deposit, Md.
Kidd, J. H.	Lieut.	25th Wis. Vol.	July 22d, "	Decatur, Ga.	Potosi, Wis.
Kendrick, R. H.	"	17th Ill. Vol.	Aug. 17th, "	Cedar Creek, Ky.	
Kenyon, G. C.	"	113th Pa. Vol.	June 10th, "	Tishamingo Cr., Miss.	Danton, Ill.
Kidder, G. C.	"	118th Pa. Vol.	"	Mechanicsville, Va.	
Kelly, H. K.	Capt.	109th Pa. Vol.	July 20th, "	Atlanta, Ga.	Philadelphia, Pa.
Knox, G.	Lieut.	4th Tenn. Vol.	" 30th, "	Newnan, Ga.	Athens, Tenn.
Kelly, J. M.	Capt.	2d Ind. Cav.	"	"	
Kessler, J. G.	Lieut.	3d N. Y. Art'y.	Feb. 2d, "	Newbern, N. C.	
Kirby, W. M.					

Names.	Rank.	Regiment.	When captured.	Where captured.	Residence.
King, T.	L. Q. M.	101st Pa. Vol.	Apr. 20th, 1864.	Plymouth, N. C.	Bradford, Pa.
Keister, W. H. H.	Lieut.	103d Pa. Vol.	"	"	Hillsville, Pa.
Kirk, J. B.	"	101st Pa. Vol.	"	"	"
Krause, J.	Capt.	3d Pa. Art'y.			
Kempton, F. H.	Lieut.	58th Mass. Art'y.	July 30th, "	Petersburg, Va.	Ft. Monroe, Va.
Kennits, H.	"	2d Mass. Vol.	"	"	
Kautz, J. D.	"	1st Ky. Cav.	Sept. 10th, 1863.	Graysville, Va.	Dent, O.
Kellogg, H.	"	6th Mich. Cav.	July 14th, "	Falling Waters, Va.	
Kronemeyer, C.	Capt.	52d N. Y. Vol.	May 8th, "	Spotsylvania, Va.	Williamsburg, N. Y
King, M. D.	Lieut.	3d O. Vol.	" 3d, "	Rome, Ga.	Barnesville, O.
Kendall, J.	Capt.	43d Ind. Vol.			
King, G. E.	"	103d Ill. Vol.	June 10th, 1864.	Brie's Cross Rds., Tenn.	Middleport, Ill.
Knight, H. B.	Lieut.	20th Mich. Vol.	May 3d, 1863.	Horse-shoe Bend, Ky.	
Kelly, J. R.	"	1st Pa. Cav.	June 24th, 1864.	Samaria Ch., Va.	Patterson, Pa.
Kirkpatrick, G. W.	"	15th Iowa Vol.	Feb. 27th, "	Canton, Miss.	Smyrna, Iowa.
Knox, J. C.	"	4th Ind. Cav.	May 9th, "	Varnell, Ga.	Ladoga, Ind.
Kepheart, J. S.	"	5th Ind. Vol.	" 18th, 1863.	Marabone, Ky.	Franklin, Ind.
Kerin, J.	"	6th U. S. Cav.	June 9th, "	Bradley Sta., Va.	Washington, D. C.
Kenyon, P. D.	Capt.	14th & 15th Ill. V. Batt.	Oct. 4th, 1864.	Acworth, Ga.	Mt. Carroll, Ind.
King, Abe	Lieut.	12th O. V. Inf.	May 8th, "	Cloyd's House, Va.	Xenia, O.
King, John	"	15th Ill. Cav.	" 3d, 1863.	Rome, Ga.	Geneva, Ill.
Kissam, Edgar	Capt.	9th N. J. Vol.			Jersey City, N. J.
Kepheart, J.	Lieut.	13th O. Vol.	July 30th, 1864.	Petersburg, Va.	Russell Sta., O.
Kellow, J.	"	2d Pa. Art'y.	"	"	Honesdale, Pa.
Kibby, G. L.	"	4th R. I. Vol.	"	"	Providence, R. I.
Kendale, W. M.	Major.	73d Ind. Vol.	May 3d, 1863.	Rome, Ga.	Plymouth, Ind.
Kost, R.	Lieut.	6th Conn. Vol.	July 8th, "	Fort Wagner, S. C.	Bridgeport, Conn.
Kenfield, F.	Capt.	17th Vt. Vol.	July 30th, 1864.	Petersburg, Va.	Morristown, Vt.
King, John	Lieut.	6th Conn. Vol.	" 18th, 1863.	Fort Wagner, S. C.	New Haven, Conn.
Kings, S. B.	Capt.	12th Pa. Cav.			

APPENDIX. 347

Lindemeyer, L.	Capt.	45th N. Y. Vol.		New York City.
Lamson, A. T.	Lieut.	104th N. Y. Vol.	July 1st, 1863.	Genesee, N. Y.
Litchfield, J. B.	Capt.	4th Me. Vol.	" 2d, "	
Lombard, H. G.	Adjt.	4th Mich. Vol.	" 1st, "	
Logan, W. S.	Capt.	17th Mich. Vol.	Gettysburg, Pa.	Richland, Mich.
Love, J. E.	"	8th Kansas Vol	May 12th, 1864.	Spottsylvania, Va.	St. Louis, Mo.
Lucas, John	"	5th Ky. Vol.	Sept. 19th, 1863.	Chickamauga, Ga.	
Lovett, L. T.	"	"	" "		
Lodge, G. R.	Lieut.	53d Ill. Vol.	July 12th, "	Jackson, Miss.	Ottawa, Ill.
Lucas, W. D.	Capt.	5th N. Y. Cav.	" 6th, "	Hagerstown, Md.	East Gainesville, N. Y.
Little, J. S.	"	143d Pa. Vol.	May 5th, 1864.	Wilderness, Va.	Nicholson, Pa.
Lowis, C. E.	Lieut.	1st N. Y. Drag.	" 7th, "	Todd's Tavern, Va.	Nunda, N. Y.
Laycock, J. B.	"	7th Pa. R. V. C.	" 5th, "	Wilderness, Va.	
Lyman, H. H.	"	147th N. Y. Vol.	" "		Pulaski, N. Y.
Larrabee, W. H	"	7th Me. Vol.	" 6th, "		Portland, Me.
Lanning, A.	Sergeant.	24th Mich. Vol.	" 5th, "		Nankin, Mich.
Leigh, S. J.	Lt.& A.D.C.				
Lee, A.	Lieut.	152d N. Y. Vol.	June 22d, "	Petersburg, Va.	Utica, N. Y.
Lynch, C. M.	Major.	145th Pa. Vol.	" "		Erie, Pa.
Lynn, J. L.	Lieut.	"	" 16th, "		West Greenville, Pa.
Lyttle, C. W.	Capt.	"	" "		Nicholson, Pa.
Lond, E. De C.	Lieut.	2d Pa. Art'y.	" 27th, "		Philadelphia, Pa.
Ludweg, M. S.	"	53d Pa. Vol.	" 22d, "		"
Lewry, D. W.	"	2d Pa. Art'y.	" "		"
Longnecker, J. H.	Adjt.	101st Pa. Vol.	July 1st, "		Woodbury, Pa.
Landen, H.	Lieut.	16th Conn. Vol.	Apr. 20th, "	Plymouth, N. C.	
Laughlin, J. M.	"	103d Pa. Vol.	" "		Callensburg, Pa.
Langworthy, D. A.	Capt.	85th N. Y. Vol.	" "		New York City.
Lafler, J. A.	Lieut.	"	" "		Penn Yan, N.Y.
Lyman, J.	"	27th Mass. Vol.	May 16th, "	Drury's Bluff, Va.	East Hampton, Mass.
Laird, J. O.	"	35th U. S. Inf.	" 23d, "	Florida, N. C.	
Litchfield, A. C.	Lieut. Col.	7th Mich. Cav.	Mar. 1st, "	Atley's Sta., Va.	Grand Rapids, Mich.

348   APPENDIX.

Names.	Rank.	Regiment.	When captured.	Where captured.	Residence.
Lyon, W. C.	Lieut.	23d O. Vol.	Feb. 3d, 1864.	Kanawha, W. Va.	Leeville, O.
Lintz, W. J.	"	8th Tenn. Vol.	Oct. 6th, 1863.	Norristown, Tenn.	
Leslee, J. L.	"	18th Pa. Cav.	Aug. 11th, "	Stafford C. H., Va.	Titusville, Pa.
Leonard, A.	"	71st N. Y. Vol.	Oct. 11th, "	Brandy Sta., Va.	
Laird, M.	"	16th Iowa Vol.	July 22d, 1864.	Atlanta, Ga.	Desmoine Town, Iowa.
Luther, J. C.	"	1st Pa. V. R. C.	May 30th, "	Cold Harbor, Va.	Ridgeway, Pa.
Lemon, M. W.	"	14th N. Y. Art'y.	June 2d, "	"	Canton, N. Y.
Lane, L. M.	"	9th Min. Vol.	" 12th, "	Ripley, Miss.	
Lamson, T. D.	"	3d Ind. Cav.	" 29th "	Stony Creek, Va.	Venny, Ind.
Loomis, A. W.	"	18th Conn. Vol.	" 15th, 1863.	Winchester, Va.	Tolland, Conn.
Locke, W. H.	"	"	"	"	Willimantic, Conn.
Lindsy, A. H.	"	"	"	"	Greenville, Conn.
Leith, S.	"	132d N. Y. Vol.	Feb. 20th, 1864.	North Carolina.	Frederick City, Md.
Long, C. H.	"	1st Md. Vol.	June 29th, "	Duffield's Dépôt, Va.	Waterbury, Vt.
Lewis, D. B.	"	12th Pa. Cav.			Union Town, Pa.
Livingston, C. H.	"	1st W. Va. Cav.	July 18th, 1863.	Wytheville, Va.	Ellenboro', W. Va.
Law, G.	Capt.	6th W. Va. Cav.	June 26th, 1864.	Springfield, Va.	Boston, Mass.
Loyd, J. K.	"	17th Mass. Vol.	Feb. 17th, "	Newbern, N. C.	Bantam, O.
Leeds, M. A.	Lieut. Col.	153d O. Vol.	July 3d, "	Winchester, Va.	Newport, Ky.
Lock, D. R	Lieut.	8th Ky. Cav.	Aug. 3d, 1863.	Elkton, Ky.	Delphos, O.
Limbard, A.	"	McLaughlin's Sqn.	" 3d, 1864.	Jug Tavern, Ga.	Terre Haute, Ind.
Lloyd, T. S. C.	"	6th Ind. Cav.	Jan. 19th, "	Big Spa, Tenn.	Buffalo, N. Y.
Lawrence, G. H.	"	2d N. Y. Mounted Rifles.	June 2d, "	Cold Harbor, Va.	
Laud, J. R.	Capt.	66th Ind. Vol.	Oct. 11th, 1863.	Colliersville, Tenn.	Leavenworth, Ind.
Lee, E. N.	"	5th Mich. Cav.	" 19th, "	Buckland Mills, Va.	
Larkin, F. A.	Lieut.	18th Ind. Vol.	June 4th, "	Edward's Dépôt,Miss.	
Locklin, A. W.	"	94th N. Y. Vol.	July 1st, "	Gettysburg, Pa.	Great Bend, N. Y.
Lang, C. H.	"	59th Mass. Vol.	" 30th, 1864.	Petersburg, Va.	Reading, Mass.
Latimer, E. C.	Capt.	27th U. S. C. T.	"	"	Canton, O.
Lenter, A. P.	"	2d Tenn. Inf.			

APPENDIX. 349

Name	Rank	Regiment	Battle	Date	Residence
Myers, T.	Lieut.	107th Pa. Vol.	Gettysburg, Pa.	July 1st, 1863.	Chambersburg, Pa.
Mooney, J.	"	"	"	"	Dushore, Pa.
Mussel, O.	Capt.	68th N. Y. Vol.	"	"	
Millis, V.	Lieut.	"	"	"	
Mosely, H. H.	"	25th O. Vol.	"	"	Summerfield, O.
Makepeace, A. I.	Capt.	19th Ind. Vol.	"	"	Anderson, Ind.
McDade, A.	Lieut.	154th N. Y. Vol.	"	"	Westfield, N. Y.
Murphy, F.	Capt.	97th N. Y. Vol.	"	"	Salisbury Centre, N. Y.
Moran, F.	Lieut.	73d N. Y. Vol.	"	" 3d, 1863.	New York City.
Mendenhall, J. A.	"	75th N. Y. Vol.	"	" 2d, "	Ringgold, O.
Mell, J. R.	"	61st N. Y. Vol.	"	" 1st, "	Deerfield, O.
Morres, W. J.	"	5th Md. Vol.	Winchester, Va.	June 15th, "	Baltimore, Md.
Metta, J. S.	"				
Merwin, S. T. C.	"	18th Conn. Vol.			Norwich, Conn.
Madera, W. B.	"	6th W. Va. Vol.			Morgantown, W. Va.
Meany, D. B.	Capt.	13th Pa. Cav.		Apr. 8th, 1864.	Philadelphia, Pa.
Matherson, E. J.	Lieut.	18th Conn. Vol.		June 15th, 1863.	Dison, Conn.
McKeag, F.	Lieut.			"	Norwich, Conn.
Morningstar, H.	"	87th Pa. Vol.		"	Hanover, Pa.
Manning, J. S.	"	116th O. Vol.		"	
Mash, P.	Capt.	67th Pa. Vol.		"	Scranton, Pa.
McNeal, D.	Lieut.	13th Pa. Cav.		"	
Matson, C. C.	Lieut. Col.	6th Ind. Cav.	Atlanta, Ga.	Aug. 7th, 1864.	Greencastle, Ind.
McCarty, W. W.	Capt.	18th O. Vol.	"	July 22d, "	McConnellsville, O.
Morgan, C. H.	Lieut.	21st Wis. Vol.	Chickamauga, Tenn.	Sept. 20th, 1863.	Oshkosh, Wis.
McGruder, W. H.	"		"	"	
McDowal, J. S.	Capt.	77th Pa. Vol.	"	Sept. 19th, "	Ft. Little, Pa.
Moses, H.	Lieut.	4th Ky. Vol.	"	" 20th, "	
Morrison, M. V. B.	"	33d O. Vol.	"	"	Chilicothe, O.
McKinson, A. H.	"	10th Wis. Vol.	"	"	Pine Hill, Wis.
Meael, L. C.	"	22d Mich. Vol.	"	"	Ann Arbor, Mich.
McKercher, D.	Colonel.	10th Wis. Vol.	"	"	New Lisbon, Wis.

350 APPENDIX.

Names.	Rank.	Regiment.	When captured.	Where captured.	Residence.
Mathews, A. S.	Adjt.	22d Mich. Vol.	Sept. 20th, 1863.	Chickamauga, Tenn.	Pontiac, Mich.
McGowan, E.	Lieut.	29th Ind. Vol.	" 19th, "	"	Newark, N. J.
Murphy, J.	"	16th U. S. Inf.	" "	"	
Mitchell, J.	"	79th Ill. Vol.	" "	"	
McCune, A. W.	"	2d O. Vet. Vol.	" 20th, "	"	Woodburn, Ill.
Muhlemen, J. R.	Major & A. A. Gen.				
McNeil, S.	Lieut.	51st O. Vol.	" "	"	Spring Mountain, O.
Metcalf, C. W.	Capt.	42d Ind. Vol.	" "	"	Dale, Ind.
Messick, J. M.	Lieut.		" "	"	Evansville, Ind.
Mackey, J. T.	"	16th U. S. Inf.	" 19th, "	"	Dallas City, Ill.
Mahoney, J. S.	"	21st O. Vol.	" 20th, "	"	Prairie Dépôt, O.
Mead, W. H.	"	6th Ky. Cav.	" "	"	
Moore, M.	Capt.	29th Ind. Vol.	" "	"	
Moore, G. W.	"	7th Tenn. Vol.	Mar. 24th, 1864.	Union City, Tenn.	Lovington, Tenn.
McConalee, W. J.	Lieut.	14th Iowa Cav.	Jan. 20th, 1863.	Vicksburg, Miss.	Wintersett, Iowa.
Morton, J. W.	Capt.	4th Mass. Cav.	Aug. 17th, 1864.	Gainesville, Fla.	
Malambre, J. M.	Lieut.	75th O. Vol.	" "	"	Dayton, O.
Morse, E.	Major.	78th Ill. Vol.	Sept. 22d, 1863.	Mission Ridge, Tenn.	Macomb, Ill.
Marshall, W. S.	Lieut.	5th Iowa Vol.	Nov. 25th, "	"	
McGovern, J.	"	75th Pa. Vol.	" "	"	
McKinley, J.	"	98th O. Vol.	Sept. 22d, "	"	
McNiece, A.	"	73d Pa. Vol.	Nov. 25th, "	"	
Mann, G.	"	80th O. Vol.	" "	"	
Moore, F.	"	73d Pa. Vol.	" "	"	
Mooney, A. H.	Capt.	16th N. Y. Cav.	Apr. 16th, 1864.	Fairfax, Va.	Plattsburg, N. Y.
McHugh, J.	"	69th Pa. Vol.	June 22d, "	Petersburg, Va.	Philadelphia, Pa.
McFadden, W. M.	"	59th N. Y. Vol	" "	"	
Monaghan, J.	Lieut.	62d Pa. Vol.	" "	"	New York City.
McIntosh, J. C.	"	145th Pa. Vol.	" 16th, "	"	Erie, Pa.
Mather, F. W.	"	7th N. Y. Art'y.	" "	"	Albany, N. Y.

APPENDIX. 351

McCray, H.	Capt.	115th Pa. Vol.	June 22d, 1864.	Petersburg, Va.	Albany, N. Y.
Mockrie, P. B.	Lieut.	7th N. Y. Art'y.	"	"	Albany, N. Y.
May, J.	Capt.	15th Mass. Art'y.	"	"	Gowanda, N. Y.
Moore, N. H.		7th N. Y. Art'y.			Rochester, Vt.
McCutcheon, E. T.	Lieut.	64th N. Y. Vol.	" 17th, "	"	Erie, Pa.
McWain, E. J.		1st N. Y. V. Art'y.	" 23d, "	"	Candia, N. H.
McCreary, D. B.	Lieut. Col.	145th Pa. Vol.	" 16th, "	"	Hollidaysburg, Pa.
Murry, S. F.	Capt.	2d U. S. S. S.	" 21st, "	"	Howard, Pa.
McKage, J.	"	184th Pa. Vol.	" 22d, "	"	Winfield, Pa.
Muffley, S. F.	Adjt.	"	"	"	James's Creek, Pa.
Mangus, H. F.	Lieut.	53d Pa. Vol.	" 16th, "	"	Boston, Mass.
McLauglin, J.	"	"	"	"	Brownington, Vt.
McGinnes, W. A.	"	19th Mass. Vol.	" 22d, "	"	Fayetteville, Vt.
Mathews, A. D.	"	1st Vt. Art'y.	" 23d, "	"	York, Pa.
Morse, A.	"	"	"	"	
Maish, L.					
McQuiddy, ——.	Capt.	87th Pa. Vol.	May 3d, 1863.	Rome, Ga.	Indianapolis, Ind.
Marshall, W. S.	"	5th Tenn. Cav.	"	"	
McDill, H.	Adjt.	51st Ind. Cav.	"	"	Springfield, O.
Maxwell, C. A.	Lieut.	80th Ill. Vol.	"	"	
Mall, D. H.	Capt.	3d O. Vol.	"	"	La Porte, Ind.
Munday, J. W.	Lieut.	73d Ind. Vol.	"	"	Logansport, Ind.
Murdock, H. S.	"	"	"	"	Adriance, Ind.
McHolland, D. A.	Capt.	"	"	"	
Morey, H.	Lieut.	10th N. Y. Cav.	Oct. 12th, 1863.	Sulphur Spa, Va	Georgetown, O.
McColgin, J.	"	7th O. Cav.	Nov. 6th,	Rodgersville, Tenn.	
Morris, J. H.	"	4th Ky. Vol.	July 30th, 1864.	Georgia.	
McLernan, P.	Major.	22d N. Y. Cav.	June 29th, "	Ream's Station, Va.	Memphis, N. Y.
Mattock, C. P.	Lieut.	17th Mc. Vol.	May 5th, "	Wilderness, Va.	
Myers, W. H.	"	76th N. Y. Vol.	"	"	Cortland, N. Y.
McIeehan, J.		146th N. Y. Vol.			Brooklyn, N. Y.
Miller, F. C.	Colonel.	147th N. Y. Vol.			Oswego, N. Y.

APPENDIX.

Names.	Rank.	Regiment.	When captured.	Where captured.	Residence.
Mitchell, H. W.	Lieut.	14th N. Y. Vol.	May 5th, 1864.	Wilderness, Va.	Meadville, Pa.
Mallison, A. C.	Capt.	12th N. J. Vol.	"	"	
Morrisy, G. H.	R. Q. M.	12th Iowa Vol.	July 11th, 1863.	Jackson, Miss.	Philadelphia, Pa.
McKay, D. S.	Lieut.	18th Pa. Cav.	Sept. 13th, "	Culpepper, Va.	Hoboken, N. J.
Mayer, L.	"	12th Pa. Cav.	June 19th "	Point of Rocks, Md.	
Merritt, H. A. D.	"	5th N. Y. Cav.	Mar. 3d, 1864.	Stevensville, Va.	
Metzger, J.	Capt.	55th Pa. Vol.	May 16th, "	Drury's Bluff, Va.	Fremont, O.
Moore, Le Roy	"	72d O. Vol.	June 12th, "	Salem, Miss.	Logansport, Ind.
McCain, J. C.	Lieut.	9th Minn. Vol.	" 17th, "	Ripley, Miss.	"
McKee, T. H.	Capt.	1st W. Va. Vol.	Sept. 10th, 1863.	Moorefield, Va.	St. Charles, Ill.
McGuire, T.	"	7th Ill. Vol.	May 7th, 1864.	Florence, Ala.	Lincoln, Ill.
Miller, J. W	Lieut.	14th Ill. Cav.	July 31st, "	Sunshine Ch., Ga.	Newark, N. J.
Murphy, J.	"	69th N. Y. Vol.	June 3d, "	Cold Harbor, Va.	Brandon, Wis.
Mallison, J.	"	4th N. Y. Vol.	" 6th, "	"	
Moulton, O.	Lieut. Col.	25th Mass. Vol.	" 3d, "	"	
Morgan, S. M.	Capt. & A. A. Gen.		" 30th, "	"	Lindy, N. Y.
McGraylis, M.	Capt.	93d Ind. Vol.	" 12th, "	Salem, Miss.	Franklin, O.
Morgan, Benj. B.	Lieut. Col.	75th O. Vol.	Aug. 19th, "	Newnansville, Fla.	Biddeford, Me.
Mullegan, J. A.	Lieut.	4th Mass. Cav.	" 17th "	Gainesville, Fla.	Moravia, N. Y.
Mead, S.	Capt.	111th N. Y. Vol.	Dec. 7th, 1863.	Mine Run, Va.	Rimersburg, Pa
McCall, O.	Lieut.	103d Pa. Vol.	Apr. 20th, 1864.	Plymouth, N. C.	Bedford, Pa.
Mullin, D. W.	Capt.	101st Pa. Vol.	"	"	
Morrow, J. M.	Lieut.		"	"	
McHeney, C.	"	85th N.Y.Vet.Vol.	"	"	East Bloomfield, N. Y.
Miller, W. G.	"	16th Conn. Vol.	"	"	
Mackey, J. F.	Capt.	103d Pa. Vol.	"	"	Clarion, Pa.
Morrow, J. J.	"	"	"	"	Plumville, Pa.
Mathews, W. F.	Lieut.	1st Md. Vol.	June 25th, 1864.	Duffield, Va.	Martinsburg, W. Va.
Merrill, H. P.	Capt.	4th Ky. Vol.	July 29th, "	Jonesboro', Ga.	
Menier, N. J.	Lieut.	93d Ind. Vol.	Aug. 11th, "	Salem, Miss.	Leopold, Ind.

APPENDIX.

Name	Rank	Regiment	Date	Place	Residence
McDonald, H. J.	Capt.	11th Conn. Vol.	May 16th, 1864.	Drury's Bluff, Va.	Kingston, N. J.
Moodey, J. E.	Lieut.	59th Mass. Vol.	June 15th, "	Chickahominy, Va.	Newburyport, Mass.
Martin, J. C.	Capt.	1st Tenn. Cav.	Nov. 6th, 1863.	Rodgersville, Tenn.	
Melkorn, M.	"	135th O. Vol.	July 7th, 1863.	Maryland H'ghts, Md.	Ada, O.
Moon, R. A.	Lieut.	6th Mich. Cav.	Oct. 12th, 1863.	Charlestown, Va.	Big Rapids, Mich.
Moore, M. M.	"	"	" 18th, "	"	
Manley, J. A.	Capt.	64th N. Y. Vol.	May 12th, 1864.	Spottsylvania, Va.	Detroit, Mich.
Miller, H.	Lieut.	17th Mich. Vol.	"	"	Davenport, Iowa.
McManus, P. W.	Adjt.	27th Mass. Vol.	" 16th, "	Drury's Bluff, Va.	Allegany Bridge, Pa.
Moses, C. C.	Capt.	58th Pa. Vol.	July 6th, 1863.	Washington, N. C.	
Mudgett, A. G.	"	11th Me. Vol	June 2d, 1864.	Drury's Bluff, Va.	Newburgh, Me.
McMahon, E.	Lieut.	72d O. Vol.	" 15th, "	Salem, Miss.	
McKinstry, J.	"	16th Ill. Cav.	Jan. 3d, "	Jonesville, Va.	Mattoon, Ill.
McEvoy, W.	Adjt.	3d Ill. Vol	Aug. 15th, 1863.	Oxford, Miss.	
McBeth, N.	Lieut.	45th O. Vol.	Nov. 15th, "	Knoxville, Tenn.	Zanesfield, O.
Merry, W. A.	"	106th N. Y. Vol.	June 10th, "	Hagerstown, Md.	Ogdensburg, N. Y.
Marney, A.	Capt.	2d Tenn. Vol.	Nov. 6th, "	Rodgersville, Tenn.	Kingston, Tenn.
Moore, D. T.	Lieut.	"	"	"	Clinton, Tenn.
Morton, G. C.	"	4th Pa. Cav.	June 11th, 1864.	Trevillian Station, Va.	
McKay, R. G.	"	5th Mich. Cav.	Sept. 23d, 1863.	Robinson River, Va.	
Molton, H.	"	1st U. S. Cav.	June 21st, "	Uppersville, Va.	
Montgomery, R. H.	"	5th U. S. Cav.	Oct. 29th, "	Elk Run, Va.	
Marrow, H. C.	A. Engineer U. S. N.		May 7th, 1864.	James River, Va.	Baltimore, Md.
Morgan, J. T.	Capt.	17th Mich. Vol.	Nov. 16th, 1863.	Campbell's Station, Va.	Ypsilanti, Mich.
Manning, G. A.	"	2d Mass. Cav.	Feb. 22d, 1864.	London Valley, Va.	Oldtown, Md.
Mather, E.	Lieut.	1st Vt. Cav.	June 1st, "	Ashley, Va.	Fair Haven, Vt.
McDonald, C.	"	2d Ill. Art'y.	" 7th, "	Big Shanty, Ga.	Tamaroa, Ill.
Moore, W. Q.	"	2d Md. Cav.	Feb. 11th, "	Tunpahoc, La.	Wilmington, Del.
McCafferty, N. J.	"	4th U. S. Art'y.	" 22d, "	West Point, Miss.	Pittsburg, Pa.
Millis, J.	"	66th Ind. Vol.	Oct. 11th, 1863.	Colliersville, Tenn.	Paoli, Ind.
McClure, T. W.	"	6th U. S. Art'y.	Apr. 12th, 1864.	Fort Pillow, Tenn.	Wabash, Ind.

APPENDIX.

Names.	Rank.	Regiment.	When captured.	Where captured.	Residence.
McNitt, R. J.	Capt.	1st Pa. Cav.	June 21st, 1864.	White House, Va.	Milroy, Pa.
Mason, J.	Lieut.	13th Pa. Cav.	Oct. 12th, 1863.	Brandy Station, Va.	
Main, C. A.	Capt.	5th Ill. Cav.	June 22d, "	Jones Co., Miss.	
McDonald, J.	Lieut.	2d E. Tenn. Vol.	Nov. 16th, "	Rodgersville, Tenn.	
Morse, C. W.	"	16th Conn. Vol.	Apr. 20th, 1864.	Plymouth, N. C.	New Hartford, Conn.
Miller, C.	Adjt.	14th Ill. Cav.	Sept. 13th, 1863.	Bean's Station, Tenn.	Chicago, Ill.
McAdams, J.	Lieut.	10th W. Va. Vol.	" 19th, "	Jackson River, Va.	
Mayer, G. W.	"	37th Ind. Vol.	Nov. 25th, 1864.	Sandersville, Ga.	Lawrenceburg, Ind.
Muri, C.	"	15th Mo. Vol.	Sept. 20th, 1863.	Chickamauga, Ga.	St. Louis, Mo.
McIntyre, ——.	Capt.	15th Wis. Vol.	Oct. 5th, 1864.	Altoona, Ga.	
McCormick, J.	Lieut.	21st N. Y. Cav.	July 19th, "	Ashley's Gap, Va.	Troy, N. Y.
Moore, L.	Capt.	72d O. Vol.	June 11th, "	Guntown, Miss.	Fremont, O.
McKay, R. G.	Lieut.	1st Mich. Cav.			Detroit, Mich.
Marshall, A. J.	"	2d Pa. Art'y.	July 30th, "	Petersburg, Va.	Nicetown, Pa.
Millard, R. J.	Capt.	19th U. S. C. T.	"	"	Fowlersville, Pa.
Mix, W. H.	Lieut.	37th Wis. Vol.	"	"	Warsaw, N. Y.
Munger, T. J.	"	73d Pa. Vol.			Madison, Wis.
McNure, A.	"	32d Me. Vol.	July 30th, 1864.	Petersburg, Va.	Philadelphia, Pa.
Mitchell, H. G.	"	57th O. Vol.	Dec. 3d, "	Statesboro', Ga.	Portland, Me.
Marshall, J. D.	"	9th Minn. Vol.	June 12th, "	Salem, Miss.	Wapakonetta, O.
McLane, ——.	"	93d Ill. Vol.	Nov. 25th, 1863.	Mission Ridge, Ga.	Rock Island, Ill.
Morriz, W. M.					
Norris, A. W.	Lieut.	107th Pa. Vol.	July 1st, "	Gettysburg, Pa.	
Norcross, J. C.	"	2d Mass. Cav.	" 12th, "	Ashley's Gap, Va.	Farmington, Me.
Niedenhoffen, C.	"	9th Minn. Vol.	" 12th, 1864.	Brie's Cross Rds., Va.	Winona, Minn.
Nyce, W.	"	2d N. Y. Cav.	Aug. 18th, 1863.	Thoroughfare Gap, Va.	Hainesville, N. J.
Nelson, W. H.		13th U. S. Inf.	July 11th, "	Jackson, Miss.	
Nutting, J. H.	Capt.	27th Mass. Vol.	May 16th, 1864.	Drury's Bluff, Va.	
Norris, O. P.	Lieut.	111th O. Vol.	Nov. 15th, 1863.	Tennessee.	
Nelson, P.	Major.	66th N. Y. Vol.	June 17th, 1864.	Petersburg, Va.	Westchester, N. Y.

APPENDIX.

Name	Rank	Regiment	Date	Place	Residence
Nelson, A.	Lieut.	66th N. Y. Vol.	June 17th, 1864.	Petersburg, Va.	Westchester, N. Y.
Nolan, L.	Capt.	2d Del. Vol.	" 22d, "	"	"
Needham, J. B.	Lieut.	4th Vt. Vol.	" 23d, "	"	Shrewsbury, Vt.
Noggle, C. L.	"	2d U. S. Inf.	" 2d, "	"	Janesville, Wis.
Nichols, C. H.	Capt.	6th Conn. Vol.		Mechanicsville, Va.	
Newbrant, J. F.	Lieut.	4th Mo. Cav.	July 10th, 1863.	Bermuda Hund'ds, Va.	Cincinnati, O.
Norwood, J.	"	76th N. Y. Vol.	May 5th, 1864.	Morrow City, Tenn.	Slatersville, N. Y.
Norton, E. E.	Capt.	24th Mich. Vol.	" "	Wilderness, Va.	Detroit, Mich.
Nealy, O. H.	Lieut.	11th U. S. Inf	" "	"	Ft. Independence, Boston Harbor, Mass.
Netlerville, W. McM.	"	12th U. S. Inf.	" "	"	Albany, N. Y.
Nash, W. H.	Capt.	1st U. S. S. S.	" "	"	New York City.
Neher, W.	Lieut.	7th Pa. R. V. Cav.	" "	"	Philadelphia, Pa.
Newsome, E.	Capt.	81st Ill. Vol.	June 13th, "	Salem, Miss.	Carbondale, Ill.
Neal, A.	Lieut.	5th Ind.'Cav.	" 31st "	Sunshine Ch., Va.	
Nuhfer, A.	Capt.	72d O. Vol.		Ripley, Miss.	Woodville, O.
Nolan, H. J.	"	14th N. Y. Cav.	" 15th, 1863.	Port Hudson, Miss.	
Niswander, D. M.	Lieut.	2d Pa. Art'y.	" 2d, 1864.	Cold Harbor, Va.	Welch Run, Pa.
Niemayer, B. H.	"	11th Ky. Cav.	Oct. 20th, 1863.	Philadelphia, E.Tenn.	
Newlin, C.	Capt.	7th Pa. Cav.	June 20th, 1864.	Marietta, Ga.	
Nyman, H. J.	Lieut.	19th Mich. Vol.	Oct. 27th, "	Adairsville, Ga.	
Nulland, W. R.	"	5th Ind. Cav.			Lafayette, Ind.
Norris, J.	Capt.	2d Pa. Art'y.			Washington, D. C.
Noyes, C. S.	"	31st Me. Vol.	July 30th, 1864.	Petersburg, Va.	Mt. Desert, Me.
Ontcolt, R. V.	Lieut.	135th O. Vol.	" 3d, "	New Mount, Va.	Cohoes, N. Y.
O'Harre, J.	"	7th N. Y. Art'y.	June 16th, "	Petersburg, Va.	Byfield, Mass.
Osborne, F.	"	19th Mass. Vol.	" 22d, "	"	Meigsville, O.
Ong, O. C.	"	2d Va. Cav.	May 12th, 1863.	Summersville, Va.	
Ottinger, W.	Capt.	8th Tenn. Vol.	Mar. 2d, 1864.	Green Creek, Tenn.	
Oliphant, D.	Lieut.	35th N. J. Vol.	July 22d, "	Decatur, Ga.	
O'Conner, W.	"	13th Pa. Cav.	Apr. 26th, "	Greenwich, Va.	Philadelphia, Pa.

APPENDIX.

Names.	Rank.	Regiment.	When captured.	Where captured.	Residence.
O'Brien, E.	Capt.	29th Mo. Vol.	Nov. 27th, 1863.	Ringgold, Ga.	Cape Girardeau, Mo.
O'Shea, E.	Lieut.	13th Pa. Cav.	June 24th, 1864.	Samaria, Va.	Philadelphia, Pa.
Olcott, D. W.	Capt.	134th N. Y. Vol.	July 1st, 1863.	Gettysburg, Pa.	New York City.
O'Kain, J.	Lieut.	7th Ill. Cav.	Nov. 3d, "	Quine's Mills, Miss.	Polo, Ind.
Oats, J. G.	"	3d O. Vol.	Jan. 12th, 1864.	Benton, Tenn.	Greenwich, O.
O'Connell, P.	"	55th Pa. Vol.	May 16th, "	Drury's Bluff, Va.	Johnstown, Pa.
Owens, W. N.	Major.	1st Ky. Cav.	Oct. 20th, 1863.	Philadelphia, Tenn.	Somerset, Ky.
Ogden, J.	Lieut.	1st Wis. Cav.	June 5th, 1864.	Dallas, Ga.	Winona, Minn.
Ogan, H. W.	Capt.	14th O. Vol.	Oct. 19th, "	Rough & R'dy Sta., Ga.	
O'Sullivan, F. J.	Lieut.	67th O. Vol.	July 18th, 1863.	Fort Wagner, S. C.	Toledo, O.
Olden, G. C.	"	112th Ill. Vol.	May 24th, 1864.	Cass Station, Ga.	
Pickenpaugh, A. C.	Lieut.	6th W. Va. Vol.	June 26th, "	Springfield, Va.	Morgantown, W. Va.
Picquet, H.	"	32d Ill. Vol.	July 22d, "	Atlanta, Ga.	Olney, Ill.
Parker, J. T.	"	13th Iowa Vol.	" "	"	Sigourney, Iowa.
Phinney, A.	"	90th Ill Vol.	" 20th, "	"	Rockford, Ill.
Province, W. M.	"	84th Ill. Vol.	" 16th, "	"	Vermont, Ill.
Purcell, T.	"	16th Iowa Vol.	" 22d, "	"	Muscatine, Iowa.
Powell, W. H.	"	2d Ill. L. Art'y.	" 18th, "	"	
Parker, G. M.	"	45th Ill. Vol.	" 1st, "	Marietta, Ga.	Carmi, Ill.
Purveance, J. S.	Major.	130th Ind. Vol.	" 23d, "	Petersburg, Va.	Huntington, Ind.
Pratt, J. E.	Capt.	4th Vt. Vol.	June 11th, "	"	Bennington, Vt.
Pemberton, H. V.	Lieut.	14th N. Y. Art'y.	" 17th, "	"	New York City.
Piffard, D. H.	"	"	" 22d, "	"	
Price, C. A.	"	5th Mich. Vol.	" 23d, "	"	Maple Rapids, Mich.
Parker, E. B.	"	1st Vt. Art'y.	" 15th, 1863.	Winchester, Va.	
Pumphry, J. B.	"	123d O. Vol.	" "	"	Marseilles, O.
Paxton, W. N.	"	140th Pa. Vol.	July 2d, "	Gettysburg, Pa.	
Porter, E.	Capt.	154th N. Y. Vol.	" "	"	Olean, N. Y.
Poole, S. V.	"	"	" "	"	Springville, N. Y.
Potts, G. P.	Lieut.	151st Pa. Vol.	" 1st, "	"	Pottsville, Pa

APPENDIX. 357

Name	Rank	Regiment	Date	Battle	Residence
Potts, J. H.	Lieut.	75th O. Vol.	July 2d, 1863.	Gettysburg, Pa.	Hamilton, N. Y.
Powers, J. L.	"	157th N. Y. Vol.	" 1st, "	"	Fort Snelling, Minn.
Pettijohn, D. B.	"	2d U. S. S. S.	" 2d, "	"	
Parsons, W. L.	Major.	2d Wis. Vol.	May 5th, 1864.	Wilderness, Va.	Trenton, N. J.
Parker, J.	Capt.	1st N. J. Vol.	" 6th, "	"	Clinton, N. Y.
Powell, J. P.	"	146th N. Y. Vol.	"	"	Garrattsville, N. Y.
Paine, L. B.	"	121st N. Y. Vol.	"	"	Brooklyn, N. Y.
Partridge, W. H.	Lieut.	67th N. Y. Vol.	June 2d, "	Bermuda Hund'ds, Va.	Unionville, Conn.
Pierce, H. H.	"	7th Conn. Vol.	Apr. 20th, "	Plymouth, N. C.	Hartford, Conn.
Pasco, H. L.	Major.	16th Conn.;Vol.	"	"	Short Tract, N. Y.
Pitt, G. W.	Lieut.	85th N. Y. Vet.	" 18th, "	"	Hinsdale, N. Y.
Peake, L. S.	"	"	" 20th, "	"	Waterloo, N. Y.
Pierson, E. C.	Capt.	8th Pa. Cav.	June 24th, "	Samaria Ch., Va.	Philadelphia, Pa.
Piggott, J. T., Jr.	Lieut.	"	Oct. 12th, 1863.	Warrenton Spa, Va.	Colchester, Conn.
Phelps, L. D.	Capt.	87th U. S. Inf.	June 2d, 1864.	Mechanicsville, Va.	Dayton, O.
Plase, W. R.	Lieut.	4th N. Y. Cav.	Sept. 6th, "	Raccoon Ford, Va.	
Pentzell, D.	"	95th O. Vol.	June 10th, "	Tishamingo Cr., Miss.	London, O.
Peetrey, J. G.	Capt.	6th Mich. Cav.	" 11th, "	Trevillian Sta., Va.	
Powers, D. H.	"	7th Ind. Vol.	Feb. 22d, "	Okolona, Miss.	Valparaiso, Ind.
Parmalee, J. A.	Major.	5th N. Y. Cav.	July 6th, 1863.	Hagerstown, Md.	Crown Point, N. Y.
Penfield, J. A.	Lieut.	6th Mich. Cav.	" 14th, "	Falling Waters, Md.	Jeddo, Me.
Potter, E. D.	"	2d O. Vol.	Sept. 19th, "	Chickamauga, Ga.	
Purlier, H.	"	42d Ill. Vol.	" 20th, "	"	
Powell, O.	"	21st O. Vol.	"	"	
Patterson, J. B.	"	13th Mich. Vol.	"	"	3d Avenue, N. Y. City.
Perley, J. P.	Capt.	19th U. S. Inf.	" 19th, "	"	Dubuque, Iowa.
Pierce, G. S.	"	10th Wis. Vol.	"	"	Menasha, Wis.
Perry, F. W.	"	11th Ky. Cav.	Oct. 20th, "	Philadelphia, Tenn.	
Pulliam, M. D.	Lieut.	116th Ill. Vol.	July 22d, "	Jackson, Miss.	Le Roy, N. Y.
Prather, Z. R.	"	100th N. Y. Vol.	May 16th, 1864.	Drury's Bluff, Va.	
Pierson, M. P.	"				
Pilsbury, S. H.	Capt.	5th Me. Vol.	July 24th, 1863.	White Plains, Va.	Biddeford, Me.

APPENDIX.

Names.	Rank.	Regiment.	When captured.	Where captured.	Residence.
Phares, W.	Lieut.	46th W. Va.	Jan. 15th, 1864.	West Virginia.	Seneca, W. Va.
Paul, A. C.	Capt.&A.A. Genl.		May 9th, "	Spotsylvania, Va.	Newport, Ky.
Pettit, G.	Capt.	120th N. Y. Vol.	June 1st, "	Mechanicsville, Va.	Lexington, N. Y.
Preston, A. L.	Lieut.	8th Mich. Cav.	Aug. 4th, "	Gainesville, Ga.	Mount Clemens, Mich.
Pendleton, D. R.	Capt.	5th Mich. Cav.	June 11th, "	Trevillian Sta., Va.	Detroit, Mich.
Porter, D. M.	"	120th Ill. Vol.	" "	North Mississippi.	
Pennypacker, E. J.	"	18th Pa. Cav.	Oct. 4th, 1863.	Buckland Mills.	Philadelphia, Pa.
Patterson, F. A.	"	3d W. Va. Cav.	June 15th, "	Winchester, Va.	Washington, D. C.
Potter, H. C.	Lieut.	18th Pa. Cav.	July 6th, "	Hagerstown, Md.	Philadelphia, Pa.
Paul, J. S.	"	122d O. Vol.	June 15th, "	Winchester, Va.	
Phillpp, F.	"	5th Pa. Cav.	Mar. 6th, 1864.	S. Mills, N. C.	Philadelphia, Pa.
Pierce, S. C.	Capt.	3d N. Y. Cav.	June 29th, "	Ream's Sta., Va.	Rochester, N. Y.
Pratsman, C. N.	Lieut.	7th Wis. Vol.	Oct. 19th, 1863.	Haymarket, Va.	Plainfield, Wis.
Potter, G. A.	"	2d Ky. Vol.	May 26th, "	Murfreesboro', Tenn.	Cincinnati, O.
Peters, G.	"	9th N. J. Vol.	" 16th, 1864.	Drury's Bluff, Va.	Elizabeth, N. J.
Pitt, J. H.	"	118th N. Y. Vol.	" "	"	Canton, N. Y.
Post, James	"	149th Pa. Vol.	" 23d, "	Hanover Junction, Va.	Shickshinny, Pa.
Page, J. F.	Capt.	5th Iowa Vol.	Nov. 25th, 1863.	Mission Ridge, Tenn.	Iowa City, Iowa.
Pace, N. C.	"	80th Ill. Vol.	May 3d, "	Rome, Ga.	Mount Vernon, Ill.
Piper, S. B.	Adjt.	3d O. Vol.	" "	"	Barnesville, O.
Phelps, J. D.	Capt.	73d Ind. Vol.	" "	"	Michigan City, Ind.
Palmer, E. L.	Lieut.	57th N. Y. Vol.	Aug. 1st, 1864.	Morrisville, Va.	Montville, Conn.
Poston, J. I.	Capt.	13th Tenn. Vol.	Apr. 12th, 1864.	Fort Pillow, Tenn.	Cageville, Tenn.
Patree, L. B.	Lieut.	126th O. Vol.	Nov. 27th, 1863.	Mine River, Va.	
Poole, J. F.	"	1st W. Va. Cav.	July 6th, "	Hagerstown, Md.	Martinsburg, W. Va.
Peterson, C. J. A.	"	1st R. I. Cav.	June 18th, "	Middleburg, Va.	
Peck, W. D.	"	2d N. Y. Cav.	" 22d, 1864.	Ream's Sta., Va.	Syracuse, N. Y.
Pelton, E. W.	"	2d Md. Vol.	Jan. 3d, "	Moorefield, Va.	Cumberland, Md.
Patterson, G. W.	"	135th O. Vol.	July 3d, "	North Mount, Va.	
Price, J. C.	"	75th O. Vol.	Aug. 17th, "	Newnan, Ga.	Alexandria, O.

APPENDIX. 359

Pain, H. C.	Lieut.	20th Ill. Vol.	Sept. 22d, 1863.	Mission Ridge, Tenn.	
Porter, B. B.	Capt.	10th N. Y. Art.	June 22d, 1864.	Samaria Ch., Va.	Taylor, N. Y.
Perrin, Z.	Lieut.	72d O. Vol.	" 12th, "	Ripley, Miss.	Clyde, O.
Platt, S. H.	"	34th Mass. Vol.			Pittsfield, Mass.
Porter, L. G.	"	81st Ill. Vol.	" 11th, "		Tamaroa, Ill.
Paine, J. A.	Capt.	2d Ind. Cav.	May 9th, "	Varnell, Ga.	Bridgetown, Ind.
Phelps, L. A.	Major.	5th W. Va. Vol.	Sept. 7th, 1863.	Guyandotte, W. Va.	Ceredo, W. Va.
Palmer, J. H.	Lieut.	12th O. Vol.	May 9th, 1864.	Cloyd's House, Va.	
Peckeville, W. F.	Capt.	55th Iowa Vol.	Nov. 25th, 1863.	Mission Ridge, Tenn.	Ripley, O.
Pope, W. A.	Lieut.	18th Wis. Vol	Oct. 5th, 1864.	Altoona, Ga.	
Pyne, D. B.	"	3d Mo. Vol.			Alden, Iowa.
Ping, T.	Capt.	17th Iowa Vol	" 13th, "	Tilton, Ga.	Ashland, Iowa.
Park, A.	Lieut.	"		"	Germainville, Iowa.
Perrin, J.	Adjt.	6th U. S. Cav.	June 9th, 1863.	Brandy Sta., Va.	Woodstock, Vt.
Pierce, Worthington	Lieut.	17th Vt. Vol.	July 30th, 1864.	Petersburg, Va.	Hyde Park, Pa.
Phillips, W. B.	"	2d Pa. Art'y.	"	"	Bridgeton, Me.
Poindexter, C. O.	"	31st Me. Vol			Lapier, Mich.
Pierson, A. P.	"	9th Mich. Cav.	Oct. 27th, "	Stone Mount, Ga.	Woodstock, Conn.
Phillips, W. E.	"	7th Conn. Vol.	July 11th, 1863.	Fort Wagner, S. C.	Tonawanda, N. Y.
Payne, L. S.	Capt.	100th N. Y. Vol	Aug. 3d, "	Morris Island, S. C.	Maple Rapids, Mich.
Price, Chas. A.	Lieut.	3d Mich. Vol.	June 22d, 1864.	Petersburg, Va.	
Quigg, D.	Major.	14th Ill. Cav.	Aug. 4th, "	Athens, Ga.	Bloomington, Ill.
Rees, M.	Lieut.	72d O. Vol.	June 11th, "	Ripley, Miss.	Rollersville, O.
Robinson, J. L.	"	7th Tenn. Cav.	Mar. 24th, "	Union City, Tenn.	Huntington, Pa.
Robbins, H.	Capt.	2d Wis. Vol.	July 1st, 1863.	Gettysburg, Pa.	
Rockwell, W. O.	Lieut.	134th N. Y. Vol.	"	"	
Robbins, N. A.	"	4th Me. Vol.			Esperance, N. Y.
Russell, J. H.	"	12th Mass. Vol.	" 2d, "	"	Union, Me.
Rockwell, J. O.	"	97th N. Y. Vol.	"	"	Boston, Mass.
Richardson, H.	"	19th Ind. Vol.	"	"	Booneville, N. Y.

360 APPENDIX.

Names.	Rank.	Regiment.	When captured.	Where captured.	Residence.
Robinson, G. L.	Lieut.	80th O. Vol.	Nov. 25th, 1863.	Chickamauga, Tenn.	Mount Clemens, Mich.
Robertson, G. W.	"	22d Mich. Vol.	Sept. 20th, "	"	
Roach, S.	"	100th Ill. Vol.	"	"	
Riggs, B. T.	Capt.	18th Ky. Vol.	"	"	Harrisburg, Ill.
Rice, J. A.	"	73d Ill. Vol.	"	"	Roscoe, O.
Retilley, W. L.	Lieut.	51st O. Vol.	"	"	
Ray, T. J.	"	49th O. Vol.	" 19th, "	"	
Reynolds, H.	"	42d Ill. Vol.	" 20th, "	"	
Rose, W. B.	"	106th Pa. Cav.	June 22d, 1864.	Petersburg, Va.	
Rourke, J.	Capt.	1st Ill. Art'y.	" 31st, "	"	Milwaukee, Wis.
Reynolds, W. H.	Major.	14th N. Y. Art'y.	" 17th, "	"	Utica, N. Y.
Ruger, J. M.	Lieut.	57th Pa. Vol.	" 22d, "	"	
Richards, L. S.	"	1st Vt. Art'y.	" 23d, "	"	West Concord, Vt.
Rounels, J. R.	"	145th Pa. Vol.	" 16th, "	"	
Rieneckar, G.	"	5th Pa. Cav.	" 29th, "	"	
Rahu, O.	"	184th Pa. Vol.	" 22d, "	"	Duncannon, Pa.
Ritter, H.	"	52d N. Y. Vol.	"	"	Philadelphia, Pa.
Reynolds, W. J.	Capt.	75th O. Vol.	Aug. 17th, "	Newnan, Ga.	
Reynolds, E. P.	Lieut.	5th Tenn. Cav.	May 22d, 1863.	Huntsville, Tenn.	McMinnville, Tenn.
Robbinson, J. F.	"	67th Pa. Vol.	June 15th, "	Winchester, Va.	Scott, Pa.
Ruff, J.	"	"	"	"	Philadelphia, Pa.
Randolph, J. F.	Capt.	123d O. Vol.	"	"	
Robbins, A.	"	"	"	"	Upper Sandusky, O.
Rosenbaum, O. H.	"	"	"	"	Sandusky City, O.
Rossman, W. C.	"	3d O. Vol.	May 3d, "	Rome, Ga.	Hamilton, O.
Russell, M.	"	51st Ind. Vol.	"	"	
Randall, W.	Lieut.	80th Ill. Vol.	"	"	
Richley, J. A.	Capt.	73d Ind. Vol.	"	"	
Roach, A. C.	Lieut.	51st Ind. Vol.	"	"	Indianapolis, Ind.
Rosencranz, A. C.	Capt.	4th Ind. Cav.	" 9th, 1864.	Dalton, Ga.	Evansville, Ind.
Rowley, G. A.	Lieut.	2d U. S. Inf.	June 2d, "	Mechanicsville, Va.	

APPENDIX. 361

Name	Rank	Regiment	Date	Place	Residence
Reid, J. A.	Lieut.	2d N. C. Vol.	Apr. 20th, 1864.	Plymouth, N. C.	Whitestown, Pa.
Robinson, B. E.	"	95th O. Vol.	June 10th, "	Tishaningo Cr., Miss.	Reynoldsburg, O.
Ryder, S. B.	Capt.	5th N. Y. Cav.	Oct. 11th, 1863.	James City, Va.	Arbane, N. Y.
Robinson, W. A.	"	77th Pa. Vol.	Sept. 20th, "	Chickamauga, Ga.	Pittsburg, Pa.
Roach, W. E.	Lieut.	49th N. Y. Vol.	June 30th, 1864.	Ream's Station, Va.	Rochester, N. Y.
Rogers, A.	Capt.	4th Ky. Cav.	Sept. 21st, 1863.	Stephen's Gap, Tenn.	Louisville, Ky.
Raymond, H. W.	Lieut.	8th N. Y. Art'y.	June 3d, 1864.	Cold Harbor, Va.	Elba, N. Y.
Ross, C. W.	"	1st Ky. Inf.	Sept. 15th, 1863.	Lagrange, Ga.	
Rose, J. E.	"	120th Ill. Vol.	June 12th, 1864.	North Ripley, Miss.	Vienna, Ill.
Roberts, E. R.	"	7th Ill. Vol.	May 7th, "	Florence, Ala.	
Reed, J. H.	"	120th Ill. Vol.	June 14th, "	North Mississippi.	
Richard, J. M.	"	1st W. Va. Vol.	" 21st, "	Virginia.	Wheeling, W. Va.
Rings, G.	Adjt.	100th O. Vol.	Sept. 8th, 1863.	Jonesboro', Tenn.	
Rothe, H.	Lieut.	15th N. Y. Art'y.	May 15th, 1864.	Spotsylvania, Va.	Alexandria, Va.
Robb, W. J.	Capt.	1st W. Va. Vol.	Jan. 31st, "	Greenland Gap, Va.	Wheeling, W. Va.
Ramsey, E. K.	Lieut.	1st N. J. Vol.	May 6th, "	Wilderness, Va.	Phœnixville, Pa.
Riley, L. H.	"	7th Pa. R. V. C'ps.	" 5th, "	"	
Ruby, S. V.					
Ross, C. H.	Adjt.	13th Ind. Vol.	June 2d, "	Mechanicsville, Va.	Zanesville, O.
Risedon, I.	Lieut.	11th Tenn. Vol.	Feb. 22d, "	Lee Creek, Va.	Huntsville, Tenn.
Robs, E. W.	"	1st Tenn. Vol.	Oct. 19th, 1863.	Ray Creek, Tenn.	
King, A.	"	12th O. Vol.	May 12th, 1864.	Cloud's Farm, Va.	
Richardson, J. A.	"	2d N. Y. Cav.	July 5th, 1863.	Emmettsburg, Va.	Stoneham, Mass.
Romaine, L.	"	2d N. J. Vol.	" "		
Roberts, G.	"	7th N. H. Vol.	Feb. 20th, 1864.	Olustee, Fla.	Dover, N. H.
Ross, G.	"	7th Vt. Vol.	" 19th, "	Wash'gton Co., W. Fla.	Vergennes, Vt.
Rathbone, T. W.	"	153d O. Vol.	July 3d, "	West Virginia.	
Rugg, C. L.	"	6th Ind. Cav.	Aug. 3d, "	Athens.	Newport, Ky.
Roger, J. R.	"	157th Pa. Vol.	Apr. 16th, "	Fairfax Court H., Va.	Lancaster City, Pa.
Reed, ——.	Capt.	107th N. Y. Vol.	Nov. 19th, "		
Roney, J. C.	Lieut.	3d O. Vol.	May 3d, 1863.	Rome, Ga.	Newark, O.
Robinson, T. B.	Capt.	16th Conn. Vol.	Apr. 20th, 1864.	Plymouth, N. C.	Bristol, Conn.

Q

362 APPENDIX.

Names.	Rank.	Regiment.	When captured.	Where captured.	Residence.
Richards, J. S.	Lieut.	93d Ill. Vol.	Nov. 25th, 1863.	Mission Ridge, Tenn.	Neponsett, Ill.
Russell, J. A.	Capt.	13th Ind. Vol.	July 22d, 1864.	Atlanta, Ga.	Washington, Iowa.
Rice, J. S.	Lieut.	57th Mass. Vol.	" 30th, "	Petersburg, Va.	Milford, Mass.
Reade, J.	"	45th Pa. Vol.	" "	"	Cherry Flats, Pa.
Richards, R. C.	Capt.	19th U. S. C. T.	" "	"	Ontario, N. Y.
Raynor, A. J.	Lieut.	2d N. J. Cav.	June 12th, "	Moscow, Tenn.	Freehold, N. J.
Raincar, L.	"	4th R. I. Vol.	July 30th, "	Petersburg, Va.	Wickford, R. I.
Reynolds, W. J.	Capt.	7th Tenn. Cav.	" "	"	Huntingdon, Tenn.
Robeson, J. S.	Lieut.	21st N. Y. Cav.	" 19th, "	Ashley's Gap, Va.	Brighton, N. Y.
Riley, W. L.	"	1st Mich. S. S.	" 30th, "	Petersburg, Va.	Ypsilanti, Mich.
Randall. W. H.	Capt.	107th N. Y. Vol.	" "	"	S. side Staten Isl, N. Y.
Reir, Geo. W.	"	31st U. S. C. T.	" 30th, "	Petersburg, Va.	London, Iowa.
Robinson, C.	Lt.&A.D.C.	31st Iowa Vol.	Feb. 14th, 1865.	Columbia, S. C.	Neversink, N. Y.
Rorick, D.	Capt.	143d N. Y. Vol.		Lexington, S. C.	
Reynolds, B. J.	Lieut.	107th Pa. Vol.	July 14th, 1864.	Petersburg, Va.	Shippensburg, Pa.
Sturgeon, W. B.	"	184th Pa. Vol.	June 22d, "	"	
Stover, M. H.	"	2d Pa. Cav.	July 12th, "	"	
Sweetland, A. A.	Capt.	14th N. Y. Vol.	June 17th, "	"	Huvelton, N. Y.
Snyder, J.	Lieut.	1st Vt. Art'y.	" 23d, "	"	Newport, Vt.
Smith, E. B.	Lieut. Col.	2d U. S. S. S.	" 21st, "	"	
Stoughton, H. R.	Major.	2d Pa. Cav.	July 12th, "	"	Pittsburg, Pa.
Steele, J.	Capt.	145th Pa. Vol.	June 16th, "	"	West Greenville, Pa.
Smart, G. F. C.	Lieut.	7th N. Y. Art'y.	" "	"	
Schurr, C.	"	5th Pa. Cav.	" 29th, "	"	
Shafer, W. H.	"	42d N. Y. Vol.	" 22d, "	"	Trenton, N. J.
Standeford, S. A.	Capt.	53d Pa. Vol.	" 16th, "	"	Huntingdon, Pa.
Smith, H. J.	Lieut.	1st Vt. Art'y.	" 23d, "	"	Newport, Vt.
Sargeant, M. G.	Capt.	2d Pa. Art'y.	July 1st, "	"	Pittston, Pa.
Schooley, D.	Lieut.	87th Pa. Art'y.	June 22d, "	"	York, Pa.
Stallman, C. H.					

APPENDIX. 363

Socks, J.	Lieut.	5th Md. Art'y.	June 15th, 1863.	Winchester, Va.	Liberty, Md.
Swedner, J.	"	"	"	"	Philadelphia, Pa.
Stewart, T. H.	"	"	"	"	York, Pa.
Stroman, C. P.	"	87th Pa. Art'y.	"	"	Racine, O.
Sibley, H. L.	"	116th O. Art'y.	"	"	Monroeville, O.
Smith, M. H.	"	123d O. Art'y.	"	"	Attica, O.
Schuyler, J. F.					Mauch Chunk, Pa.
Simpson, G. W.	"	67th Pa. Art'y.	"	"	York, Pa.
Schroeder, E.	"	5th Md. Art'y.	"	"	Latrobe, Pa.
Smith, J.	Capt.	67th Pa. Art'y.	"	"	Easton, Pa.
Schortz, D.	"	12th Pa. Cav.	"	"	Arcanum, O.
Sheppard, E. A.	Major.	110th O. Vol.	"	"	Terre Haute, Ind.
Smith, O. J.	Lieut. Col.	6th Ind. Cav.	Aug. 3d, 1864.	Atlanta, Ga.	Davenport, Iowa.
Sanders, A. H.	Colonel.	16th Iowa Vol.	July 22d, "	"	Aledo, Ill.
Shedd, W.	Capt.	30th Ill. Vol.	"	"	Collins's Station, Ill.
Strang, H. W.	"	16th Iowa Vol.	"	"	Lyons, Iowa.
Smith, J. H.	"	57th O. Vol.	"	"	
Skilton, A. S.	Lieut.	37th O. Vol.	"	"	Toledo, O.
Shuttz, W.	Capt.	1st Ill. Art'y.	"	"	Elkhorn, Ill.
Smythe, S. S.	Lieut.	48th Ill. Vol.	"	"	
Smith, A. B.	"	10th Ind. Vol.	"	"	Lebanon, Ind.
Scott, Geo.	Adjt.	74th Ill. Vol.	July 21st, 1864.	Jonesboro', Va.	Pecatonica, Ill.
Swift, F.	Capt.	126th O. Vol.	" 6th, "	"	Smithfield, O.
Sutherland, G. W.	"	85th N. Y. Vol.	Sept. 1st, "	Mine Run, Va.	Olean, N. Y.
Starkweather, W. L.	Lieut.	101st Pa. Vol.	Nov. 27th, 1863.	Plymouth, N. C.	Carlisle, Pa.
Shaefer, Jas.	Capt.	16th Conn. Vol.	Apr. 20th, 1864.	"	N'th Manchester, Conn.
Strong, E. E.	Lieut.	2d Mass. H. Art'y.	"	"	Springfield, Mass.
Sampson, I. B.	Lieut.		"	"	Worcester, Mass.
Sinclair, R. B.	"		"	"	Pittsburg, Pa.
Spence, D. M.			"	"	Orrsville, Pa.
Stoke, G. W.	Capt.	103d Pa. Vol.	"	"	Oakland, Pa.
Smulin, F.					

364 APPENDIX.

Names.	Rank.	Regiment.	When captured.	Where captured.	Residence.
Stewart, A., Jr.	Capt. & A. A. Genl		Apr. 20th, 1864.	Plymouth, N. C.	Uniontown, Pa.
Sweeney, J.	Ass't Eng'r U.S.N.		"	"	
Starr, G. H.	Capt.	104th N. Y. Vol.	July 3d, 1863.	Gettysburg, Pa.	Rochester, N. Y.
Schell, G. L.	"	88th Pa. Vol.	" 1st, "	"	Philadelphia, Pa.
Seely, H. B.	Adjt.	86th N. Y. Vol.	" 2d "	"	So. Troupsburg, N. Y.
Schroeders, E.	Lieut.	74th Pa. Vol.	" 1st, "	"	
Sears, D. C.	"	94th N. Y. Vol.	"	"	Somerville, N. Y.
Smith, J. A.	"	154th N. Y. Vol.	"	"	
Schull, G.	"	45th N. Y. Vol.	"	"	
Sampson, J. B.	"	12th Mass. Vol.	"	"	N. Bridgewater, Mass.
Spring, W.	Capt.	45th N. Y. Vol.	"	"	Chicago, Ill.
Schroeder, C. H.	Lieut.	12th Ill. Vol.	"	"	Machias, N. Y.
Stevens, C. G.	"	154th Ill. Vol.	"	"	Springfield, Mass.
Swift, R. R.	Capt.	27th Mass. Vol.	May 16th, 1864.	Drury's Bluff, Va.	Amherst, Mass.
Skinner, J. L.	Lieut.	"	"	"	Warrensburg, N. Y.
Stone, D.	Capt.	118th N. Y. Vol.	"	"	
Spindler, J.	Lieut.	73d Ill. Vol.	Sept. 20th, 1863.	Chickamauga, Ga.	
Spencer, S. A.	Lieut.	82d Ind. Vol.	"	"	
*Spafford, A. C.	Capt.	41st O. Vol.	" 19th, "	"	Lancaster, Pa.
Schroade, J. C.	"	77th Pa. Vol.	" 20th, "	"	
Singer, G. P.	Lieut.	33d O. Vol.	"	"	Port Huron, Mich.
Spauldeng, F. G.	"	22d Mich. Vol.	" 19th, "	"	
Smythe, W. H.	Capt.	16th U. S. Inf.	" 20th, "	"	Chicago, Ill.
Schummerhone, J.	Lieut.	42d Ind. Vol.	" 23d, "	"	Xenia, Ill.
Schwainforth, F.	"	24th Ill. Vol.	" 20th, "	"	Wilmington, O.
Sanger, A. W.	"	21st Ill. Vol.	" 23d, "	"	
Spencer, F.	"	17th O. Vol.	"	"	
Simpson, J. D.	"	10th Ind. Vol.	"	"	
Stover, J. C.	Capt.	3d Tenn. Vol.	Jan. 3d, 1864.	Knoxville, Tenn.	

APPENDIX. 365

Name	Rank	Regiment	Date	Place	Residence
Stevens, J. H.	Lieut.	5th Me. Vol.	Dec. 14th, 1863.	Milford Ford, Va.	North Lebanon, Me.
Stevens, F.	"	190th Pa. Vol.	June 13th, 1864.	Malvern Hill, Va.	Newburg, N. Y.
Stuart, C.	"	24th N. Y. Vol.	" 1st, "	Mechanicsville, Va.	
Shanan, M.	"	140th N. Y. Vol.	May 5th, "	Wilderness, Va.	
Stevens, J. R.	Capt.	40th N. Y. Vol.	" 6th, "	"	Brooklyn, N. Y.
Speece, L. B.	Major.	7th Pa. V. R. C'ps.	" 5th, "	"	Wilkesbarre, Pa.
Shelton, W. H.	Lieut.	1st N. Y. Art'y.	" "	"	Bloomfield, N. Y.
Smith, M. S.	"	16th Me. Vol.	" "	"	E. Livermore, Me.
Snowwhite, E.	"	7th Pa. V. R. C'ps.	" "	"	Palmyra, Pa.
Swan, E. J.	Capt.	76th N. Y. Vol.	" "	"	Cherry Valley, N. Y.
Sweet, W. H. S.	Lieut.	146th N. Y. Vol.	" "	"	Utica, N. Y.
Schofield, E.	Capt.	11th Pa.V.R.C'ps.	" "	"	Brookville, Pa.
Steel, J. M.	Lieut.	1st W. Va. Vol.	" "	"	Wellsville, O.
Sitler, J. R.	"	2d Pa. Cav.	Sept. 11th, 1863.	Moorefield, Va.	Harmonsburg, Pa.
Shaw, J. C.	"	7th O. Vol.	May 7th, 1864.	Todd's Tavern, Va.	
Sheerd, D. G.	"	5th Ky. Cav.	Nov. 6th, 1863.	Rolgersville, Tenn.	Jamestown, Ky.
Shannon, A. L.	"	3d Ind. Cav.	May 5th, "	Nashville, Tenn.	Hanover, Ind.
Smith, C. B.	"	4th N. Y. Cav.	June 29th, 1864.	Reum's Station, Va.	New York City.
Smith, A. M.	"	1st Tenn. Cav.	Sept. 16th, 1863.	Raccoon Ford, Va.	
Sutter, C.	"	39th N. Y. Vol.	July 31st, 1864.	Chattahoochie R., Ga.	New York City.
Spaulding, E. J.	"	2d U. S. Cav.	Dec. 2d, 1863.	Mine Run, Va.	Galesburg, Mich.
Shaffer, H. C.	"	2d N. Y. Cav.	June 9th, "	Brandy Station, Va.	
Swayzie, W. A.	Capt.	3d O. Vol.	Oct. 10th, "	Culpepper, Va.	Columbus, O.
Sharp, E. E.	Lieut.	51st Ind. Vol.	May 3d, "	Rome, Ga.	Kokoma, Ind.
Smith, D. D.	Capt.	1st Tenn. Vol.	" "	"	
Segar, T. W.	Lieut.	81st Ill. Vol.	" "	"	
Smith, J. C.	"	24th Ind. Bat.	July 3d, 1864.	Atlanta, Ga.	Chester, Ill.
Saber, G. E.	Adjt.	2d R. I. Cav.	Aug. 3d, 1863.	Jackson, La.	Burlington, Ind.
Sullivan, J.	Lieut.	7th R. I. Cav.	July 13th, "	Jackson, Miss.	
Smith, J. B.	"	5th W. Va. Cav.	May 13th, 1864.	Middletown, Va.	
Sandon, W.		1st Wis. Cav.	" 9th, "	Dalton, Ga.	Ontario, Wis.
Sutcher, C. B.	Capt.	16th Ill. Vol.	" 12th, "	"	

Names.	Rank.	Regiment.	When captured.	Where captured.	Residence.
Sharp, G. A.	Lieut.	19th Pa. Cav.	Feb. 13th, 1864.	Holly Spa, Miss.	Philadelphia, Pa.
Stone, L. L.	R. Q. M.	2d Vt. Vol.	Oct. 26th, 1863.	Warrenton, Va.	Mt. Indoes Falls, Vt.
Smith, L. S.	Lieut.	14th N. Y. Cav.	June 14th, "	Port Hudson, La.	Littleton, N. H.
Sanford, O. L.	Major.	7th Conn. Vol.	" 2d, 1864.	Bermuda Hund'ds, Va.	
Smith, J. P.	Lieut.	49th Pa. Vol.	" 1st, "	Cold Harbor, Va.	Spring Mills, Pa.
Stevens, J. G.	"	52d Pa. Vol.	July 3d, "	Fort Johnson, S. C.	
Smith, T. A.	Major.	7th Tenn. Cav.	May 24th, "	Union City, Tenn.	Lexington, Tenn.
Swope, C. T.	Lieut.	4th Ky. Vol.	July 31st, "	Jonesboro', Ga.	
Stewart, A. S.	"	"	" "	" "	
Strickland, E. P	"	114th Ill. Vol.	May 11th, "	Tishamingo Cr., Miss.	Morristown, Tenn.
Smith, P.	"	4th Tenn. Cav.	Aug. 1st, "	Franklin, Ga.	Carmel, Ind.
Stanton, J. W.	"	5th Ind. Cav.	July 31st, "	Sunshine Ch., Va.	Sheldon, Ill.
Soper, M. H.	Major.	"	" "	" "	Greensburg, Ind.
St. John, W. H.	Lieut.	"	" "	" "	Newburgh, O.
Shepard, E.	"	6th O. Cav.	Sept. 1st, 1863.	Barber'sCrossRds., Va.	
Scripture, F. E.	R. Q. M.	7th N. Y. Art'y.	May 27th, 1864.	Bowling Green, Va.	
Simmons, A. B.	Lieut.	5th Ind. Cav.	July 31st, "	Chattahoochee R., Ga.	Union City, Ind.
Starr, H. P.	"	22d N. Y. Cav.	May 8th, "	Chancellorsville, Va.	Rochester, N. Y.
Spring, B.	"	75th O. Vol.	Aug. 17th, "	Newnan, Ga.	
Shurtz, E.	Capt.	8th Iowa Cav.	July 30th, "	" "	Urbana, O.
Stover, A. C.	Lieut.	95th O. Vol.	June 10th, "	Tishamingo Cr., Miss.	
Stansbury, M. L.	Capt.	"	" "	Briers' Cr. Rds., Miss.	
Schofield, R.	"	1st Vt. Cav.	July 12th, 1863.	Hagerstown, Md.	Brattleboro', Vt
Stone, C. P.	Lieut.	"	June 1st, 1864.	Ashland, Va.	
Scudder, A. A.	R. Q. M.	35th Pa. Vol.	Feb. 14th, "	Brentsville, Va.	Rockford, Ill.
Scoville, H. C.	Lieut.	92d Ill. Vol.	Apr. 20th, "	Ringgold, Ga.	
Stebbins, J.	"	77th N. Y. Vol.	May 12th, "	Spottsylvania, Va.	
Schwartz, C. S.	"	2d N. J. Cav.	June 10th, "	Tishamingo Cr., Miss.	Philadelphia, Pa.
Sailor, J.	"	13th Pa. Cav.	" 24th, "	Samaria Church, Va.	Newport, Pa.
Smyser, H. C.	"	2d Md. Vol.	May 29th, "	Newton, Va.	Ashland Furnace, Pa.
Scott, R. F.	"	11th Ky. Cav.	Oct. 20th, 1863.	Philadelphia, Tenn.	Kirksville, Ky.

APPENDIX. 367

String, T. B.	Capt.	11th Ky. Cav.	Nov. 11th, 1863.	Maysville, Tenn.	Louisville, Ky.
Stewart, R. R.	Lieut.	2d N. Y. Cav.	May 19th, 1864.	Spotsylvania, Va.	New York City
Stribling, M. W.	"	61st O. Vol.	" 25th, "	Dalton, Ga.	Circleville, O.
Sutcher, C. B.	Capt.	16th Ill. Vol.	" 12th, "	"	
Shoemaker, F. M.	"	100th O. Vol.	Sept. 8th, 1863.	Limestone, Tenn.	Waterville, O.
Smith, J.	Lieut.	5th Pa. Cav.	June 24th, 1864.	Ream's Sta., Va.	
Stout, J. O.	"	McLauglin's Sqd'n Ohio Cav.	Oct. 5th, "	Decatur, Ga.	Wooster, O.
Shepstrong, M. N.	"	60th O. Vol.	May 25th, "	Dallas, Ga.	New Madison, O.
Snodgrass, J. G.	Capt.	110th O. Vol.	July 9th, "	Monocacy, Md.	Portland, Me.
Sargent, H. R.	"	32d Me. Vol.	" 30th, "	Petersburg, Va.	Carmel, Hamilton Co., [Ind.
Stanton, J. W.	Lieut.	5th Ind. Cav.			Dennysville, Mc.
Sheehan, J. P.	"	31st Me. Vol.			Bloomington, Ind.
Shull, J. F.	"	28th U. S. C. T.	July 30th, 1864.	Petersburg, Va.	Woodbury, N. J.
Smith, S. B.	"	30th U. S. C. T.	"	"	Lewistown, Pa.
Stauber, B. F.	"	20th Pa. Cav.	" 19th, "	Paris, Va.	Albany, N. Y.
Schulter, H.	"	43d N. Y. Vol.	May 6th, "	Wilderness, Va.	Providence, R. I.
Sherman, S. U.	Capt.	4th R. I Vol.			Knoxville, Pa.
Seely, L. D.	Lieut.	45th Pa. Vol.	July 30th, "	Petersburg, Va.	Norristown, Pa.
Stewart, R. T.	Capt.	138th Pa. Vol.	" 9th, "	Monocacy, Md.	Meadow Gap, Pa.
Stevens, Frank	Lieut.	12th Pa.V.R.C'ps.			Pottsville, Pa.
Scott, D. W.	Capt.	23d U. S. C. T.	July 30th, 1864.	Petersburg, Va.	
Shroeder, H.	Lieut.	82d Ill. Vol.	" 1st, 1863.	Gettysburg, Pa.	
Sexton, A. F.	"	8th Iowa Cav.	" 30th, 1864.	Newnan, Ga.	
Senter, A. P.	Capt.	2d E. Tenn. Cav.	Nov. 6th, 1863.	Rodgersville, Tenn.	
Scofield, T. D.	Lieut.	27th Mich. Vol.	July 30th, 1864.	Petersburg, Va.	
Sanders, C. B.	"	30th U. S. C. T.	"	"	
Simondson, P. A.	"	23d U. S. C. T.	"	"	
Shaefer, N. W.	"	24th Ind. Cav.	" 31st, "	Macon, Ga.	
Tuthill, P. A.	"	104th N. Y. Vol.	July 1st, 1863.	Gettysburg, Pa.	Nunda, N. Y.
Templeton, O. F.	Capt.	107th Pa. Vol.	" "	"	Laceyville, Pa.

368 APPENDIX.

Names.	Rank.	Regiment.	When captured.	Where captured.	Residence.
Thonsen, B. E.	Lieut.	9th O. Vol.	Sept. 20th, 1863.	Chickamauga, Ga.	Cincinnati, O.
Toter, A. J.	"	2d O. Vol.	"	"	Steubenville, O.
Teneyck, S.	Capt.	18th U. S. Inf.	May 25th, 1864.	Hanover Junction, Va.	
Tainter, H. S.	Lieut.	82d N. Y. Vol.	" 24th, "	Raymond, Miss.	Canton, Pa.
Tanner, D.	"	118th Ill. Vol.	June 22d, "	Petersburg, Va.	Philadelphia, Pa.
Tompkins, H. V.	"	59th N. Y. Vol.	"	"	Newark, O.
Trout, B. W.	"	106th Pa. Vol.	"	"	
Tyler, L. D. C.	Capt.	135th O. Vol.	July 3d, 1864.	North Mount, Va.	
Thomas, D.	Major.	39th Ky. Vol	June 9th, 1863.	Boyd Co., Ky.	Lafayette, Ind.
Thornbury, J. M.	Lieut.	5th Ind. Cav.	July 31st, "	Sunshine Ch., Va.	Calumet, Ind.
Thompson, C. H.	Major.	73d Ind. Vol.	May 3d, "	Rome, Ga.	
Tillottson, H. H.	Lieut.				
Thomas, A. V.	"	10th Vt. Vol.	June 1st, 1864.	Cold Harbor, Va.	Almond, N. Y.
Tompson, J. S.	"	1st N. Y. Drag.	" 11th, "	Trevillian Sta., Va.	"
Thorp, T. J.	Lieut. Col.	85th N. Y. Vol.	Apr. 20th, "	Plymouth, N. C.	Hartford, Conn.
Terwilliger, J. E.	Lieut.	16th Conn. Vol.			Preston City, Conn.
Turner, M. C.	Capt.	1st Conn. Cav.	June 4th, "	Hanover Court H., Va.	New York City.
Tyler, L. E.	Lieut.	95th N. Y. Vol.	May 5th, "	Wilderness, Va.	
Timpson, S. C.	Capt.	67th Pa. Vol.	June 15th, 1863.	Winchester, Va.	Cambridge, O.
Thayer, H. O.	Lieut.	122d O. Vol.	"	"	Stoddardsville, Pa.
Taylor, A. A.	"	67th Pa. Vol.	" 16th, "	"	
Thompson, R.	Capt.	4th N. H. Vol.	" 1864.	Bermuda Hund'ds,Va.	Gardner, Kansas.
Tilbrand, H.	Lieut.	5th Ky. Vol.	Sept. 20th, 1863.	Chickamauga, Ga.	Davenport, Iowa.
Thorn, R. F.	"	16th Iowa Vol.	July 22d, 1864.	Atlanta, Ga.	Muscatine, Iowa.
Timm, A.	Capt.				
Turner, J. H.	Lieut.	18th Wis. Vol.	Oct. 5th, "	Altoona, Ga.	Adrian, Mich.
Todd, O.	"	9th Minn. Vol.	June 11th, "	Ripley, Miss.	Carver, Minn.
Tiffany, A. W.	"	55th Ind. Vol.	Dec. 14th, 1863.	Bean's Station, Tenn.	
Taylor, H	"	2d N. Y. Cav.	Sept. 18th, "	Liberty Mills, Va.	Brooklyn, N. Y.
Temple, H.	"	16th Ill. Cav.	Jan. 3d, 1864.	Jonesville, Va.	Chicago, Ill.
True, W. M.					

Name	Rank	Regiment	Date	Place	Residence
Thompson, J. J. T.	Ass't Surg.	12th O. Vol.	May 12th, 1864.	Cloyd's Farm, Va.	Maysville, Ky.
Tibbles, H. G.	Capt.	"	" 18th, "	Meadow Bluff, Va.	Dayton, O.
Taylor, J.	Lieut.	2d Pa. V. R. C'ps.	" 5th, "	Wilderness, Va.	
Tubbs, A.					
Tower, D. W.	Lieut.	17th Iowa Vol.	Oct. 13th, 1864.	Tilton, Ga.	Farmington, Iowa.
Tomson, F.	"	"			Oskaloosa, Iowa.
Tipton, A. F.		8th Iowa Cav.	July 11th, 1863.	Fort Wagner, S. C.	Elkader, Iowa.
Tourtillotte, J.	Capt.	7th Conn. Vol.	May 24th, "	Raymond, Miss.	Putnam, Conn.
Turner, David	Lieut.	118th Ill. Vol.	" 6th, 1864.	Wilderness, Va.	Warsaw, Ill.
Tobel, C.	"	15th N. Y. Art'y.	Aug. 20th, "	Lovejoy Sta., Ga.	New York City.
Thomson, J.	Capt.	4th O. Cav.	July 30th, "	Petersburg, Va.	
Toby, J. P. F.	Lieut.	31st Me. Vol.	June 12th, "		Machiasport, Me.
Tinker, S. H.	"	93d Ind. Vol.		Ripley, Miss.	Allensville, Ind.
Unthank, C. L.	Capt.	11th Ky. Cav.	May 24th, "	Cass Sta., Ga.	
Ullenbaugh, G.	Lieut.	1st O. Vol.	Sept. 23d, 1863.	Chickamauga, Ga.	
Urwiler, S. C.	Capt.	67th Pa. Vol.	June 15th, "	Winchester, Va.	Philadelphia, Pa.
Ulem, J.	Lieut.	3d O. Vol.	May 3d, "	Rome, Ga.	Wooster, O.
Uptigrove, J. R.	"	73d Ind. Vol.	" "	"	
Underdown, J. D.	Capt.	2d Tenn. Vol.	Nov. 6th, "	Rogers, Tenn.	
Ulfar, H. A.	Capt. & A. A. Genl.		June 6th, 1864.	Bethsuida Ch., Va.	
Underwood, J. W.	Capt.	57th O. Vol.	July 22d, "	Atlanta, Ga.	
Von Keiser, A.	Capt.	30th N. Y. Batt.	June 21st, "	H. R. Gap, Va.	
Van Netter, R. N.	Lieut.	1st Mich. Cav.	July 6th, 1863.	Hagerstown, Md.	Watervliet, Mich.
Von Valack, D. D.	"	12th U. S. Inf.	May 5th, 1864.	Wilderness, Va.	
Vandeshif, J. W.	Capt.	45th N. Y. Vol.	July 1st, 1863.	Gettysburg, Pa.	East Brooklyn, N. Y.
Veltfort, Geo.	Lieut.	54th N. Y. Vol.	" "	"	New York City.
Vickers, D.	Major.	4th N. J. Vol.	May 6th, 1864.	Wilderness, Va.	Philadelphia, Pa.
Von Rottenburg, H. N.	Lieut.	103d N. Y. Vol.	June 2d, "	Morris Island, S. C.	Dykeman's Sta., N. Y.

370   APPENDIX.

Names.	Rank.	Regiment.	When captured.	Where captured.	Residence.
Von Helmrich, G.	Lieut. Col.	4th Mo. Cav.	June 14th, 1864.	Shelby Creek, Miss.	St. Louis, Mo.
Vinay, F.	Lieut.	85th N. Y. Vol.	Apr. 20th, "	Plymouth, N. C.	New York City.
Van Doren, D.	"	72d O. Vol.	June 11th, "	Salem, Miss.	Fremont, O.
Van Ness, G. A.	"	73d Ind. Vol.	May 3d, 1863.	Rome, Ga.	Nogansport, Ind.
Van Rensalaer, C.	"	148th N. Y. Vol.	June 15th, 1864.	Petersburg, Va.	Seneca Falls, N. Y.
Vaugn, Z.	Capt.	1st Mc. Cav.	May 11th, "	South Anna B'dge, Va.	Freeman, Me.
Van Buren, G. M.	"	6th N. Y. Cav.	July 6th, 1863.	Williamsport, Md.	Struyvesant Falls, N. Y.
Van Alin, W. C.	Lieut.	45th Pa. Vol.	" 30th, 1864.	Petersburg, Va.	Fleming, Pa.
Von Bulow, A.	"	3d N. J. Cav.	" 6th, "	"	New York City.
Von Ilaack, A.	Capt.	68th N. Y. Vol.			
West, O. W.	Lieut.	1st N. Y. Drag.	May 7th, 1864.	Todd's Tavern, Va.	Dansville, N. Y.
Warner, J. B.	"	8th Mich. Cav.	Aug. 5th, "	Brown's Bridge, Va.	Marshall, Mich.
Williams, G.	"	"	" 7th, "	Covington, Va.	
Whitney, M. G.	Capt.	29th Mo. Vol.	Nov. 27th, 1863.	Ringgold, Ga.	St. Louis, Mo.
Winters, J.	Lieut.	72d O. Vol.	June 11th, 1864.	Ripley, Miss.	Townsend, O.
Warner, J.	"	33d N. J. Vol.	July 20th, "	Atlanta, Ga.	Newark, N. J.
Wheeler, J. F	"	149th N. Y. Vol.	"	"	Salina, N. Y.
West, J. H.	Capt.	11th Ky. Vol.	" 31st, "	"	Big Hill, Ky.
Waidmann, F.	Lieut.	16th Iowa Vol.	" 22d, "	"	Davenport, Iowa.
Walker, J.	"	8th Tenn. Vol.	Aug. 6th, "	"	Bull's Gap, Tenn.
Western, C. S.	"	21st Wis. Vol.	Sept. 20th, 1863.	Chickamauga, Ga.	Chelton, Wis.
Willets, W.	"	22d Mich. Vol.	"	"	Birmingham, Mich.
Wands, H. P.	Capt.		"	"	St. Clair, Mich.
Welker, W. H.	Lieut.	21st O. Vol.	"	"	"
Welshimer, P.	Capt.	21st Ill. Vol.	"	"	Neoga, Ill.
Weatherbu, J.	Lieut.	51st O. Vol.	"	"	
Weesner, T. A.	"	14th & 15th Ill.Vet. Batt.	Oct. 3d, 1864.	Moon Station, Ga.	Port Washington, O. Greenfield, Ill.
Wyman, E. F.	Capt.&C.S.		July 11th, "	Maryland.	Augusta, Me.
West, D. J.	Lieut.	6th Conn. Vol.	" 18th, "	Fort Morgan, S. C.	Bridgeport, Conn.

APPENDIX. 371

Name	Rank	Regiment	Date	Place	Residence
Ware, Eton W.	Lieut.	9th Me. Vol.	July 11th, 1863.	Fort Morgan, S. C.	Bangor, Me.
White, Daniel	Colonel.	31st Me. Vol.	" 30th, 1864.	Petersburg, Va.	"
Washburne, W.	Capt.	35th Mass. Vol.	" "	"	Boston, Mass.
Wing, G. H.	Lieut.	14th N. Y. Arty.	" "	"	Glenn's Falls, N. Y.
Wilder, G. O.	Adjt.	15th Mass. Vol.	" "	"	Holliston, Mass.
Willis, A. R.	Capt.	8th Me. Vol.	June 22d, 1864.	"	Biddeford, Me.
Wilcox, C. W.	Lieut.	9th N. H. Vol.	May 16th, "	Drury's Bluff, Va.	
Westbrook, U. S.	Capt.	135th O. Vol.	" 12th, "	Spottsylvania, Va.	Zanesville, O.
Weeks, E. J.	Lieut.	67th Pa. Vol.	July 3d, "	North Mount, Va.	Phœnixville, Pa.
Wodard, J. E.	"	18th Conn. Vol.	June 15th, 1863.	Winchester, Va.	Norwich, Conn.
Weakly, T. J.	"	110th O. Vol.	" "	"	New Carlisle, O.
Wright, B. F.	Capt.	146th N. Y. Vol.	May 5th, 1864.	Wilderness, Va.	Utica, N. Y.
Wilson, W. M., Jr.	"	122d O. Vol.	" 6th, "	"	Zanesville, O.
Watson, J. C.	Lieut.	126th O. Vol.	" "	"	New Salem, O.
Woodruff, F. M.	"	76th N. Y. Vol.	" 5th, "	"	Oswego Falls, N. Y.
Wright, D. L.	"	51st Ind. Vol.	" 3d, 1863.	Rome, Ga.	Indianapolis, Ind.
Whiting, J. D.	"	3d O. Vol.	" "	"	New York City.
Wright, W. R.	Capt.	80th Ill. Vol.	" "	"	Upper Alton, Ill.
Wilson, A.	"	3d O. Vol.	" "	"	Wooster, O.
Wolbach, A. R.	Lieut.	73d Ind. Vol.	" "	"	
Woodrow, J. C.	"	14th W. Va. Vol.	Jan. 3d, 1864.	Greenland Gap, Va.	Middlebourne, W. Va.
Williamson, J. B.	"	18th Pa. Cav.	Oct. 11th, 1863.	Brandy Sta., Va.	Latrobe, Pa.
Weaver, J. R.	"	"	" "	"	Houston, Pa.
Wilson, H.	"	118th Ill. Vol.	May 24th, "	Raymond, Miss.	Warsaw, Ill.
Worthen, T. A.	"	55th Ind. Vol.	June 27th, 1864.	Kennesaw Mt., Ga.	Azalia, Ind.
Wakefield, H. B.	Capt.	66th Ind. Vol.	Oct. 11th, 1863.	Colliersville, Tenn.	New Albany, Iowa.
Whitman, W. S.	Lieut.	45th O. Vol.	Nov. 15th, "	Knoxville, Tenn.	Cincinnati, O.
Wiltshire, J. W.	"	114th O. Vol.	July 9th, 1864.	Monocacy, Md.	Perrysburg, O.
Weddle, Geo.	"	19th Iowa Vol.	Oct. 13th, "	Tilton, Ga.	Mount Pleasant, Iowa.
Woodrow, C. W.	Capt.	2d Pa. Arty.	June 2d, "	Mechanicsville, Va.	Murey, Pa.
Webb, G. W.	Lieut.	4th Pa. Cav.	Oct. 12th, 1863.	Sulphur Spa., Va.	Allegany City, Pa.
White, A. B.					

372　APPENDIX.

Names.	Rank.	Regiment.	When captured.	Where captured.	Residence.
Warwick, Jos. F.	Lieut.	101st Pa. Vol.	Apr. 20th, 1864.	Plymouth, N. C.	Beaver, Pa.
Willis, H. H.	"	40th N. Y. Vol.	June 1st, "	Mechanicsville, Va.	Aurora, Ill.
Winship, J.	"	88th Ill. Vol.	Aug. 20th, "	East Point, Ga.	Chicago, Ill.
Whitney, J. N.	"	2d R. I. Cav.	July 2d, 1863.	Port Hudson.	Raymond, Me.
Wilson, R.	"	113th Ill. Vol.	June 11th, 1864.	Tishamingo Cr., Miss.	Chicago, Ill.
Whitten, B. F.	"	9th Me. Vol.	" 1st, "	Cold Harbor, Va.	
Whiteside, J. C.	Capt.	94th N. Y. Vol.	July 1st, 1863.	Gettysburg, Pa.	Wyoming, N. Y.
Warren, J. W.	Lieut.	1st Wis. Cav.	" 23d, 1864.	Campbellton, Ga.	Beaver Dam, Wis.
Wanzer, G. G.	Major.	24th N. Y. Cav.	May 6th, "	Wilderness, Va.	Rochester, N. Y.
Wadsworth, M. C.	Lieut.	16th Me. Vol.	July 1st, 1863.	Gettysburg, Pa.	Pittston, Me.
Warchaw, F.	"	54th N. Y. Vol.	" "	"	New York City.
Wilson, W. C.	Capt.	104th N. Y. Vol.	" "	"	Spencer, Mass.
White, H. G.	"	94th N. Y. Vol.	" "	"	Lysander, N. Y.
Widdess, C. C.	"	150th Pa. Vol.	" "	"	Germantown, Pa.
Whiston, D.	Lieut.	13th Mass. Vol.	" "	"	
Welsh, W. H. H.	"	87th Pa. Vol.	" "	"	York, Pa.
White, C. W.	Capt.	5th W. Va. Cav.	" "	"	Baltimore, Md.
Wilson, J.	"	57th O. Vol.	July 12th, 1864.	Atlanta, Ga.	
Williams, W. H.	"	41st N. Y. Vol.	Sept. 16th, 1863.	Virginia.	
Watson, W. I.	Lieut.	21st Wis. Vol.	" 20th, "	Chickamauga, Ga.	Waupaca, Wis.
Winner, C. N.	"	1st O. Vol.	" 19th, "	"	
Wasson, J. M.	"	40th O. Vol.	" 21st, "	"	
Webb, G. W.	Capt.	2d Pa. Art'y.	June 2d, 1864.	Mission Ridge, Tenn.	
Welch, J. C.	"	12th O. Vol.	May 9th, "	Cold Harbor, Va.	Dayton, O.
Wheeler, J. D.	Lieut.	85th N. Y. Vol.	Apr. 20th, "	Newbern Dépôt, Va.	Angelica, N. Y.
*Wenrick, J. E.	Capt.	15th Conn. Vol.	" "	Plymouth, N. C.	New Haven, Conn.
Williams, W.	Lieut.	19th Pa. Cav.	" 8th, "	Memphis, Tenn.	Philadelphia, Pa.
Willis, W.	"	8th Mich. Cav.	Aug. 6th, "	Macon, Ga.	
Williams, M. T.	"	51st Ind. Vol.	May 3d, 1863.	Rome, Ga.	
Wiley, M.	Capt.	15th Ky. Vol.	June 29th, "	Jackson, Miss.	
		1st Tenn. Vol.	Aug. 30th, 1864.	Sweet Water, Ga.	

Whittaker, E. B.	Capt.	72d Pa. Vol.	June 22d, 1864.	Morning Sun, O.
Wallace, J.	Lieut. Col.	47th O. Vol.	July 22d, "	Westerville, O.
Ward, T. H.	Lieut.	59th U. S. C. T.	June 12th, "	Briers'Cross Rds., Miss.
Wheaton, J.	"	"	"	"
Wright, R. J.	Capt.	6th O. Vol.	May 17th, "	Springfield, O.
Wilcox, W. H. H.	Lieut.	10th N. Y. Cav.	Oct. 12th, 1863.	New York City.
Wallace, R. P.	"	120th O. Vol.	May 24th, "	Loudonville, O.
Walpole, H. H.	Capt.	122d N. Y. Vol.	" 11th, 1864.	
Wright, J. W.	Lieut.	10th Iowa Vol.	Nov. 25th, 1863.	Des Moines City, Iowa.
Whittemore, B. W.	"	5th N. Y. Cav.	June 29th, 1864.	
Wallace, J. J.	"	7th Tenn. Cav.	Mar. 24th, "	Dowagiac, Mich.
Wentworth, H. A.	"	14th N.Y.H.Art'y.	June 2d, "	Randolph, N. Y.
Wall, M. W.	Capt.	69th N. Y. Vol.	" 22d, "	
Walker, W. H.	Lieut.	4th O. Vol.	July 9th, "	Arcadia, O.
Wilson, E. S.	"	1st Mass. Cav.	May 10th, "	Havana, Cuba
Warren, D. H.	Ass't Surg.	8th Iowa Cav.	July 30th, "	Glencoe, O.
Wilson, R. P.	Lieut.	5th U. S. Cav.	May 10th, "	Philadelphia, Pa.
Willetts, W.	"	22d Mich. Vol.		Birmingham, Mich.
White, Harry	Major.			Indiana, Pa.
White, G. M.	Capt.	1st W. Va. Vol.		Wellsburg, W. Va.
Whitney, J. De W.		O. Vet. Inf.		New York City.
Yaw, E. C.	Lieut.	67th N. Y. Vol.	May 6th, 1864.	Naples, N. Y.
York, J. H.	"	63d Ind. Vol.	June 27th, "	
Yontz, H. C.	Capt.	126th O. Vol.	" 14th, 1863.	New Salem, O.
Young, D. G.	"	81st Ill. Vol.	" 11th, 1864.	De Soto, Ill.
Young, W. J.	Lieut.	111th Ill. Vol.	July 22d, "	Xenia, Ill.
York, F. D.	"	2d N. C. U. Vol.	Apr. 20th, "	Friendship, N. Y.
Young, J. W.	Major.	76th N. Y. Vol.	May 5th, "	Wilderness, Va.
Yates, C. H.	Lieut.	96th Ill. Vol.	Sept. 22d, 1863.	Mission Ridge, Tenn.
*Young, A.	"	4th Pa. Cav.	June 24th, 1864.	Cherry Valley, N. Y.
Young, T. P.	"	4th Ky. Vol.	July 31st, "	Newark, N. J.

(Battle/location column: Petersburg, Va.; Atlanta, Ga.; Briers'Cross Rds., Miss.; Richmond, Va.; Bealton Station, Va.; Raymond, Miss.; Spotsylvania, Va.; Mission Ridge, Tenn.; Ream's Station, Va.; Union City, Tenn.; Cold Harbor, Va.; Petersburg, Va.; Chattahoochee R., Ga.; Beaver Dam, Ga.; Macon, Ga.; Beaver Dam, Ga.; Wilderness, Va.; Kennesaw Mt., Ga.; Martinsburg, Va.; Ripley, Miss.; Atlanta, Ga.; Plymouth, N. C.; Wilderness, Va.; Mission Ridge, Tenn.; Yellow Tavern, Va.; Newnan, Ga.)

Names.	Rank.	Regiment.	When captured.	Where captured.	Residence.
Zarracher, F. K.	Capt.	18th Pa. Cav.	May 5th, 1864.	Wilderness, Va.	Philadelphia, Pa.
Zeigler, Aaron	Lieut.	7th Pa. V. R. C'ps.	"	"	Myerstown, Pa.
Zeis, H.	Capt.	80th Ill. Vol.	" 3d, 1863.	Rome, Ga.	
Zimm, A.	Lieut.	15th Iowa Vol.	July 22d, 1864.	Atlanta, Ga.	
Zobel, C.	"	15th N. Y. Art'y.	May 6th, "	Wilderness, Va.	
Zeigler, J. D.	"	114th Ill. Vol.	Apr. 10th, "	Briers' CrossRds., Miss.	

THE END.

www.ingramcontent.com/pod-product-compliance
Lightning Source LLC
Chambersburg PA
CBHW032043220426
43664CB00008B/836